NEHRU'S INDIA

NEHRU'S INDIA

Select Speeches

edited with an Introduction
by

MUSHIRUL HASAN

OXFORD
UNIVERSITY PRESS

OXFORD
UNIVERSITY PRESS

YMCA Library Building, Jai Singh Road, New Delhi 110 001

Oxford University Press is a department of the University of Oxford. It furthers the
University's objective of excellence in research, scholarship, and education
by publishing worldwide in

Oxford New York

Auckland Cape Town Dar es Salaam Hong Kong Karachi
Kuala Lumpur Madrid Melbourne Mexico City Nairobi
New Delhi Shanghai Taipei Toronto

With offices in
Argentina Austria Brazil Chile Czech Republic France Greece
Guatemala Hungary Italy Japan Poland Portugal Singapore
South Korea Switzerland Thailand Turkey Ukraine Vietnam

Oxford is a registered trade mark of Oxford University Press
in the UK and in certain other countries

Published in India by Oxford University Press, New Delhi

The publishers would like to thank Priyanka Gandhi Vadra and the Jawaharlal Nehru
Memorial Fund for permission to include the following extracts from
Selected Works of Jawaharlal Nehru (Second series): vol. 2, 1996, pp. 501–2;
vol. 3, 1985, pp. 66–73, 137–8; vol. 15 (part II), 1993, pp.14–17;
vol. 31, 2002, pp. 126–33, 170–83; vol. 34, 2005, pp. 114–24.

ISBN 13: 978-0-19-568787-3
ISBN 10: 0-19-568787-6

Typeset in AGaramond 10.5/12 at Le Studio Graphique, Gurgaon 122 001
Printed in India at Deunique, New Delhi-110 018
Published by Oxford University Press
YMCA Library Building, Jai Singh Road, New Delhi 110 001

CONTENTS

INTRODUCTION

Mushirul Hasan

The Constituent Assembly of India met in the Constitution Hall, New Delhi at midnight on August 14, 1947 with Dr Rajendra Prasad in the chair.

MR PRESIDENT: The first item on the agenda is the singing of the *Vande Mataram*. Shrimati Kripalani sang the first verse.

MR PRESIDENT: After this I propose that we all stand in silence to honour the memory of those who have died in the struggle for freedom in India and elsewhere.

MR PRESIDENT: Pandit Jawaharlal Nehru will now move the motion [Pledge by Members], which stands in his name.

PANDIT JAWAHARLAL NEHRU: Long years ago we made a tryst with destiny, and now the time comes when we shall redeem our pledge, not wholly or in full measure, but very substantially. At the stroke of the midnight hour, when the world sleeps India will awake to life and freedom. A moment comes, which comes but rarely in history, when we step out from the old to the new, when an age ends, and when the soul of a nation, long suppressed, finds utterance. It is fitting that in this solemn moment we take the pledge of dedication to the service of India and her people and to the still larger cause of humanity.

CHOUDHRY KHALIQUZZAMAN: [Mr Khaliquzzaman seconded the Pledge]. Mr President, after midnight today a great revolution is to take place in India; a revolution for which India had been working for the last one hundred years in her fight for freedom.... Now the time has come when we shall have to shoulder great responsibilities when there will be no room for clapping and for high-sounding slogans.

DR S. RADHAKRISHNAN: Mr President it is not necessary for me to speak at any length on this Resolution so impressively moved by Pandit Jawaharlal Nehru and seconded by Mr Khaliquzamman. History and legend will grow around this day. It marks a milestone in the march of our democracy. A significant date it is in the drama of the Indian people who are trying to rebuild and transform themselves.

The next morning—The Appointed Day—Governor General Mountbatten swore in Jawaharlal Nehru as the first prime minister of free India. The crowds on the spacious roads outside Raisina Hill were spectacular. The streets rent with spontaneous rejoicing. At six in the evening independent India's first prime minister, hoisted the Indian tricolour at India Gate. Delhi bubbled with joyous excitement. Only Gandhi celebrated independence in Calcutta by fasting. The Mahatma was sitting in a Muslim's house in Calcutta on the day of freedom, his heart heavy with sorrow over the communal carnage that marked the Partition of India.

The Constituent Assembly that drafted India's Constitution began its work in New Delhi in December 1946. From the mid-1930s onwards the Congress had called for a Constituent Assembly elected by adult franchise. However, under the Cabinet Mission's provisions for transfer of power, provincial assemblies of British India indirectly elected the Constituent Assembly in 1946. Thus, its complexion reflected the complexion of the provincial assemblies. The Congress ruled the Constituent Assembly by virtue of its overwhelming victory in the provincial elections the year before and during partition on 15 August 1947. Thus 82 per cent of the members of the Assembly were from the Congress. In effect it was a one-party Assembly and the Muslim League boycotted it. It wanted two Assemblies, one for Hindustan and one for Pakistan. The Congress viewpoint was the reverse, no matter what religion, all Indians are one, and, therefore, the Congress could just as well represent them all. Jawaharlal Nehru wrote in 1939: 'The Congress has within its fold many groups, widely differing in their viewpoints and ideologies. This is natural and inevitable if the Congress is to be the mirror of the nation.'

The Congress-led nationalist movement was ideologically and socially diverse, and it included the viewpoints and representatives of competing ideological strands—ranging from reactionary to revolutionary—and gave space to the minorities as well as the right-wing Hindu positions. The Congress Working Committee recommended women, minorities, and experts in constitutional law and national affairs to the Assembly.

The leader of India's untouchables, B.R. Ambedkar, chaired the drafting committee and steered the passage of the Constitution through nearly three years of debate over its various provisions. Politically, the Assembly was controlled by the quartet of Nehru, Sardar Vallabhbhai Patel, Rajendra Prasad and Maulana Abul Kalam Azad. They constituted a virtual 'oligarchy' with their control over the Congress legislative party and the Assembly's eight committees. The drafting was left to more than a dozen distinguished lawyers and experts in constitutional law. Every provision of the Constitution was freely debated and its fate decided on the floor of the House, but the influence of the Congress in the deliberations was unmistakable.

The Assembly's task was to draft a Constitution that would serve the goal of social revolution, a national renaissance. What form of political framework and institutions would foster a social revolution was the main question before the Assembly. Nehru famously defined the aims of the Assembly in a speech that came to be known as the 'Objectives Resolution'. For him the Constituent Assembly represented a moment of radical political choice. Unlike previous constitutional models, the Indian Constitution envisaged a comprehensive design of transformation of a traditional society, and fifty years later that vision with its notion of rights and justice survives.

With 395 articles and eight schedules the Constitution of India is among the longest in the world. It was approved on 25 November 1949 and adopted by acclamation on 26 January 1950. It has undergone 104 amendments. The radically new feature, when compared with colonial rule, was a sovereign legislature elected under universal suffrage without communal representation, but with reservation for Scheduled Castes and Tribes, and explicit guarantee of Fundamental Rights. It provided for a parliamentary system of government, with an executive responsible to parliament, but with an indirectly elected President as the head of state. It also provided for an independent judiciary with certain powers of judicial review of laws passed by parliament.

This volume claims neither to be a compendium of all of Jawaharlal Nehru's speeches or writings, nor a chronological record of his prolific output. It is instead a thematic arrangement of some of his most crucial, engaging, and moving speeches. Though I have eschewed a chronological basis of organization, most of the speeches are drawn from what could be termed his 'Prime Minister Years'.

There is sound basis for ignoring the writings and speeches from an earlier period, engaged as they were primarily with the question of national liberation. Though to be sure the character of the future independent India was a keenly contested one for most of Nehru's early career too, with various ideological trends, even within the Congress, jostling for hegemony, it remained at best fuzzy and even distant.

The idea of a free India looked within grasp and an imminent reality with the formation of the Constituent Assembly. The map of new India began to be drawn up in right earnest, and the nation-building project was underway. The architect of this new edifice was to be Jawaharlal Nehru. The volume hopes to capture some of the rough and tumble of the early days of that tentative planning, begun a couple of years before the actual dream of free India was realized; the heat and dust—or the 'prose' as Nehru called it—of attempting to translate that blueprint into reality; and finally—and perhaps, crucially—Nehru's intellectual concerns that were rooted in his cosmopolitanism and an incredible openness to cross-cultural osmosis. This spirit he hoped the institutions he envisaged and invested in—the Indian Council for Cultural Relations, Sahitya Akademi, the numerous museums and art galleries—would foster in his fellow-citizens.

The opening sections delineate Nehru's vision for free India. This vision was however far from settled; it was being etched out in conjunction and contention with other voices. We see Nehru responding to various political actors defending his blueprint for India's future, appealing to them for cooperation, occasionally even chiding them for what he perceived as unfair criticism.

The charter of free India was embodied in the Objectives Resolution Nehru placed before the Constituent Assembly. It was the core of what would later become the country's constitution, holding within it the seeds of all that we, as a nation, may uphold: social justice, secularism, federalism, and several others. Nehru emphasized that the Objectives Resolution was to be the basis of something new and remarkable:

We have been cutting our way and clearing the ground on which we intend to erect the edifice of a constitution. It, however, seems proper that before we proceed further we should clearly understand where we are going and what we intend building. It is apparent that on such occasions details are unnecessary. In building, you will, no doubt, use each brick after mature consideration. Usually, when one desires to construct a building, one must have a plan for the structure that one wishes to erect and then collect the material required.... The Resolution that I am placing before you defines our aims, describes an outline of the plan and points the way which we are going to tread.

More than a mere legal document, the Resolution is suffused with a kind of *volkgeist* which its dry language betrays: 'And so I cannot say that this Resolution at all conveys the passion that lies in the hearts and minds of the Indian people today.'

For Nehru, the Objectives Resolution carries of course the weight of a 5000-year-old civilization, but he also sought to trace its lineage to the American and French revolutions and finally—and not unexpectedly at all—the Russian Revolution. And yet, the course he envisioned India would take was to be wholly indigenous and suited to its own conditions. Rejecting any modular form of democracy, he observed:

We are not going to just copy, I hope, a certain democratic procedure or an institution of a so-called democratic country. We may improve upon it.... The House will notice that in this Resolution, although we have not used the word 'democratic' because we thought it is obvious that the word 'Republic' contains the word... we have given the content of democracy in this Resolution and not only the content of democracy but the content of economic democracy in this Resolution without mentioning the word 'Socialism' for fear of offending some.

Thus neither democracy nor socialism was mere procedural matter for Nehru. His strategy was to radicalize the founding principles by swamping them with the content of democracy and socialism, without really naming them as such.

But regardless of whether he called his programme socialist or not, its content ensured that Nehru countenanced fierce opposition from those entrenched interests and power centres his programme sought to supplant. The leading of these were the Princes whose principalities faced the threat of extinction with the introduction of universal suffrage and democracy. The republican in Nehru militated against the idea of monarchical form of governance while the democrat in him assured the princes and their advocates that he would not stand in the way of such a government in any of the states if its subjects so wished.

The resolution is both a repository of the aspirations and dreams of millions as well as the instrument towards the realization of those dreams. It was meant as a message of intent of the new nation—a message to its people, the members of the assembly, and the world community. Already in this resolution, there were intimations of the role India was to play in the world arena under Nehru.

The last point of the resolution clearly called for India to take her rightful position in the comity of nations. Nehru urged the Assembly to recognize the historical role that destiny had bestowed on the nation as a leader of Asia, by virtue of the vigorous freedom struggle waged by Indians and the subsequent decolonization:

When some petty matter divides us and we have difficulties and conflicts amongst ourselves over these small matters, let us remember not only this Resolution but this great responsibility that we shoulder, the responsibility of the freedom of 400 million people of India, the responsibility of the leadership of a large part of Asia, the responsibility of being some kind of guide to vast numbers of people all over the world.

It is not always easy to extricate the national concerns from the international ones in Nehru's writings and speeches, for his vision was typically Janus-faced—at once looking back at the centuries-old civilization and the modern future, and simultaneously cast inside and turned to the external world.

Nehru's first foreign policy challenge came over the question of India's entry into the Commonwealth. He was accused variously of sacrificing India's interests at the altar of Commonwealth, of making India subservient to the British Crown, of legitimizing by association, openly racist regimes such as that of South Africa, and finally, obstructing India's ties with its Asian neighbours. In his speech in the Assembly, he attempted to allay these fears. First, he assured the House that the King would have no powers over the Republic of India or her subjects; second, he expected great benefits to accrue from cooperating with and entering into alliances with other Commonwealth countries; and further, that no advantage was so great as to merit compromising with the pledges that the country's founding fathers had taken, no privilege too weighty to vitiate the principles on which the new nation was to be built. To the charge of hobnobbing with racist regimes, he said:

When we have entered into an alliance with a nation or a group of nations, it does not mean that we accept their other policies etc., it does not mean that we commit ourselves in any way to something that they may do. In fact, this House knows that we are carrying on a struggle in regard to racial discrimination in various parts of the world.

The only safe principle to follow in foreign policy was to allow each country to live its life in its own way, subject to certain limitations of course. His philosophy is encapsulated in these words: 'I am afraid I'm a bad bargainer. I'm not used to the ways of the marketplace. I hope I'm a good fighter...'

Nehru and Non-alignment were synonymous with each other. Non-alignment, he argued, was not passive apathy but an active resistance to the carving of the world into two antagonistic blocs and the refusal to join either.

Is my country so small so insignificant, so lacking in worth or strength, that it cannot say what it wants to say, that it must say ditto to this or that? Why should my policy be the policy of this country or that country? It is going to be my policy and my country's policy.

Nehru was severely criticized by his own colleagues for his Pakistan policy, which was considered to be feeble, especially in the light of clear evidence of Pakistani belligerence and the mass migrations into West Bengal from across the border. Nehru counsels restraint, moderation and friendship, and heartily rebukes the Hindu Mahasabha for making irresponsible suggestions—suggestions, which he says could only be the products of perverse minds. He understands that his proposal for a joint declaration with the Government of Pakistan will be viewed as a weakness but he recalls Gandhi's warning about countries that look at one another with bloodshot eyes.

It is always well to be conciliatory and to stretch your hand to those who grasp it; because though their government may not do so, the people will always grasp an outstretched hand, not only the people of a particular country but the people of all the countries of the world.

Nehru laments the demise of the older, gentler traditions of diplomacy, which appear to have been overtaken by a vacuous verbal warfare. India and Pakistan cannot forever carry on as enemies, he says.

Under Nehru's stewardship, India emerged as a vastly respected voice in the international arena. The Five-nation resolution proposed by Nehru on behalf of Ghana, the United Arab Republic, Indonesia, Yugoslavia and India, was a fervent plea to break the deadlock that seemed to grip the United Nations as a result of the high tensions between the United States and Soviet Union. We see him at his combative best when responding to the Australian Prime Minister who moved an amendment to the Five-nation resolution. Nehru could not accept that the question of world peace be left to the four superpowers—the US, USSR, France and UK—as the Australian PM suggested. This would have undermined the sanctity and status of the United Nations Assembly. And when the wording of the Draft resolution was changed at the behest of some of the more powerful countries, Nehru and his friends refused to be associated with it any longer:

The resolution was drafted under great stress of feeling, almost, at what it described as 'the recent deterioration in international relations'.... Therefore, the resolution referred to the 'grave and urgent responsibility that rests on the United Nations to initiate helpful efforts.' As the draft resolution has been changed, it seems to us that that essential urgency has gone, and the passionate feeling that something should be done has faded away in the wording of the resolution as it is.

The set of three speeches delivered at the United Nations exemplify the great regard Nehru attached to morality in international policy. Other shorter speeches, minutes of the Commonwealth meetings and messages underline his faith in building Asian solidarities; his unremitting interest and role in defusing tensions and promoting world peace. Nehru's advocacy of peace is not that of a pacifist:

I am not a pacifist. Unhappily the world today finds that it cannot do without force. We have to project ourselves and to prepare ourselves for any contingency. We have to meet aggression or any other kinds of evil. To surrender to evil is always bad. But in resisting evil we must not allow ourselves to be swept away by our own passions and fears and act in a manner which is itself evil.

One would do well to remember that a free India emerged out of Partition, and the movement for freedom was paralleled by a growing communalization of its polity. Thus it was quite natural that 'secular' and 'communal' issues would engage those who were drawing up the road map to future. The question of separate electorates and communal reservation was foremost on the agenda. Nehru personally abhorred separate electorates, attributing the tragedy of Partition to it, and considering it antithetical to nationalism and democracy. So when the matter of reservation came up, Nehru felt relieved that there would be no reservation but for the Scheduled Castes.

In a full-blooded democracy, if you seek to give safeguards to a minority, and a relatively small minority, you isolate it. Maybe you protect it to a slight extent, but at what cost? At the cost of isolating it and keeping it from the main current in which the majority is going....

However, he warned against any injustice towards the minorities. He placed a great deal of faith on what he believed to be the innate generosity and goodness of people, both the majority and minority to create an atmosphere of goodwill and communal harmony. He spoke on this theme in response to a resolution moved by another Congress leader, M. Ananthasayanam Ayyangar, in the Constituent Assembly. In his speech, Nehru seized the opportunity to draw attention to 'certain communal elements' in the Draft Constitution, namely the proposal of some reservation of seats for minorities or for the Scheduled Castes. While he recognized the historical deprivations of certain groups such as the tribals, he admitted that a mere granting of voting rights would neither benefit them nor would it be democracy in any true sense. But again, he doubted whether reservations were the best antidote. He was of course guided by the bitterness of partition and communalism of the period but it is doubtful if the last word had been said on Nehru's views on reservations.

The concern with communal harmony and a firmly secular state is also evident in his speech broadcast on All India Radio four days after Independence and his convocation addresses at Allahabad University and Aligarh Muslim University included in this collection.

Barely four days after Independence, he addressed a nation still reeling under the Partition bloodbath and mass exodus. This speech is remarkable for its simplicity and lucidity. The reader will be able, simply by reading it, to gauge the measure of his sorrow and bewilderment at the large-scale violence. But its purpose is not to merely communicate the scale of tragedy; it is also to reassure the public that anarchy will not be allowed a free run—that things will soon be under control and that the government will care for those who had lost their properties and families. Finally, there is a call for restraint. Throughout the tone remains personal, yet authoritative.

Addressing a convocation of the Allahabad University in late 1947, he elaborated on the role a university ought to play in the life of a nation, especially one still recovering from horrific violence and chaos, as India was in the aftermath of partition violence. He envisaged the universities as lighthouses that would lead the country out of this morass. He invested great hope in the new generation's ability to heal old wounds and to dedicate itself to work for the fulfilment of the national objectives. Barely a month later, he addressed a convocation at the Aligarh Muslim University—the ideological vanguard of the Pakistan movement.

The questions weighing on his mind are the same: India's partition and the urgency of ending communal discord. His address is not tinged with suspicion but by a frank acknowledgement that the subject of Pakistan must be on the minds of his audience. He admits that he finds the idea of a theocratic state unsuited to the modern age, and tentatively laid out for the first time, in the barest of details, a preliminary idea of an Asian confederation: 'Any closer association must come out of a normal process and in a friendly way which does not end Pakistan as a State, but makes it an equal part of a large union in which several countries might be associated.'

The kernel of the model of nation-building that the Nehruvian State embarked upon, in other words the nation's vision, can be found in his broadcast to the nation on 15 August 1947. He clearly laid out the challenges facing the newly independent nation: internal strife, grinding poverty, low productivity, inflation, long-entrenched interests and so on. He then outlined the ways out of this quagmire. Two of his prescriptions were particularly vital: a rapid change of the antiquated land tenure system and large-scale industrialization. Nehru virtually unfolded his blueprint before the nation: 'The Government of India have in hand at present several vast schemes for developing river valleys by controlling the flow of rivers, building dams and reservoirs and irrigation works and developing hydro-electric power.'

Big dams and hydroelectric plants—the 'temples of modern India'—were of course to become the hallmarks of the Nehruvian era. Regardless of the ecological wisdom of large dams, one cannot fail to be struck by the fact that *this* is an

Independence Day speech, and already Nehru had his course clearly drawn out, and his task neatly chalked out. His 'National Vision' speech a few years later is of course more detailed, sketching out his plans—the Five Year Plan to be precise. The centrality of the Five Year Plans in the country's economy till at least the 1980s can hardly be overemphasized—the public sector, control over the private sector, abolition of the zamindari and jagirdari systems, introducing new agricultural techniques, and several others. And it is here in this speech that Nehru first attempted to familiarize the people with it 'because it affects each one of you', even urging them to study the Plan, or at least the summaries that were circulated for the benefit of the public. Nehru's notions of centralized planning did not erode his democratic instincts.

Nehru was nothing if not an extraordinary communicator. He communicated not to entertain, amuse or provoke, but to edify, enlist, and mobilize the masses into action, to join his project of nation building, as partners and comrades. On the occasion of India becoming a Republic, he urged citizens to work harder: 'Only hard work can produce wealth for us and rid us of our poverty. Each one of us, man or woman, young or old, must therefore, toil and work. Rest is not for us. We did not win our freedom so that we might afterwards [rest] ... but in order to work harder to hold and strengthen that freedom...' Again, at a public meeting in Allahabad, he exhorted the people to help his government fight the food crisis by refraining from hoarding and by becoming more productive. He ended his appeal thus: 'The most important problem is, I think, how to change the atmosphere in this country so that the common people are involved in the task of nation-building and all of us may be able to work together.'

While the early speeches of this section outline the faintest details of Nehru's model of development for the country, the heart of the collection catalogues his speeches in which these themes receive a fuller treatment. How is modern India to be built? What are to be the foundations of its economy? How would the production relations be organized? What is to be the relation between the small-scale, cottage industry (the preferred Gandhian way) and the big industry (a route Nehru personally advocated for rapid progress)? Was reorganization of Indian states along linguistic principles the right direction to take?

These speeches are like despatches from the field, dwelling on the shape government policies would adopt in the early years of free India. They give us a sense of the daily business of governance and how the vision articulated in the early years was being realized on the ground. Nehru himself formulates the shift thus:

I have myself been concerned with the theoretical aspects of planning for a fairly considerable time. I realize that there is a great deal of difference between the theory of it and the practice of it; as in almost everything in life the theory is full of poetry ... from the poetry of rather vague planning in air, we have come down to the prose of the statement.

Nehru acknowledges that the prose may appeal less than poetry; we see him therefore engaging in debate with a variety of actors over the path his government is pursuing in the sphere of economic planning and development. To an industry unhappy with the taxation regime of the government, he explains the character of the State he is building, a 'social' rather than a 'police' State. Such a State—involved in solving the social problems, from health to education—perforce demands a greater burden to be shared by industry. Profit motive, pure and simple, he terms a vulgarity, which the country has neither the will nor means to support at that juncture in history.

On the other side of the spectrum were the Socialists and Communists whom Nehru castigated for their 'obsession' with obsolete technology and methods, despite an agreement with their programme for overhauling the feudal land system. He had little patience with their agenda of nationalization of all existing industries, most of which he feared employed outdated technology. He favoured, instead, the construction of new enterprises, the shining examples of which were the great river valley projects initiated by him. These, he believed, would change the face of the country and would, ultimately, hold the key to transforming Indian economy and industry. The country's progress, he believed, largely depended on industrial peace, on relations of mutual trust between management and labour. Recognizing the central role of the government as arbiter of disputes, Nehru's cabinet moved a resolution that proposed the establishment of a mechanism to advise on fair conditions for labour and fair returns to capital and industrial courts. But in the end, he hoped, as he expressed to a gathering at the Indian Merchant's Chamber in Bombay, that the two parties involved would themselves mitigate the conflict and work in a spirit of cooperation.

One of the most lucid explications of the 'mixed economy' path the country was embarking upon under Nehru's leadership can be found in his address to the Indian Chemical Manufacturers. Reacting to the charge that this 'mixed economy' was fettering the growth of industry, and that Nehru must choose between the free enterprise embodied in the United States system or go the Soviet nationalization way whole hog, Nehru says: 'That is a very hard choice indeed and I do not see why I should be forced to make it.' No country, he argues, can afford to blindly apply any axiom or dogma without weighing its worth and suitability to its peculiar conditions. The way forward for India, given its specific situation, is the mixed economy model. Dismissing industry's desire for the so-called free enterprise model, he reminds them of the feebleness of Indian industry: 'If private industry has full play, one of the first casualties will be private enterprise itself.'

The need, then, is to be constantly sensitive to the specificities of a society. And thus, in proposing the 'socialistic pattern of society', 'we shall have our own socialism'. Aware of the weight of its historical legacy—the proletarian struggles of Europe—he appropriates the term and imparts a new meaning to it. But in doing so, he feels the need to distinguish himself from the Communists, the natural claimants to the legacy of socialism, whom he euphemistically refers to as 'adventurists'. Nehru's socialism will come through peaceful methods rather than violent conflicts espoused by the Communists—and the prime examples of peaceful transformation are the abolition of princedoms through privy purses and the dissolution of big landed estates.

From the 1950s onwards, the national political imagination came to be seized by an intense mobilization around the language issue, with demand for the linguistic reorganization of states. Nehru was not particularly interested where the internal lines of states would be drawn; his prime concern was for linguistic minorities, especially in light of the existence of bilingualism, and trilingualism, even in clearly marked linguistic areas of great languages. Though he believed in the development of languages of the people, erecting boundaries on the basis of language seemed to him to be rather 'parochial'. He simply could not appreciate the passions that the language issue aroused, as it did amongst the people of Bihar, Bengal, and Orissa. The idea of a monolingual state was abhorrent to him as he feared the domination of the linquistic majority over the minority language: and he says so clearly in the Lok Sabha in the course of a debate over the States Reorganization Committee: 'May I say quite briefly and precisely that I dislike that principle absolutely 100 per cent, as it has tended to go?'

Nehru's prescription was simple, if a little naïve; he advocated the unfettered growth of all languages. He firmly believed that the development of one language nurtures and sustains other languages. This was the moving principle behind the founding of Sahitya Akademi, which would translate the works of one language into another, and thus encourage many languages and literatures. Nehru of course spoke in the House with the authority of the founding President of the Akademi.

But did Nehru fear that AMU would, in independent India, become a hot bed of communal politics? His answer is quite clear:

For my part, I do not like the intrusion of communal spirit anywhere, and least of all in educational institutions. Education is meant to free the spirit of man and not to imprison it in set frames. I do not like the university being called the Muslim University just as I do not like the Benaras University to be called the Hindu University. This does not mean that a university should not specialize in particular cultural subjects and studies. I think it is right that this University should lay special stress on certain aspects of Islamic thought and culture.

With his implicit faith in the redemptive potential of modern industries and technological advances, Nehru's interest in matters of Science may appear natural. One may not be too surprised by the fact that he ensured his presence at the opening sessions of the Indian Science Congress for almost the entire period of his premiership. What is surely refreshing is his insistence upon the inseparability of ethics from science. Emptied of morality, science can be turned into a force of evil, he argued. In a world still trying to come to terms with the horrors of Hiroshima and Nagasaki, Nehru called upon the congregation of scientists, both Indian and international, to alloy the temper of peace with that of science.

Addressing another conference of the Indian Science Congress, Nehru— arriving straight from the opening ceremony of the Hirakud Dam and prior to that, from the ruins of the ancient Nalanda University in Bihar—muses on the deeper philosophical questions—of science's relation with the values of truth, compassion and tolerance. This speech traverses with ease between centuries, mapping the continuities between the remote past of Buddha's time, the engineering feat of the Hirakud Dam and the Science Congress. He emphasizes the worth of emulating the tolerance of the Buddha period. He recalls Buddha's message:

If you reverence your faith, while you reverence your faith, you should reverence the faith of the other who differs from you. In reverencing the faith of others, you will exalt your own faith and will get your own faith honoured by the other. This must be the motto that must guide the scientist.

The scientist is supposed to be an objective seeker after truth, and science has grown because, in large measure, the great scientists have sought truth in that way. But no man, I suppose today, not even a scientist, can live in the world of his own, in some kind of ivory tower, cut off from what is happening, cut off from the effects of his own work, which are so powerfully affecting the destiny of morals and ethics. If it divorces itself completely from the realm of morality and ethics, then the power it possesses may be used for evil purposes...I plead with the scientists here and elsewhere to adhere to the temper of science, to remember that this temper of science is essentially one of tolerance, one of humility, to the great truths which they are seeking to discover and which they are seeking to discover in future, but always remembering that somebody else also may have a bit of the truth.

It is apt that the closing sections of this volume consist of speeches that illumine Nehru, the man behind the politician and administrator, an intellectual and philosopher, much in the mode of Plato's philosopher-King, whom he was so fond of citing. These speeches show him as a keen builder of cultural institutions of enduring value. It is evident that he gave much thought to the question of how a nation might forge and take pride in a national identity; how it may preserve the rich heritage that history had bequeathed it. But his vision was never trapped in the exclusivist, culturological mode; far from it, his vision was supremely inclusive and driven by a belief in the existence, even the necessity of cultures constantly interacting with each other, of cultures working on and transforming the other and their own through a live contact. A self-confessed 'amateur' historian, the text of his lecture at the silver jubilee session of the Indian Historical Records Commission transmits the enthusiasm and animation he felt for the discipline of History.

There is something uncanny about the way in which Nehru, a self-taught and amateur historian, pre-empts some of the methodological debates of historiography. He makes a fervent plea for social history—for a greater research on the daily lives of ordinary men and women who lived in the past (family budgets from hundreds of years ago, he suggests could show us how life was organized in that age!). Only this could clothe the dry bones with flesh and blood. His second appeal to the gathering of historians and archivists is to rescue history from the charmed circle of fellow-historians; to understand that history must be written not for specialists alone but also for the general interested lay reader in a popular and accessible mode.

At the inaugural address of the Asian History Congress, Nehru once more pressed for the need for Asian historians to bring new perspectives to history writing, as much of the contemporary histories were guilty of unabashed eurocentricism, which negatively affected the appreciation of Asian histories.

Nehru's inclusive understanding of the concept of culture is reflected in his inaugural speech at the Indian Council for Cultural Relations (ICCR). He warned against the chauvinism of cultural nationalism, as represented in the German word, "*kultur*"; cultural relations should not be defined by conquest and domination. No culture is pristine and untouched by the influence of others. A culture and civilization's advance can be measured by the degree of openness it exhibits towards the ideas of other cultures. Thus he identified the Indian tradition as characterized primarily by the synthesis of a variety of streams: the Gita, Upanishads, teachings of Buddha, the rejuvenating Islamic trends, new ideas of liberalism and industrial technology that came in the wake of colonialism, and the ideas of Socialism, Marxism and social justice that India's encounter with the West engendered.

For Nehru, material progress alone did not suffice, the quality and depth of a people was just as important. He feared that the modern, technological life was corroding the life of the mind, stultifying creative imagination and rendering the modern man and woman intellectually desolate. It is these lost aesthetic sensibilities that museums and art galleries as storehouses of beautiful objects, would revitalize. But as congealed history, he warned the organizers of centenary celebrations of Madras Government Museum, museums must not merely inventorize the oddities of our culture, but those artefacts and items that would help us in relating the past to the present; only as living history, would they appeal to the common man. Thus museums should not be merely frozen tableaus from the past but, along the lines of the Deutsches Museum in Munich, he suggests, they could be developed as windows to modern life, modern activity, the growth of science from the pre-scientific period. He wished them to be pedagogical tools, for students and lay public alike, though of course he thought young adults and children to be more receptive to new thoughts and influences.

This volume concludes with some moving, warm and vivid portraits of a few of Nehru's contemporaries, colleagues and comrades of the freedom struggle, and others whom he idealized. These were people who shared Nehru's vision for India. As the leader of the House, it fell on him the unpleasant business of announcing the death of a colleague or friend. Of Sarojini Naidu, who began her career as a poetess before being drawn to the national struggle, he says: '...she did not write much poetry with pen and paper [after joining the movement], but her whole life became a poem and a song. And she did that amazing thing: she infused artistry and poetry into our national struggle.' In her, Nehru surely recognized a kindred spirit: 'She herself was a composite both of various currents of culture in India as well as various currents of culture both in the East and the West. And so she was, while being a very great national figure, also truly an internationalist...' This is something that could be said equally of Nehru; and he notes with alarm, the gradual fading away of these qualities and the rise of narrow nationalism. In Sarojini Naidu's death, Nehru laments the loss of a vital and ideal link between the East and the West.

Maulana Abul Kalam Azad too embodied this synthesis of cultures—the Persianate, Arabic, and Indian. Nehru condoled his death not simply as the passing away of a man, but the passing away of an age, characterized by a certain grace, tolerance, patience and courtesy, which he felt was dissipating fast. In a warm remembrance speech in the Lok Sabha, he compared Azad to the 'great men of Renaissance' or the 'encyclopaedists who preceded the French revolution.'

Another profile included here is that of Gandhi. Here he writes a Foreword to a biography of Gandhi by D.G. Tendulkar. He admits that it is not for him to assess the Mahatma's historical role in the long story of humanity, given his personal closeness to the man; but neither can those who remained untouched by the magic of his charisma and personality accomplish this task. Nonetheless, he recounted some of Gandhi's leadership qualities. Even though Gandhi adhered to his ideas and to his conception of truth, yet he succeeded in moulding and moving enormous masses of human beings. He was not inflexible, but much alive to the necessities of the moment. He adapted himself to changing circumstances. Nehru was certain that much ink and paper would be expended on discussing and critiquing Gandhi's life theories and activities, but for him the Mahatma cannot be reduced to theory. He will remain forever 'a radiant and beloved figure'. The image of Gandhi that will forever endure in Nehru's mind is that of Gandhi leading the Dandi march, determined, staff in his hand.

During a debate in the Lok Sabha over the linguistic re-organization of states, Nehru argued against monolingualism (and the homogeneity of culture it engenders). He informed the House that he sent his daughter, Indira, to Santiniketan so that she could imbibe the culture of Bengal. But it is in his tribute to Rabindranath Tagore on his birth centenary at Visva Bharati that one gets a real sense of the reasons that may have moved Nehru to send Indira to Santiniketan. The institution built by Tagore, or Gurudev, exemplified the values that Nehru himself held so dear: the confluence of nationalism and internationalism, tradition and modernity, the importance of developing the spirit over sheer material gains, the necessity of breaking own the narrow barriers of caste, race and creed. 'I have a fear', he says, 'that in this year of Gurudeva's birth centenary his message and ideals might be swept away in the flood of words and eloquence and that we may imagine that we have done our duty by him. That is a dangerous delusion which comes over us often. I should like you specially here at Santiniketan and the Visva Bharati to remember that the test of your homage is not what you may say about him but the way you live, the way you grow, and the way you act up to his message.'

Though the focus is decidedly on Nehru the nation builder and institution builder, this volume reveals the wide range of his interests, and his remarkable erudition in dealing with subjects ranging from domestic politics to the ethics and morality of science, from India's role in world affairs to his thoughts on culture. Through it all, one is struck by how aware and alive Nehru was to the continuity between the past, the present and his hopes and vision for the future. Hence, the constant reference to the weight of the past, the greatness of the civilization he had inherited, not as a burden to be carried but as a reference point for judging the moral worth and wisdom of his decisions.

Nehru may be a cosmopolitan par excellence, but deracinated he was not. He believed his cosmopolitanism to be a gift from Asoka and the Buddhist period. While Asoka is the paradigmatic ruler for him; the Buddhist period is a veritable 'golden age', marked by a unique internationalism, tolerance, compassion and a vigorous openness to 'foreign' influences and ideas. It is to Asoka and the 'golden period' that he constantly harks back, be it in the adoption of the Asoka chakra in the national flag or the policy of Panch Shila.

In conclusion, one cannot but be regaled by the literary quality of Nehru's words: they come across clear and honest. Now you hear him delighted, now solemn, now youthful and energetic, full of hopes for his country, and now piqued at the delays in the fruition of his ideas. It is a voice that we shall gain much from by returning to more often.

Sovereignty and the Making of the Indian Republic

INDEPENDENCE RESOLUTION[1]

Friday, 13 December 1946

The Constituent Assembly of India met in the Constitution Hall, New Delhi, at Eleven of the Clock, Mr Chairman (The Hon'ble Dr Rajendra Prasad) in the Chair.

RESOLUTION REGARDING AIMS AND OBJECTS

MR CHAIRMAN: Pandit Jawaharlal Nehru will now move the Resolution which stands in his name.

THE HON'BLE PANDIT JAWAHARLAL NEHRU (United Provinces: General)[2]: Mr Chairman, this Constituent Assembly has not been in session for some days. It has done much formal business, but more is yet to be done. We have been cutting our way and clearing the ground on which we intend to erect the edifice of a constitution. It, however, seems proper that before we proceed further we should clearly understand where we are going and what we intend building. It is apparent that on such occasions details are unnecessary. In building, you will, no doubt, use each brick after mature consideration. Usually, when one desires to construct a building, one must have a plan for the structure that one wishes to erect and then collect the material required. For a long time we have been having various plans for a free India in our minds, but now, when we are beginning the actual work, I hope, you will be at one with me when I say, that we should present a clear picture of this plan to ourselves, to the people of India and to the world at large. The Resolution

---

[1] 13 December 1946, *Constituent Assembly Debates, Official Report*, vol. 1, pp. 56–65, 316–23.

[2] English translation of Hindustani speech begins.

that I am placing before you defines our aims, describes an outline of the plan and points the way which we are going to tread.

You all know that this Constituent Assembly is not what many of us wished it to be. It has come into being under particular conditions and the British Government has a hand in its birth. They have attached to it certain conditions. We accepted the State Paper, which may be called the foundation of this Assembly, after serious deliberations and we shall endeavour to work with its limits. But you must not ignore the source from which this Assembly derives its strength. Governments do not come into being by State Papers. Governments are, in fact the expression of the will of the people. We have met here today because of the strength of the people behind us and we shall go as far as the people—not of any party or group but the people as a whole—shall wish us to go. We should, therefore, always keep in mind the passions that lie in the hearts of the masses of the Indian people and try to fulfil them.

I am sorry there are so many absentees. Many members who have a right to come and attend the meeting are not here to-day. This, in one sense, increases our responsibility. We shall have to be careful that we do nothing which may cause uneasiness in others or goes against any principle. We do hope that those who have abstained, will soon join us in our deliberations, since this Constitution can only go as far as the strength behind it can push it. It has ever been and shall always be our ardent desire to see the people of India united together so that we may frame a constitution which will be acceptable to the masses of the Indian people. It is, at the same time, manifest that when a great country starts to advance, no party or group can stop it. This House, although it has met in the absence of some of its members, will continue functioning and try to carry out its work at all costs.

The Resolution that I am placing before you is in the nature of a pledge. It has been drafted after mature deliberation and efforts have been made to avoid controversy. A great country is sure to have a lot of controversial issues; but we have tried to avoid controversy as much as possible. The Resolution deals with fundamentals which are commonly held and have been accepted by the people. I do not think this Resolution contains anything which was outside the limitations laid down by the British Cabinet or anything which may be disagreeable to any Indian, no matter to what party or group he belongs. Unfortunately, our country is full of differences, but no one, except perhaps a few, would dispute the fundamentals which this Resolution lays down. The Resolution states that it is our firm and solemn resolve to have a sovereign Indian republic. We have not mentioned the word 'republic' till this time; but you will well understand that a free India can be nothing but a republic.

On this occasion, when the representatives of the Indian States are not present, I desire to make it clear how this Resolution will affect the Indian States. It has also been suggested, and the suggestion may take the form of an amendment laying down that since certains sections of the House are not present, the consideration of the Resolution may be postponed. In my opinion, such an amendment is not in keeping with the spirit of the times, because if we do not approve the first objective that we are placing before ourselves, before our country and before the world at large, our deliberations will become meaningless and lifeless, and the people will have no interest in our work. Our intention regarding the States must be clearly understood. We do desire that all sections of India should willingly participate in the future Indian Union but in what way and with what sort of government rests with them. The Resolution does not go into these details. It contains only the fundamentals. It imposes nothing on the States against their will. The point to be considered is how they will join us and what sort of administration they will have. I do not wish to express my personal opinion on the matter. Nevertheless I must say that no State can have an administration which goes against our fundamental principles or gives less freedom than obtaining in other parts of India. The Resolution does not concern itself with what form of government they will have or whether the present Rajas and Nawabs will continue or not. These things concern the people of the States. It is quite possible that the people may like to have their Rajas. The decision will rest with them. Our republic shall include the whole of India. If a part within it desires to have its own type of administration, it will be at liberty to have it.

I do not wish that anything should be added to or subtracted from the Resolution. It is my hope that this House will do nothing that may appear in Papers, so that, at no time, should people, who are concerned with these problems but who are not present here, be able to say that this House indulged in irregular talk.

I desire to make it clear that this Resolution does not go into details. It only seeks to show how we shall lead India to gain the objectives laid down in it. You will take into consideration its words and I hope you will accept them; but the main thing is the spirit behind it. Laws are made of words but this Resolution is something higher than the law. If you examine its words like lawyers you will produce only a lifeless thing. We are at present standing midway between two eras; the old order is fast changing, yielding place to the new. At such a juncture we have to give a live message to India and to the world at large. Later on we can frame our Constitution in whatever words we please. At present, we have to send out a message to show what we have resolved to attempt to do. As to what form or shape this Resolution, this declaration will ultimately take, we shall see later. But one thing is, however, certain: it is not a law; but is something that breathes life in human minds.

I hope the House will pass the Resolution which is of a special nature. It is an undertaking with ourselves and with the millions of our brothers and sisters who live in this great country, If it is passed, it will be a sort of pledge that we shall have to carry out. With this expectation and in this form, I place it before you. You have copies of it in Hindustani with you. I will therefore not take more of your time to read it one way, or, I will, however, read it in English and speak further on it in that language.[3]

I beg to move:

1. This Constituent Assembly declares its firm and solemn resolve to proclaim India as an Independent Sovereign Republic and to draw up for her future governance a Constitution;

2. Wherein the territories that now comprise British India, the territories that now form the Indian States, and such other parts of India as are outside British India and the States as well as such other territories as are willing to be constituted into the Independent Sovereign India, shall be a Union of them all; and

3. Wherein the said territories, whether with their present boundaries or with such others as may be determined by the Constituent Assembly and thereafter according to the Law of the Constitution, shall possess and retain the status of autonomous Units, together with residuary powers, and exercise all powers and functions of government and administration, save and except such powers and functions as are vested in or assigned to the Union, or as are inherent or implied in the Union or resulting therefrom; and

4. Wherein all power and authority of the Sovereign Independent India, its constituent parts and organs of government, are derived from the people; and

5. Wherein shall be guaranteed and secured to all the people of India justice, social, economic and political; equality of status, of opportunity, and before the law; freedom of thought, expression, belief, faith, worship, vocation, association and action, subject to law and public morality; and

6. Wherein adequate safeguards shall be provided for minorities, backward and tribal areas, and depressed and other backward classes; and

---

[3] English translation of Hindustani speech ends.

7. Whereby shall be maintained the integrity of the territory of the Republic and its sovereign rights on land, sea, and air according to justice and the law of civilized nations, and

8. This ancient land attains its rightful and honoured place in the world and makes its full and willing contribution to the promotion of world peace and the welfare of mankind.

Sir, this is the fifth day of this first session of the Constituent Assembly. Thus far we have laboured on certain provisional and procedural matters which are essential. We have a clear field to work upon; we have to prepare the ground and we have been doing that these few days. We have still much to do. We have to pass our Rules of Procedure and to appoint Committees and the like, before we can proceed to the real step, to the real work of this Constituent Assembly, that is, the high adventure of giving shape, in the printed and written word, to a Nation's dream and aspiration. But even now, at this stage, it is surely desirable that we should give some indication to ourselves, to those who look to this Assembly, to those millions in this country who are looking up to us and to the world at large, as to what we may do, what we seek to achieve, whither we are going. It is with this purpose that I have placed this Resolution before this House. It is a Resolution and yet, it is something much more than a resolution. It is a Declaration. It is a firm resolve. It is a pledge and an undertaking and it is for all of us I hope a dedication. And I wish this House, if I may say so respectfully, should consider this Resolution not in a spirit of narrow legal wording, but rather to look at the spirit behind the Resolution. Words are magic things often enough, but even the magic of words sometimes cannot convey the magic of the human spirit and of a Nation's passion. And so, I cannot say that this Resolution at all conveys the passion that lies in the hearts and the minds of the Indian people today. It seeks very feebly to tell the world of what we have thought or dreamt of so long, and what we now hope to achieve in the near future. It is in that spirit that I venture to place this Resolution before the House and it is in that I trust the House will receive it and ultimately pass it. And may I, Sir, also, with all respect, suggest to you and to the House that when the time comes for the passing of this Resolution let it be not done in the formal way by the raising of hands, but much more solemnly, by all of us standing up and thus taking this pledge anew.

The House knows that there are many absentees here and many members who have a right to come here, have not come. We regret that fact because we should have liked to associate with ourselves as many people, as many representatives from the different parts of India and different groups as possible. We have undertaken a tremendous task and we seek the co-operation of all people in that task; because the future of India that we have envisaged is not confined to any group or section or province or other, but it comprises all the four hundred million people of India, and it is with deep regret that we find some benches empty and some colleagues, who might have been here, absent. I do feel, I do hope that they will come and that this House, in its future stages, will have the benefit of the co-operation of all. Meanwhile, there is a duty cast upon us and that is to bear the absentees in mind, to remember always that we are here not to function for one party or one group, but always to think of India as a whole and always to think of the welfare of the four hundred millions that comprise India. We are all now, in our respective spheres, partymen, belonging to this or that group and presumably we shall continue to act in our respective parties. Nevertheless, the time comes when we have to rise above party and think of the Nation, think sometimes of even the world at large of which our Nation is a great part. And when I think of the work of this Constituent Assembly, it seems to me, the time has come when we should, so far as we are capable of it, rise above our ordinary selves and party disputes and think of the great problems before us in the widest and most tolerant and most effective manner so that, whatever we may produce, should be worthy of India as a whole and should be such that the world should recognize that we have functioned, as we should have functioned, in this high adventure.

There is another person who is absent here and who must be in the minds of many of us today—the great leader of our people, the father of our Nation (*applause*)—who has been the architect of this Assembly and all that has gone before it and possibly of much that will follow. He is not here because, in pursuit of his ideals, he is ceaselessly working in a far corner of India. But I have no doubt that his spirit hovers over this place and blesses our undertaking.

As I stand here, Sir, I feel the weight of all manner of things crowding around me. We are at the end of an era and possibly very soon we shall embark upon a new age; and my mind goes back to the great past of India, to the five thousand years of India's history, from the very dawn of that history which might be considered almost the dawn of human history, till today. All that past crowds around me and exhilarates me and, at the same time, somewhat oppresses me. Am I worthy of that past? When I think also of the future, the greater future I hope, standing on this sword's edge of the present between this mighty past and the mightier future, I tremble a little and feel overwhelmed by this mighty task. We have come here at a strange moment in India's history. I do not know but I do feel that there is some magic in this moment of transition from the old to the new, something of that magic which one sees when the night turns into day and even though the day may be a cloudy one, it is day after all, for when the clouds move away, we can see the sun later on. Because of all this I find a little difficulty in addressing this House and putting all my ideas before it and I feel also that in this long succession of thousands of years, I see the mighty figures that have come and gone and I see also the long succession of our comrades who have laboured for the freedom of India. And now we stand on the verge of this passing age, trying, labouring, to usher in the new. I am sure the House will feel the solemnity of this movement and will endeavour to treat this Resolution which it is my proud privilege to place before it in that solemn manner. I believe there are a large number of amendments coming before the House. I have not seen most of them. It is open to the House, to any member of this House, to move any amendment and it is for the House to accept it or reject it, but I would, with all respect, suggest that this is not moment for us to be technical and legal about small matters when we have big things to face, big things to say and big things to do, and therefore I would hope that the House would consider this Resolution in this big manner and not lose itself in wordy quarrels and squabbles.

I think also of the various Constituent Assemblies that have gone before and of what took place at the making of the great American nation when the fathers of that nation met and fashioned out a constitution which has stood the test of so many years, more than a century and a half, and of the great nation which has resulted, which has been built up on the basis of that Constitution. My mind goes back to that mighty revolution which took place also over 150 years ago and to that Constituent Assembly that met in that gracious and lovely city of Paris which has fought so many battles for freedom, to the difficulties that Constituent Assembly had and to how the King and other authorities came in its way, and still it continued. The House will remember that when these difficulties came and even the room for a meeting was denied to the then Constituent Assembly they betook themselves to an open tennis court and met there and took the oath, which is called the Oath of the Tennis Court, that they continued meeting in spite of Kings, in spite of the others, and did not disperse till they had finished the task they had undertaken. Well, I trust that it is in that solemn spirit that we too are meeting here and that we, too, whether we meet in this chamber or other chambers, or in the fields or in the market-place, will go on meeting and continue our work till we have finished it.

Then my mind goes back to a more recent revolution which gave rise to a new type of State, the revolution that took place in Russia and out of which has arisen the Union of the Soviet Socialist Republics, another mighty country which is playing a tremendous part in the world, not only a mighty country but for us in India, a neighbouring country.

So our mind goes back to these great examples and we seek to learn from their success and to avoid their failures. Perhaps we may not be able to avoid failures because some measure of failure is inherent in human effort. Nevertheless, we shall advance, I am certain, in spite of obstructions and difficulties, and achieve and realize the dream that we have dreamt so long. In this Resolution which the House knows, has been drafted with exceeding care, we have tried to avoid saying too much or too little. It is difficult to frame a resolution of this kind. If you say too little, it becomes just a pious resolution and nothing more. If you say too much, it encroaches on the functions of those who are going to draw up a constitution, that is, on the functions of this House. This Resolution is not a part of the constitution we are going to draw up, and it must not be looked at as such. This House has perfect freedom to draw up that Constitution and when others come into this House, they will have perfect freedom too to fashion that constitution. This Resolution therefore steers between these two extremes and lays down only certain fundamentals which I do believe, no group or party and hardly any individual in India can dispute. We say that it is our firm and solemn resolve to have an independent sovereign republic. India is bound to be sovereign, it is bound to be independent and it is bound to be republic. I will not go into the arguments about monarchy and the rest, but obviously we cannot produce monarchy in India out of nothing. It is not there. If it is to be an independent and sovereign State, we are not going to have an external monarchy and we cannot have a research for some local monarchies. It must inevitably be a republic. Now, some friends have raised the question: 'Why have you not put in the word "democratic" here.' Well, I told them that it is conceivable, of course, that a republic may not be democratic but the whole of our past is witness to this fact that we stand for democratic institutions. Obviously we are aiming at democracy and nothing less than a democracy. What form of democracy, what shape it might take is another matter? The democracies of the present day, many of them in Europe and elsewhere, have played a great part in the world's progress. Yet it may be doubtful if those democracies may not have to change their shape somewhat before long if they have to remain completely democratic. We are not going just to copy, I hope, a certain democratic procedure or an institution of a so-called democratic country. We may improve upon it. In any event, whatever system of Government we may establishment here must fit in with the temper of our people and be acceptable to them. We stand for democracy. It will be for this House to determine what shape to give to that democracy, the fullest democracy, I hope. The House will notice that in this Resolution, although we have not used the word 'democratic' because we thought it is obvious that the word 'republic' contains that word and we did not want to use unnecessary words and redundant words, we have done something much more than using the word. We have given the content of democracy in this Resolution and not only the content of democracy but the content, if I may say so, of economic democracy in this Resolution. Others might take objection to this Resolution on the ground that we have not said that it should be a Socialist State. Well, I stand for Socialism and, I hope, India will stand for Socialism and that India will go towards the constitution of a Socialist State and I do believe that the whole world will have to go that way. What form of Socialism again is another matter for your consideration. But the main thing is that in such a Resolution, if, in accordance with my own desire, I had put in, that we want a Socialist State, we would have put in something which may be agreeable to many and may not be agreeable to some and we wanted this Resolution not to be controversial in regard to such matters. Therefore we have laid down, not theoretical words and formulae, but rather the content of the thing we desire. This is important and I take it there can be no dispute about it. Some people have pointed out to me that our mentioning a republic may somewhat displease the Rulers of Indian States. It is possible that this may displease them. But I want to make it clear personally and the House knows that I do not believe in the monarchical system anywhere, and that in the world today monarchy is a fast disappearing institution. Nevertheless it is not a question of my personal belief in this matter. Our view in regard to these Indian States has been, for many years, first of all that the people of those States must share completely in the freedom to come. It is quite inconceivable to me that there should be different standards and degrees of freedom as between the people in the States and the people outside the States. In what manner the States will be parts of that Union, that is a matter for this House to consider with the representatives of the States. And I hope in all matters relating to the States, this House will deal with the real representatives of the States. We are perfectly willing, I take it, to deal in such matters as appertain to them, with the Rulers or their representatives also, but finally when we make a constitution for India, it must be through the representatives of the people of the States as with the rest of India, who are present here. (*Applause.*) In any event, we may lay down or agree that the measure of freedom must be the same in the States as elsewhere. It is a possibility and personally I should like a measure of uniformity too in regard to the apparatus and machinery of Government. Nevertheless, this is a point to be considered in co-operation and in consultation with the States. I do not wish, and I imagine this Constituent Assembly will not like, to impose anything on the States against their will. If the people of a particular State desire to have a certain form of administration, even though it might be monarchical, it is open to them to have it. The House will remember that even in the British Commonwealth of Nations, today, Eire is a Republic and yet in many ways it is a member of the British Commonwealth. So, it is a conceivable thing. What will happen, I do not know because that is partly for this House and partly for others to decide. There is no incongruity or impossibility about a certain definite form of administration in the States, provided there is complete freedom and responsible Government there and the people really are in charge. If monarchical figure-heads are approved by the people of the State, of a particular State, whether I like it or not, I certainly will not like to interfere. So I wish to make it clear that so far as this Resolution or Declaration is concerned, it does not interfere in any way with any future work that this Constituent Assembly may do, with any future negotiations that it may undertake. Only in one sense, if you like, it limits our work, if you call that a limitation, that is, we adhere to certain fundamental propositions which are laid down in the Declaration. Those fundamental propositions, I submit, are not controversial in any real sense of the word. Nobody challenges them in India and nobody ought to challenge them and if anybody does challenge, well, we accept that challenge and we hold our position. (*Applause.*)

Well, Sir, we are going to make a constitution for India and it is obvious that what we are going to do in India, is going to have a powerful effect on the rest of the world, not only because a new free independent nation comes out into the arena of the world, but because of the very fact that India is such a country that by virtue, not only of her large size and population, but of her enormous resources and her ability to exploit those resources, she can immediately play an important and a vital part in the world affairs. Even today, on the verge of freedom as we are today, India has begun to play an important part in world affairs. Therefore, it is right that the framers of our Constitution should always bear this larger international aspect in mind.

We approach the world in a friendly way. We want to make friends with all countries. We want to make friends in spite of the long history of conflict in the past, with England also. The House knows that recently I paid a visit to England. I was reluctant to go for reasons which the House knows well. But I went because of a personal request from the Prime Minister of Great Britain. I went and I met with courtesy everywhere. And yet at this psychological moment in India's history when we wanted, when we hungered for messages of cheer, friendship and co-operation from all over the world and more especially from England, because of the past contact and conflict between us, unfortunately, I came back without any message of cheer, but with a large measure of disappointment. I hope that the new difficulties that have arisen, as everyone knows, because of the recent statements made by the British Cabinet and by others in authority there, will not come in our way and that we shall yet succeed in going ahead with the co-operation of all of us here and those who have not come. It has been a blow to me, and it has hurt me that just at the moment when we are going to stride ahead, obstructions were placed in our way, new limitations were mentioned which had not been mentioned previously and new methods of procedure were suggested. I do not wish to challenge the *bona fides* of any person, but I wish to say that whatever the legal aspect of the thing might be, there are moments when law is a very feeble reed to rely upon, when we have to deal with a nation which is full of the passion for freedom. Most of us here during the past many years, for a generation or more, have often taken part in the struggle for India's freedom. We have gone through the valley of the shadow. We are used to it and if necessity arises, we shall go through it again. (*Hear, hear.*) Nevertheless, through all this long period, we have thought of the time when we shall have an opportunity, not merely to struggle, not merely to destroy, but to construct and create. And now, when it appeared that the time was coming for constructive effort in a free India to which we looked forward with joy, fresh difficulties are placed in our way at such a moment. It shows that, whatever force might be behind all this, people who are able and clever and very intelligent, somehow lack the imaginative daring which should accompany great offices. For, if you have to deal with any people, you have to understand them imaginatively; you should understand them emotionally; and of course, you have also to understand them intellectually. One of the unfortunate legacies of the past has been that there has been no imagination in the understanding of the Indian problem. People have often indulged in, or have presumed to give us advice, not realizing that India, as she is constituted today, wants no one's advice and no one's imposition upon her. The only way to influence India is through friendship and co-operation and goodwill. Any attempt at imposition, the slightest trace of patronage, is resented and will be resented. (*Applause.*) We have tried, I think honestly, in the last few months in spite of the difficulties that have faced us, to create an atmosphere of co-operation. We shall continue that endeavour. But I do very much fear that that atmosphere will be impaired if there is not sufficient and adequate response from others. Nevertheless, because we are bent on great tasks, I hope and trust, that we shall continue that endeavour and I do hope that if we continue, that we shall succeed. Where we have to deal with our own countrymen, we must continue that endeavour even though in our opinion some countrymen of ours take a wrong path. For, after all, we have to work together in this country and we have inevitably to co-operate, if not today, tomorrow or the day after. Therefore, we have to avoid in the present anything which might create a new difficulty in the creation of that future which we are working for. Therefore, so far as our own countrymen are concerned, we must try our utmost to gain their co-operation in the largest measure. But, co-operation cannot mean the giving up of the fundamental ideals on which we have stood and on which we should stand. It is not co-operation to surrender everything that has given meaning to our lives. Apart from that, as I said, we seek the co-operation of England even at this stage which is full of suspicion of each other. We feel that if that co-operation is denied, that will be injurious to India, certainly to some extent probably more so to England, and to some extent, to the world at large. We have just come out of the World War and people talk vaguely and rather wildly of new wars to come. At such a moment this New India is taking birth—renascent, vital, fearless. Perhaps it is a suitable moment for this new birth to take place out of this turmoil in the world. But we have to be clear-eyed at this moment—we, who have this heavy task of constitution-building. We have to think of this tremendous prospect of the present and the greater prospect of the future and not get lost in seeking small gains for this group or that. In this Constituent Assembly we are functioning on a world stage and the eyes of the world are upon us and the eyes of our entire past are upon us. Our past is witness to what we are doing here and though the future is still unborn, the future too somehow looks at us, I think, and so, I would beg of this House to consider this Resolution in this mighty prospect of our past, of the turmoil of the present and of the great and unborn future that is going to take place soon. Sir, I beg to move. (*Prolonged Cheers.*)

THE HON'BLE PANDIT JAWAHARLAL NEHRU (United Provinces: General)[4]: Mr President, six weeks have passed since I moved this Resolution. I had thought then that the Resolution would be discussed and passed within two or three days, but later the House decided to postpone it in order to give time to others to think over it. The decision to postpone an important Resolution like this was probably not to the liking of others like me, but I did not doubt that the decision was sound and proper. The anxiety and impatience in our hearts was not for the passage of the Resolution, which was simply a symbol, but to attain the high aims which were enshrined in it. It is also our intense desire to march on with all others and reach our goal with millions of Indians. Therefore, it was advisable to postpone the Resolution and to afford ample opportunity not only to this House but also to the country in general to think over it. The sense of all amendments and specially the amendment moved by Dr Jayakar was generally for postponement. I am grateful to Dr Jayakar for the withdrawal of his amendment and I thank the others also who have withdrawn their amendments. Many Members have spoken on the

---

[4] English translation of Hindustani speech begins.

Resolution. Their number may be thirty of forty or more. Almost all of them have supported it without any criticism. Some of them, of course, have drawn our attention to some particular matters. I am of opinion that if a plebiscite of the crores of people of India is taken, all of them will be found to stand for the Resolution; though there might be some who would lay more or less emphasis on some particular aspect of the Resolution. The Resolution was meant to clothe in words the desire of crores of Indians and it was very carefully worded so as to avoid strongly controversial issues. There is no need to say a great deal about this but with your permission, I would like to draw your attention to some points. One of the reasons for the postponement of the Resolution was that we wished that our brothers who had not come here, should be in a position to decide to come in. They have had a full month to consider the matter but I regret that they have not yet decided to come. However as I have already said at the outset, we will keep the door open for them and they will be welcomed up to the last moment, and we will give them and others, who have a right to come in, every opportunity for coming in. But it is clear that while the door remains open, our work cannot be held up. It has, therefore, become indispensable for us to proceed further and carry the Resolution to its logical conclusion. I have hopes that even at this stage those, who are absent, would decide to come in.

Some of us, even though they are in agreement with this Resolution, were in favour of postponing some other business too so that the absentees might not find any obstacle in their way to come in. I am in sympathy with this suggestion but in spite of this, I am at a loss to understand how this suggestion could be put forward. That is a question of waiting; not that of postponing the Resolution. We have waited for six long weeks. This is no matter of weeks; ages have slipped by while we have been waiting. How long are we to wait now? Many of us who waited have since passed away and many are nearing the end of their lives. We have waited enough and now we cannot wait any longer. We are to further the work of the Assembly, speed up the pace and finish our work soon. You should bear in mind that this Assembly is not only to pass resolutions, I may point out that the Constitution, which we frame, is not an end by itself, but it would be only the basis for further work.

The first task of this Assembly is to free India through a new constitution to feed the starving people and clothe the naked masses and to give every Indian fullest opportunity to develop himself according to his capacity. This is certainly a great task. Look at India today. We are sitting here and there is despair in many places, and unrest in many cities. The atmosphere is surcharged with these quarrels and feuds which are called communal disturbances, and unfortunately we sometimes cannot avoid them. But at present the greatest and most important question in

India is how to solve the problem of the poor and the starving. Wherever we turn, we are confronted with this problem. If we cannot solve this problem soon, all our paper constitutions will become useless and purposeless. Keeping this aspect in view, who could suggest to us to postpone and wait?

A point has been raised from one side that some ideas contained in the Resolution do not commend themselves to the Rulers of the States, because they conflict with the powers of the Princes. A suggestion has also been made to postpone the decision about the States in the absence of their representatives. It is a fact they are not present here but if we wait for them it is not possible for us to finish the work even at the end of the Constituent Assembly according to the plan. This is impossible. Our scheme was not that they should come in at the end. We invited them to come in at the beginning. If they come, they are welcome. Nobody is going to place any obstacles. If there is any hesitation, it is on their part only. A month ago you formed a Committee to get into touch with their representatives. We were always anxious to discuss with them although we did not get any opportunity for it. That is no fault of ours. We did not ask for time. We want to finish our work as early as possible. I am informed they complain of the following words contained in the Resolution.

'Sovereignty belongs to the people and rests with the people.'

That is to say, the final decision should rest with the people of the States. They object to this. It is certainly a surprising objection. It may not be very surprising if those people who have lived in an atmosphere of medievalism do not give up their cherished illusions, but in the modern age how can a man believe for a moment in the divine and despotic rights of a human being? I fail to understand how any Indian, whether he belongs to a State or to any other part of the country, could dare utter such things. It is scandalous now to put forward an idea which originated in the world hundreds of years ago and was buried deep in the earth long before our present age. However, I would respectfully tell them to desist from saying such things. They are putting a wrong thing before the world and by doing so they are lowering their own status and weakening their own position. At least this Assembly is not prepared to damage its very foundation and, if it does so, it will shake the very basis of our whole constitution.

We claim in this Resolution to frame a free and democratic Indian Republic. A question may be asked what relation will that Republic bear to other countries of the world? What would be its relations with England, the British Commonwealth and other countries? This Resolution means that we are completely free and are not included in any group except the Union of Nations which is now being formed in the world. The truth is that the world has totally changed. The meanings of words too are changing. Today any man who can think a little, will come to the conclusion that the only way to remove the doubts and dangers from the world, is to unite all the nations and ask them to work together and help each other. The organization of the United Nations is not free from big gaps and fissures. Thousands of difficulties lie ahead and a great deal of suspicion exists between countries. I have already said that we are not thinking in terms of isolating ourselves from the world. We will work in complete co-operation with other countries. It is not an easy thing to work in co-operation with England or the British Commonwealth, and yet we are prepared to do so. We will forget our old quarrels, strive to achieve our complete independence and stretch our hands of friendship to other countries, but that friendship shall in no case mar or weaken our freedom.

This is not a resolution of war; it is simply to put our legitimate rights before the world; and in doing so if we are challenged, we will not hesitate in accepting that challenge. But after all, this is resolution of goodwill and compromise, among the people of India, whatever their community or religion and with the different countries of the world including England and the British Commonwealth of Nations. The Resolution claims to be on friendly terms with all and it has been put before you with that motive and intention. I hope you will accept it.

A friend has suggested that it would be advisable to move the Resolution just on the eve of the Independence Day which is due to come after four days only. But I will ask him if it is proper to delay a proper thing even for a moment? Not a moment's postponement is advisable and we should finish our work as soon as possible.

This Resolution which has been put before you is in a new form and in a new shape, but I would like to tell you that it has a long trail of resolutions, pledges and declarations including the world-famed resolutions of 'Independence' and 'Quit India' behind it. It is high time to fulfil our pledges which we made from time to time. How are these pledges to be fulfilled? The right answer lies with you and I hope you will not only accept the Resolution but also fulfil it as you fulfil a solemn pledge.

One thing more I would like to tell you. We have been confronted and will again be confronted with various questions. Persons of various groups, communities, and interests would look at it from different points of view, and diverse questions and problems would be raised by them, but we should all bear in mind that we should not, on the eve of Independence, allow ourselves to be carried away by petty matters. If India goes down, all will go down; if India thrives, all will thrive and if India lives, all will live including the parties, communities and groups.

With your permission I would like to say something in English also.[5]

Mr President, it was my proud privilege, Sir, six weeks ago, to move this Resolution before this Hon'ble House. I felt the weight and solemnity of that occasion. It was not a mere form of words that I placed before the House, carefully chosen as those words were. But those words and the Resolution represented something far more; they represented the depth of our being; they represented the agony and hopes of the nation coming at last to fruition. As I stood here on that occasion I felt the past crowding round me, and I felt also the future taking shape. We stood on the razor's edge of the present, and as I was speaking, I was addressing not only this Hon'ble House, but the millions of Indians, who were vastly interested in our work. And because I felt that we were coming to the end of an age, I had a sense of our forbears watching this undertaking of ours and possibly blessing it, if we moved aright; and the future, of which we became trustees, became almost a living thing, taking shape and moving before our eyes. It was a great responsibility to be trustees of the future, and is was some responsibility also to be inheritors of the great past of ours. And between that great past and the great future which we envisage, we stood on the edge of the present and the weight of that occasion, I have no doubt, impressed itself upon this Hon'ble House.

So, I placed this Resolution before the House, and I had hoped that it could be passed in a day or two and we could start our other work immediately. But after a long debate this House decided to postpone further consideration of this Resolution. May I confess that I was a little disappointed because I was impatient that we should go forward? I felt that we were not true to the pledges that we had taken by lingering on the road. It was a bad beginning that we should postpone even such an important Resolution about objectives. Would that imply that our future work would go along slowly and be postponed from time to time? Nevertheless, I have no doubt, that the decision this House took in its wisdom in postponing this Resolution, was a right decision, because we have always balanced two factors, one, the urgent necessity in reaching our goal, and the other, that we should reach it in proper time and with as great a unanimity as possible. It was right, therefore, if I may say with all respect, that this House decided to adjourn consideration of this Motion and thus not only demonstrated before the world our earnest desire to have all those people here who have not so far come in here, but also to assure the country and every one else, how anxious we were to have the co-operation of all. Since then six weeks have passed, and during these weeks there

---

[5] English translation of Hindustani speech ends.

has been plenty of opportunity for those, who wanted to come, to come. Unfortunately, they have not yet decided to come and they still hover in this state of indecision. I regret that, and all I can say is this, that we shall welcome them at any future time when they may wish to come. But it should be made clear without any possibility of misunderstanding that no work will be held up in future, whether any one comes or not. (*Cheers.*) There has been waiting enough. Not only waiting six weeks, but many in this country have waited for years and years, and the country has waited for some generations now. How long are we to wait? And if we, some of us, who are more prosperous can afford to wait, what about the waiting of the hungry and the starving? This Resolution will not feed the hungry or the starving, but it brings a promise of many things—it brings the promise of freedom, it brings the promise of food and opportunity for all. Therefore, the sooner we set about it the better. So we waited for six weeks, and during these six weeks the country thought about it, pondered over it, and other countries also, and other people who are interested have thought about it. Now we have come back here to take up the further consideration of this Resolution. We have had a long debate and we stand on the verge of passing it. I am grateful to Dr Jayakar and Mr Sahaya for having withdrawn their amendments. Dr Jayakar's purpose was served by the postponing of this Resolution, and it appears now that there is no one in this House who does not accept fully this Resolution as it is. It may be, some would like it to be slightly differently worded or the emphasis placed more on this part or on that part. But taking it as a whole, it is a resolution which has already received the full assent of this House, and there is little doubt that it has received the full assent of the country. (*Cheers.*)

There have been some criticisms of it, notably, from some of the Princes. Their first criticism has been that such a Resolution should not be passed in the absence of the representatives of the States. In part I agree with that criticism, that is to say, I should have liked all the States being properly represented here, the whole of India—every part of India being properly represented here—when we pass this Resolution. But if they are not here it is not our fault. It is largely the fault of the Scheme under which we are functioning, and we have this choice before us. Are we to postpone our functioning because some people cannot be here? That would be a dreadful thing if we stopped not only this Resolution, but possibly so much else, because representatives of the States are not here. So far as we are concerned, they can come in at the earliest possible moment, we will welcome them if they send proper representatives of the States. So far as we are concerned, even during the last six weeks or a month, we have made some effort to get into touch with the Committee representing the States Rulers to find a way for their proper representation here. It is not our fault that there has been any delay. We are anxious to get every one in, whether it is the representatives of the Muslim League or the States or any one else. We shall continue to persevere in this endeavour so that this House may be as fully representative of the country as it is possible to be. So, we cannot postpone this Resolution or anything else because some people are not here.

Another point has been raised: the idea of the sovereignty of the people, which is enshrined in this Resolution, does not commend itself to certain rulers of Indian States. That is a surprising objection and, if I may say so, if that objection is raised in all seriousness by anybody, be he a Ruler or a Minister, it is enough to condemn the Indian States system of every Ruler or Minister that exists in India. It is a scandalous thing for any man to say, however highly placed he may be, that he is here by special divine dispensation to rule over human beings today. That is a thing which is an intolerable presumption on any man's part, and it is a thing which this House will never allow and will repudiate if it is put before it. We have heard a lot about this Divine Right of Kings, read a lot about it in past histories and we had thought that we had heard the last of it and that it had been put an end to and buried deep down into the earth long ages ago. If any individual in India or elsewhere raises it today, he would be doing so without any relation to the present in India. So, I would suggest to such persons in all seriousness that, if they want to be respected or considered with any measure of friendliness, no such idea should be even hinted at, much less said. On this there is going to be no compromise. (*Hear, hear.*)

But, as I made plain on the previous occasion when I spoke, this Resolution makes it clear that we are not interfering in the internal affairs of the States. I even said that we are not interfering with the system of monarchy in the States, if the people of the States so want it. I gave the example of the Irish Republic in the British Commonwealth and it is conceivable to me that within the Indian Republic, there might be monarchies if the people so desire. That is entirely for them to determine. This Resolution and, presumably, the Constitution, that we make, will not interfere with that matter. Inevitably it will be necessary to bring about uniformity in the freedom of the various parts of India, because it is inconceivable to me that certain parts of India should have democratic freedom and certain others should be denied it. That cannot be. That will give rise to trouble, just as in the wide world today there is trouble because some countries are free and some are not. Much more trouble will there be if there is freedom in some parts of India and lack of freedom in other parts of India.

But we are not laying down in this Resolution any strict system in regard to the governance of the Indian States. All that we say is this that they, or such of them, as are big enough to form unions or group themselves into small unions, will be autonomous units with a very large measure of freedom to do as they choose, subject no doubt to certain central functions in which they will co-operate with the Centre, in which they will be represented in the Centre and in which the Centre will have control. So that, in a sense, this Resolution does not interfere with the inner working of those Units. They will be autonomous and, as I have said, if those Units choose to have some kind of constitutional monarchy at their head, they would be welcome to do so. For my part, I am for a Republic in India as anywhere else. But whatever my views may be on that subject, it is not my desire to impose my will on others; whatever the views of this House may be on this subject, I imagine that it is not the desire of this House to impose its will in these matters.

So, the objection of the Ruler of an Indian State to this Resolution becomes an objection, in theory, to the theoretical implications and the practical implications of the doctrine of sovereignty of the people. To nothing else does any one object. That is an objection which cannot stand for an instant. We claim in this Resolution to frame a constitution for a Sovereign, Independent, Indian Republic—necessarily Republic. What else can we have in India? Whatever the States may have or may not have, it is impossible and inconceivable and undesirable to think in any other terms but in terms of the Republic in India.

Now, what relation will that Republic bear to the other countries of the world, to England and to the British Commonwealth and the rest? For a long time past we have taken a pledge on Independence Day that India must sever her connection with Great Britain, because that connection had become an emblem of British domination. At no time have we thought in terms of isolating ourselves in this part of the world from other countries or of being hostile to countries which have dominated over us. On the eve of this great occasion, when we stand on the threshold of freedom, we do not wish to carry a trail of hostility with us against any other country. We want to be friendly to all. We want to be friendly with the British people and the British Commonwealth of Nations.

But what I would like this House to consider is this: When these words and these labels are fast changing their meaning and in the world today there is no isolation, you cannot live apart from the others. You must co-operate or you must fight. There is no middle way. We wish for peace. We do not want to fight any nation if we can help it. The only possible real objective that we, in common with other nations, can have is the objective of co-operating in building up some kind of world structure, call it 'One World', call it what you like. The beginnings of this world structure have been laid down in the United Nations Organization. It is feeble yet; it has many defects; nevertheless, it is the beginning of the world structure. And India has pledged herself to co-operate in that work.

Now, if we think of that structure and our co-operation with other countries in achieving it, where does the question come of our being tied up with this Group of Nations or that Group? Indeed, the more groups and blocks are formed, the weaker will that great structure become.

Therefore, in order to strengthen that big structure, it is desirable for all countries not to insist, not to lay stress on separate groups and separate blocks. I know that there are such separate groups and blocks today and because they exist today, there is hostility between them, and there is even talk of war among them. I do not know what the future will bring to us, whether peace or war. We stand on the edge of a precipice and there are various forces which pull us on one side in favour of co-operation and peace, and on the other, push us towards the precipice of war and disintegration. I am not prophet enough to know what will happen, but I do know that those who desire peace must deprecate separate blocks which necessarily become hostile to other blocks. Therefore India, in so far as it has a foreign policy, has declared that it wants to remain independent and free of all these blocks and that it wants to co-operate on equal terms with all countries. It is a difficult position because, when people are full of fear of each other, any person who tries to be neutral is suspected of sympathy with the other party. We can see that in India and we can see that in the wider sphere of world politics. Recently an American statesman criticized India in words which show how lacking in knowledge and understanding even the statesmen of America are. Because we follow our own policy, this group of nations thinks that we are siding with the other and that group of nations thinks that we are siding with this. That is bound to happen. If we seek to be a free, independent, democratic republic, it is not to dissociate ourselves from other countries, but rather as a free nation to co-operate in the fullest measure with other countries for peace and freedom, to co-operate with Britain, with the British Commonwealth of Nations, with the United States of America, with the Soviet Union, and with all other countries, big and small. But real co-operation would only come between us and these other nations when we know that we are free to co-operate and are not imposed upon and forced to co-operate. So long as there is the slightest trace of compulsion, there can be no co-operation.

Therefore, I commend this Resolution to the House and I commend this Resolution, if I may say so, not only to this House but to the world at large so that it can be perfectly clear that it is a gesture of friendship to all, and, that behind it there lies no hostility. We have suffered enough in the past. We have struggled sufficiently, we may have to struggle again, but under the leadership of a very great personality we have sought always to think in terms of friendship and goodwill towards others, even those who opposed us. How far we have succeeded, we do not know, because we are weak human beings. Nevertheless, the impress of that message has found a place in the hearts of millions of people of this country, and even when we err and go astray, we cannot forget it. Some of us may be little men, some may be big, but whether we are small men or big, for the moment we represent a great cause and therefore something of the shadow of greatness falls upon us. Today in this Assembly we represent a mighty cause and this Resolution that I have placed before you gives some semblance of that cause. We shall pass this Resolution, and I hope that this Resolution will lead us to a constitution on the lines suggested by this Resolution. I trust that the Constitution itself will lead us to the real freedom that we have clamoured for and that real freedom in turn will bring food to our starving people, clothing for them, housing for them and all manner of opportunities of progress, that it will lead also to the freedom of the other countries of Asia, because in a sense, however unworthy we have become—let us recognize it—the leaders of the freedom movement of Asia, and whatever we do, we should think of ourselves in these larger terms. When some petty matter divides us and we have difficulties and conflicts amongst ourselves over these small matters, let us remember not only this Resolution but this great responsibility that we shoulder, the responsibility of the freedom of 400 million people of India, the responsibility of the leadership of a large part of Asia, the responsibility of being some kind of guide to vast numbers of people all over the world. It is a tremendous responsibility. If we remember it, perhaps we may not bicker so much over this seat or that post, over some small gain for this group or that. The one thing that should be obvious to all of us is this that there is no group in India, no party, no religious community, which can prosper if India does not prosper. If India goes down, we go down, all of us, whether we have a few seats more or less, whether we get a slight advantage or we do not. But if it is well with India, if India lives as a vital free country, then it is well with all of us to whatever community or religion we might belong.

We shall frame the Constitution, and I hope it will be a good constitution, but does anyone in this House imagine that, when a free India emerges, it will be bound down by anything that even this House might lay down for it? A free India will see the bursting forth of the energy of a mighty nation. What it will do and what it will not, I do not know, I do know that it will not consent to be bound down by anything. Some people imagine, that what we do now, may not be touched for 10 years or 20 years, if we do not do it today, we will not be able to do it later. That seems to me a complete misapprehension. I am not placing before the House what I want done and what I do not want done, but I should like the House to consider that we are on the eve of revolutionary changes, revolutionary in every sense of the word, because when the spirit of a nation breaks its bonds, it functions in peculiar ways and it should function in strange ways. It may be that the Constitution this House may frame may not satisfy that free India. This House cannot bind down the next generation, or the people who will dully succeed us in this task. Therefore, let us not trouble ourselves too much about the petty details of what we do, those details will not survive for long, if they are achieved in conflict. What we achieve in unanimity, what we achieve by co-operation is likely to survive. What we gain here and there by conflict and by overbearing manners and by threats will not survive long. It will only leave a trail of bad blood. And so now I commend this Resolution to the House and may I read the last para of this Resolution? But one word more, Sir, before I read it. India is a great country, great in her resources, great in her man-power, great in her potential, in every way. I have little doubt that a Free India on every plane will play a big part on the world stage, even on the narrowest plane of material power, and I should like India to play a great part in that plane. Nevertheless today there is a conflict in the world between forces in different planes. We hear a lot about the atom bomb and the various kinds of energy that it represents and in essence today there is a conflict in the world between two things, the atom bomb and what it represents and the spirit of humanity. I hope that while India will no doubt play a great part in all the material spheres, she will always lay stress on the spirit of humanity, and I have no doubt in my mind, that ultimately in this conflict, that is confronting the world, the human spirit will prevail over the atom bomb. May this Resolution bear fruit and may the time come when in the words of the Resolution, this ancient land attains its rightful and honoured place in the world and makes its full and willing contribution to the promotion of world peace and the welfare of mankind.

MR PRESIDENT: The time has now arrived when you should give your solemn votes on this Resolution. Remembering the solemnity of the occasion and the greatness of the pledge and the promise which this Resolution contains, I hope every Member will stand up in his place when giving his vote in favour of it.

FRAMING OF THE CONSTITUTION[1]

Mr Vice-President, Sir, we are on the last lap of our long journey. Nearly two years ago, we met in this hall and on that solemn occasion it was my high privilege to move a Resolution which has come to be known as the Objectives Resolution. That is rather a prosaic description of that Resolution because it embodied something more than mere objectives, although objectives are big things in the life of a nation. It tried to embody, in so far as it is possible in cold print to embody, the spirit that lay behind the Indian people at the time. It is difficult to maintain the spirit of a nation or a people at a high level all the time and I do not know if we have succeeded in doing that. Nevertheless I hope that it is in that spirit that we have to approach the framing of the Constitution and it is in that spirit that we shall consider it in detail, always using that Objectives Resolution as the yard measure with which to test every clause and phrase in this Constitution. It may be, of course, that we can improve even on that Resolution; if so, certainly we should do it, but I think that Resolution in some of its clauses laid down the fundamental and basic content of what our Constitution should be. The Constitution is after all some kind of legal body given to the ways of Governments and the life of a people. A Constitution if it is out of touch with the people's life, aims and aspirations, becomes rather empty: if it falls behind those aims, it drags the people down. It should be something ahead to keep people's eyes and minds up to a certain high mark. I think that the Objectives Resolution did that. Inevitably since then in the course of numerous discussions, passions were roused about what I would beg to say are relatively unimportant matters in this larger context of giving shape to a nation's aspirations

[1] 8 November 1948, *Constituent Assembly Debates: Official Report*, vol. 7, pp. 317–21.

and will. Not that they were unimportant, because each thing in a nation's life is important, but still there is a question of priority, there is a question of relative importance, there is a question also of what comes first and what comes second. After all there may be many truths, but it is important to know what is the first truth. It is important to know what in a particular context of events is the first thing to be done, to be thought of and to be put down, and it is the test of a nation and a people to be able to distinguish between the first things and the second things. If we put the second things first, then inevitably the first and the most important things suffer a certain eclipse.

Now I have ventured with your permission, Sir, to take part in this initial debate on this Draft Constitution, but it is not my intention to deal with any particular part of it, either in commendation of it or in criticism, because a great deal of that kind has already been said and will no doubt be said. But in view of that perhaps I could make some useful contribution to this debate by drawing attention to certain fundamental factors again. I had thought that I could do this even more because in recent days and weeks, I have been beyond the shores of India, have visited foreign lands, met eminent people and statesmen of other countries and had the advantage of looking at this beloved country of ours from a distance. That is some advantage. It is true that those who look from a distance do not see many things that exist in this country. But it is equally true that those who live in this country and are surrounded all the time with our numerous difficulties and problems sometimes may fail to see the picture as a whole. We have to do both; to see our problems in their intricate detail in order to understand them and also to see them in some perspective so that we may have that picture as a whole before our eyes.

Now this becomes even more important during a period of swift transition such as we have gone through. We who have lived through this period of transition with all its triumphs and glories and sorrows and bitterness are affected by all these changes; we are changing ourselves; we do not notice ourselves changing or the country changing so much and it is a little helpful to be out of this turmoil for a while and to look at it from a distance and to look at it also to some extent with the eyes of other people. I have had that opportunity given to me. I am glad of that opportunity, because for the moment I was rid of the tremendous burden of responsibility which all of us carried and which in a measure some of us who have to shoulder the burden of Government have to carry more. For a moment I was rid of those immediate responsibilities and with a mind somewhat free, I could look at that picture and I saw from that distance the rising Star of India far above the horizon (*hear, hear*) and casting its soothing light, in spite of all that has happened, over many countries of the world, who looked up to it with hope, who considered that out of this new Free India would come various forces which would help Asia, which would help the world somewhat to right itself, which would co-operate with other similar forces elsewhere, because the world is in a bad way, because this great continent of Asia and Europe and the rest of the world are in a bad way and are faced with problems which might almost appear to be insurmountable. And sometimes one has the feeling as if we were all actors in some terrible Greek tragedy which was moving on to its inevitable climax of disaster. Yet when I looked at this picture again from afar and from here, I had a feeling of hope and optimism not merely because of India, but because also of other things that I saw that the tragedy which seemed inevitable was not necessarily inevitable, that there were many other forces at work, that there were innumerable men and women of goodwill in the world who wanted to avoid this disaster and tragedy, and there was certainly a possibility that they will succeed in avoiding it.

But to come back to India, we have, ever since I moved this Objectives Resolution before this House—a year and eleven months ago, almost exactly—passed through strange transitions and changes. We function here far more independently than we did at that time. We function as a sovereign independent nation, but we have also gone through a great deal of sorrow and bitter grief during this period and all of us have been powerfully affected by it. The country for which we were going to frame this Constitution was partitioned and split into two. And what happened afterwards is fresh in our minds and will remain fresh with all its horrors for a very long time to come. All that has happened, and yet, in spite of all this, India has grown in strength and in freedom, and undoubtedly this growth of India, this emergence of India as a free country, is one of the significant facts of this generation, significant for us and for the vast numbers of our brothers and sisters who live in this country, significant for Asia, and significant for the world, and the world is beginning to realize—chiefly I think and I am glad to find this—that India's role in Asia and the world will be a beneficent role; sometimes it may be with a measure of apprehension, because India may play some part which some people, some countries, with other interests may not particularly like. All that is happening, but the main thing is this great significant factor that India after a long period of being dominated over has emerged as a free sovereign democratic independent country, and that is a fact which changes and is changing history. How far it would change history will depend upon us, this House in the present and other Houses like this coming in the future who represent the organized will of the Indian people.

That is a tremendous responsibility. Freedom brings responsibility; of course there is no such thing as freedom without responsibility. Irresponsibility itself means lack of freedom. Therefore we have to be conscious of this tremendous burden of responsibility which freedom has brought: the discipline of freedom and the organized way of working freedom. But, there is something even more than that. The freedom that has come to India by virtue of many things, history, tradition, resources, our geographical position, our great potential and all that, inevitably leads India to play an important part in world affairs. It is not a question of our choosing this or that; it is an inevitable consequence of what India is and what a free India must be. And, because we have to play that inevitable part in world affairs, that brings another and a greater responsibility. Sometimes, with all my hope and optimism and confidence in my nation, I rather quake at the great responsibilities that are being thrust upon us, and which we cannot escape. If we get tied up in our narrow controversies, we may forget it. Whether we forget it or not, that responsibility is there. If we forget it, we fail in that measure. Therefore, I would beg of this House to consider these great responsibilities that have been thrust upon India, and because we represent India in this as in many other spheres, on us in this House, and to work together in the framing of the Constitution or otherwise, always keeping that in view, because the eyes of the world are upon us and the hopes and aspirations of a great part of the world are also upon us. We dare not be little; if we do so, we do an ill-service to this country of ours and to those hopes and aspirations that surround us from other countries. It is in this way that I would like this House to consider this Constitution: first of all to keep the Objectives Resolution before us and to see how far we are going to act up to it, how far we are going to build up, as we said in that Resolution, 'an Independent Sovereign Republic, wherein all power and authority of the Sovereign Independent India, its constituent parts and organs of Government, are derived from the people, and wherein shall be guaranteed and secured to all of the people of India justice, social, economic and political; equality of status, of opportunity, and before the law; freedom of thought and expression, belief, faith, worship, vocation, association and action, subject to law and public morality; and this ancient land can attain its rightful and honoured place in the world and make its full and willing contribution to the promotion of world peace and the welfare of mankind.'

I read that last clause in particular because that brings to our mind India's duty to the world. I should like this House when it considers the various controversies—there are bound to be controversies and there should be controversies because we are a living and vital nation, and it is right that people should think differently and it is also right that, thinking differently when they come to decisions, they should act unitedly in furtherance of those decisions. There are various problems, some very important problems, on which there is a very little controversy and we pass them—they are of the greatest importance—with a certain unanimity. There are other problems, important no doubt, possibly of a lesser importance, on which we spend a great deal of time and energy and passion also, and do not arrive at agreements in that spirit with which we should arrive at agreements. In the country today, reference has been made—I will mention one or two matters—to linguistic provinces and to the question of language in this Assembly and for the country. I do not propose to say much about these questions, except to say that it seems to me and it has long seemed to me inevitable that in India some kind of re-organization should take place of provinces, etc., to fit in more with the cultural, geographical and economic condition of the people and with their desires. We have long been committed to this. I do not think it is good enough just to say linguistic provinces; that is a major factor to be considered, no doubt. But there are more important factors to be considered, and you have therefore to consider the whole picture before you proceed to break up what we have got and re-fashion it into something new. What I would like to place before the House, important from the point of view of our future life and governance at this question is, I would not have thought that this was a question of that primary importance, which must be settled here and now today. It is eminently a question which should be settled in an atmosphere of good-will and calm and on a rather scholarly discussion of the various factors of the case. I find, unfortunately, it has raised a considerable degree of heat and passion and when heat and passion are there, the mind is clouded. Therefore, I would beg of this House to take these matters into consideration when it thinks fit, and to treat it as a thing which should be settled not in a hurry when passions are roused, but at a suitable moment when the time is ripe for it.

The same argument, if I may say so, applies to this question of language. Now, it is an obvious thing and a vital thing that any country, much more so a free and independent country, must function in its own language. Unfortunately, the mere fact that I am speaking to this House in a foreign language and so many of our colleagues here have to address the House in foreign language itself shows that something is lacking. It is lacking; let us recognize it; we shall get rid of that lacuna undoubtedly. But, if in trying to press for a change, an immediate change, we get wrapped up in numerous controversies and possibly even delay the whole Constitution, I submit to this House it is not a very wise step to take. Language is and has been a vital factor in an individual's and a nation's life and because it is vital, we have to give it every thought and consideration. Because it is vital, it is also an urgent matter; and because it is vital, it is also a matter in which urgency may ill-serve our purpose. There is a slight contradiction. Because, if we proceed in an urgent matter to impose something, may be by a majority, on an unwilling minority in parts of the country or even in this House, we do not really succeed in what we have started to achieve. Powerful forces are at work in the country which will inevitably lead to the substitution of the English language by an Indian language or Indian languages in so far as the different parts of the country are concerned; but there will always be one all-India language. Powerful forces are also working at the formation of that all-India language. Language ultimately grows from the people; it is seldom that it can be imposed. Any attempt to impose a particular form of language on an unwilling people has usually met with the strongest opposition and has actually resulted in something the very reverse of what the promoters thought. I would beg this House to consider the fact and to realize, if it agrees with me, that the surest way of developing a natural all-India language is not so much to pass resolutions and laws on the subject as to work to that end in other ways. For my part I have a certain conception of what an all-India language should be. Other people's conception may not be quite the same as mine. I cannot impose my conception on this House or on the country just as any other person will not be able to impose his or her conception unless the country accepts it. But I would much rather avoid trying to impose my or anyone else's conception but to work to that end in co-operation and amity and see how, after we have settled these major things about the Constitution, etc., after we have attained an even greater measure of stability, we can take up each one of these separate questions and dispose of them in a much better atmosphere.

The House will remember that when I brought that motion of the Objectives Resolution before this House, I referred to the fact that we were asking for or rather we were laying down that our Constitution should be framed for an Independent Sovereign Republic. I stated at that time and I have stated subsequently this business of our being a Republic is entirely a matter for us to determine of course. It has nothing or little to do with what relations we should have with other countries, notably the United Kingdom or the Commonwealth that used to be called the British Commonwealth of Nations. That was a question which had to be determined again by this House and by none else, independently of what our Constitution was going to be. I want to inform the House that in recent weeks when I was in the United Kingdom, whenever this subject or any allied subject came up for a private discussion—there was no public discussion or decision because the Commonwealth Conference which I attended did not consider it at all in its sessions—but inevitably there were private discussions, because it is a matter of high moment not only for us but for other countries as to what, if any, relation we should have, what contacts, what links we should bear with these other countries. Therefore the matter came up in private discussion. Inevitably the first thing that I had to say, in all these discussions was this that I could not as an individual—even though I had been honoured by this high office of Prime Ministership—I could not in any way or in any sense commit the country—even the Government which I have the honour to represent could not finally decide this matter. This was essentially a matter which the Constituent Assembly of India alone can decide. That I made perfectly clear. Having made that clear, I further pointed out this Objectives Resolution of this Constituent Assembly, I said it is open of course to the Constituent Assembly to vary that Resolution as it can vary anything else because it is Sovereign in this and other matters. Nevertheless that was the direction which the Constituent Assembly gave to itself and to its Drafting Committee for Constitution, and so long as it remains as it is, and I added that so far as I knew it would remain as it is (*cheers*)— that Constitution would be in terms of that Objectives Resolution. Having made that clear, Sir, I said that it has often been said on our behalf that we desire to be associated in friendly relationship with other countries, with the United Kingdom and the Commonwealth. How in this context it can be done or it should be done is a matter for careful consideration and ultimate decision naturally on our part or by the Constituent Assembly, on their part by their respective Governments or peoples. That is all I wish to say about this matter at this stage because possibly in the course of this session this matter no doubt will come up before the House in more concrete form. But in whatever form it may come up whether now or later, the point I should like to stress is this, that it is something apart from and in a sense independent of the Constitution that we are considering. We pass that Constitution for an Independent Sovereign Democratic India, for a Republic as we choose, and the second question is to be considered separately at whatever time it suits this House. It does not in any sense fetter this Constitution of ours or limit it because this Constitution coming from the people of India through their representatives represents their free will with regard to the future governance of India.

Now, may I beg again to repeat what I said earlier and that is this: that destiny has cast a certain role on this country. Whether anyone of us present here can be called men or women of destiny or not I do not know. That is a big word which does not apply to average human beings, but whether we are men or women of destiny or not, India is a country of destiny (*cheers*), and so far as we represent this great country with a great destiny stretching out in front of her, we also have to function as men and women of destiny, viewing all our problems in that long perspective of destiny and of the World and of Asia, never forgetting the great responsibility that freedom, that this great destiny of our country has cast upon us, not losing ourselves in petty controversies and debates which may be useful but which will in this context be either out of place or out of tune. Vast numbers of minds and eyes look in this direction. We have to remember them. Hundreds of millions of our own people look to us and hundreds of millions of others also look to us; and remember this, that while we want this Constitution to be as solid and as permanent a structure as we can make it, nevertheless there is no permanence in constitutions. There should be a certain flexibility. If you make anything rigid and permanent, you stop a Nation's growth, the growth of a living vital organic people. Therefore it has to be flexible. So also, when you pass this Constitution you will, and I think it is proposed, lay down a period of years—whatever that period may be—during which changes to that Constitution can be easily made without any difficult process. That is a very necessary proviso for a number of reasons. One is this: that while we, who are assembled in this House, undoubtedly represent the people of India, nevertheless I think it can be said, and truthfully, that when a new House, by whatever name it goes, is elected in terms of this Constitution, and every adult in India has the right to vote—man and woman—the House that emerges then will certainly be fully representative of every section of the Indian people. It is right that that House elected so—under this Constitution of course it will have the right to do anything—should have an easy opportunity to make such changes as it wants to. But in any event, we should not make a Constitution such as some other great countries have, which are so rigid that they do not and cannot be adapted easily to changing conditions. Today especially, when the world is in turmoil and we are passing through a very swift period of transition, what we may do today may not be wholly applicable tomorrow. Therefore, while we make a Constitution which is sound and as basic as we can, it should also be flexible and for a period we should be in a position to change it with relative facility.

May I say one word again about certain tendencies in the country which still think in terms of separatist existence or separate privileges and the like? This very Objectives Resolution set out adequate safeguards to be provided for minorities, for tribal areas, depressed and other backward classes. Of course that must be done, and it is the duty and responsibility of the majority to see that this is done and to see that they win over all minorities which may have suspicions against them, which may suffer from fear. It is right and important that we should raise the level of the backward groups in India and bring them up to the level of the rest. But it is not right that in trying to do this we create further barriers, or even keep on existing barriers, because the ultimate objective is not separatism but building up an organic nation, not necessarily a uniform nation because we have a varied culture, and in this country ways of living differ in various parts of the country, habits differ and cultural traditions differ. I have no grievance against that. Ultimately in the modern world there is a strong tendency for the prevailing culture to influence others. That may be a natural influence. But I think the glory of India has been the way in which it has managed to keep two things going at the same time: that is, its infinite variety and at the same time its unity in that variety. Both have to be kept, because if we have only variety, then that means separatism and going to pieces. If we seek to impose some kind of regimented unity, that makes a living organism rather lifeless. Therefore, while it is our bounden duty to do everything we can to give full opportunity to every minority or group and to raise every backward group or class, I do not think it will be a right thing to go the way this country has gone in the past by creating barriers and by calling for protection. As a matter of fact nothing can protect such a minority or a group less than a barrier which separates it from the majority. It makes it a permanently isolated group and it prevents it from any kind of tendency to bring it closer to the other groups in the country.

I trust, Sir, that what I have ventured to submit to the House will be borne in mind when these various clauses are considered and that ultimately we shall pass this Constitution in the spirit of the solemn moment when we started this great endeavour.

The Assembly then adjourned for Lunch till Three of the Clock.

THE NATIONAL FLAG [1]

Mr President, it is my proud privilege to move the following resolution:

Resolved that the National Flag of India shall be horizontal tricolour of deep saffron (*Keshri*), white and dark green in equal proportion. In the centre of the white band, there shall be a Wheel in navy blue to represent the Charkha. The design of the Wheel shall be that of the Wheel (*Chakra*) which appears on the abacus of the Sarnath Lion Capital of Asoka. [2]

The diameter of the Wheel shall be approximate to the width of the white band. The ratio of the width to the length of the Flag shall ordinarily be 2:3.

This resolution, Sir, is in simple language, in a slightly technical language and there is no glow or warmth in the words that I have read. Yet I am sure that many in this House will feel that glow and warmth which I feel at the present moment, for behind this resolution and the Flag which I have the honour to present to this House for adoption lies history, the concentrated history of a short span in a nation's existence. Nevertheless, sometimes in a brief period we pass through the track of centuries. It is not so much the mere act of living that counts but what one does in this brief life that is ours; it is not so much the mere existence of a nation that counts but what that nation does during the various periods of its existence; and I do venture to claim that in the past quarter of a century or so India has lived and

---

[1] Speech in the Constituent Assembly, 22 July 1947, *Constituent Assembly Debates, Official Report,* vol. IV, 1947, pp. 761–7, *Selected Works of Jawaharlal Nehru,* (Second series), vol. 3, 1985, pp. 66–73, 137–8.

[2] The wheel represents the Buddhist Dharma *Chakra* and was used as an emblem by Asoka in the 3rd century BC.

acted in a concentrated way and the emotions which have filled the people of India represent not merely a brief spell of years but something infinitely more. They have gone down into history and tradition and have added themselves on to that vast history and tradition which is our heritage in this country. So, when I move this resolution, I think of this concentrated history through which all of us have passed during the last quarter of a century. Memories crowd in upon me. I remember the ups and downs of the great struggle for freedom of this great nation. I remember and many in this House will remember how we looked up to this Flag not only with pride and enthusiasm but with a tingling in our veins; also how, when we were sometimes down and out, then again the sight of this Flag gave us courage to go on. Then, many who are present here today, many of our comrades who have passed, held on to this Flag, some amongst them even unto death and handed it over, as they sank, to others to hold it aloft. So in this simple form of words, there is much more than will be clear on the surface. There is the struggle of the people for freedom with all its ups and downs and trials and disasters and there is, finally today as I move this resolution, a certain triumph about it—a measure of triumph in the conclusion of that struggle.

Now, I realize fully, as this House must realize, that this triumph of ours has been marred in many ways. There have been, especially in the past few months, many happenings which cause us sorrow, which has gripped our hearts. We have seen parts of this dear motherland of ours cut off from the rest. We have seen large numbers of people suffering tremendously, large numbers wandering about like waifs and strays, without a home. We have seen many other things which I need not repeat to this House, but which we cannot forget. All this sorrow has dogged our footsteps. Even when we have achieved victory and triumph, it still dogs us and we have tremendous problems to face in the present and in the future. Nevertheless it is true I think—I hold it to be true—that this moment does represent a triumph and a victorious conclusion of all our struggles, for the moment.

There has been a very great deal of bewailing and moaning about various things that have happened. I am sad, all of us are sad, at heart because of those things. But let us distinguish that from the other fact of triumph, because there is triumph in victory, in what has happened. It is no small thing that that great and mighty empire which has represented imperialist domination in this country has decided to end its days here. That was the objective we aimed at.

We have attained that objective or shall attain it very soon. Of that there is no doubt. We have not attained the objective exactly in the form in which we wanted it. The troubles and other things that accompanied our achievement are not to our liking. But we must remember that it is very seldom that people realize the dreams that they have dreamt. It is very seldom that the aims and objectives with which we start are achieved in their entirety in life, in an individual's life or in a nation's life.

We have many examples before us. We need not go into the distant past. We have examples in the present or in the recent past. Some years back, a great war was waged, a world war bringing terrible misery to mankind. That war was meant for freedom and democracy and the rest. The war ended in the triumph of those who said they stood for freedom and democracy. Yet, hardly had that war ended when there were rumours of fresh wars and fresh conflicts.

Three days ago, this House and this country and the world was shocked by the brutal murder in a neighbouring country of the leaders of the nation.[3] Today one reads in the papers of an attack by an imperialist power on a friendly country in Southeast Asia.[4] Freedom is still far off in this world and nations, all nations in greater or lesser degree, are struggling for their freedom. If we in the present have not exactly achieved what we aimed at, it is not surprising. There is nothing in it to be ashamed of. For I do think our achievement is no small achievement. It is a very considerable achievement, a great achievement. Let no man run it down because other things have happened which are not to our liking. Let us keep these two things apart. Look at any country in the wide world. Where is the country today, including the great and big powers, which is not full of terrible problems, which is not in some way, politically and economically, striving for freedom which somehow or other eludes its grasp? The problems of India in the wider context do not appear to be terrible. The problems are not anything new to us. We have faced many disagreeable things in the past. We have not held back. We shall face all the other disagreeable things that face us in the present or may do so in the future and we shall not flinch and we shall not falter and we shall not quit.

So, in spite of everything that surrounds us, it is in no spirit of downheartedness that I stand up in praise of this nation for what it has achieved. It is right and proper that at this moment we should adopt the symbol of this achievement, the symbol of freedom. Now what is this freedom in its entirety and for all humanity? What is freedom and what is the struggle for freedom and when does it end? As soon as you take one step forward and achieve something, further steps come up before you. There will be no full freedom in this country or in the world as long as a single human being is un-free. There will be no complete freedom as long as there is

---

[3] Aung San, Deputy Chairman of the Council of Ministers of Burma, and four other ministers were assassinated on 19 July 1947.

[4] On 21 July 1947, Batavia, the Capital of Indonesia, was bombed by Dutch planes.

starvation, hunger, lack of clothing, lack of necessaries of life and lack of opportunity of growth for every single human being, man, woman and child in the country. We aim at that. We may not accomplish that because it is a terrific task. But we shall do our utmost to accomplish that task and hope that our successors, when they come, will have an easier path to pursue. But there is no ending to that road to freedom. As we go ahead just as we sometimes in our vanity aim at perfection, perfection never comes. But if we try hard enough we do approach the goal step by step. When we increase the happiness of the people, we increase their stature in many ways and we proceed to our goal. I do not know if there is an end to this or not, but we proceed towards some kind of consummation which in effect never ends.

So I present this Flag to you. This resolution defines the Flag which I trust you will adopt. In a sense this Flag was adopted, not by a formal resolution, but by popular acclaim and usage, adopted much more by the sacrifice that surrounded it in the past few decades. We are in a sense only ratifying that popular adoption. It is a Flag which has been variously described. Some people, having misunderstood its significance, have thought of it in communal terms and believe that some part of it represents this community or that. But I may say that when this Flag was devised there was no communal significance attached to it. We thought of a design for a Flag which was beautiful, because the symbol of a nation must be beautiful to look at. We thought of a Flag which would in its combination and in its separate parts would somehow represent the spirit of the nation, the tradition of the nation, that mixed spirit and tradition which has grown up through thousands of years in India. So, we devised this Flag. Perhaps I am partial but I do think that it is a very beautiful Flag to look at purely from the point of view of artistry, and it has come to symbolize many other beautiful things, things of the spirit, things of the mind, that give value to the individual's life and to the nation's life, for a nation does not live merely by material things, although they are highly important. It is important that we should have the good things of the world, the material possessions of the world, that our people should have the necessaries of life. That is of the utmost importance. Nevertheless, a nation, and especially a nation like India with an immemorial past, lives by other things also, the things of the spirit. If India had not been associated with these ideals and things of the spirit during these thousands of years, what would India have been? It has gone through a very great deal of misery and degradation in the past, but somehow even in the depths of degradation, the head of India has been held high, the thought of India has been high, and the ideals of India have been high. So we have gone through these tremendous ages and we stand up today in proud thankfulness for our past and even more so for the future that is to come for which we are going to work and for which our successors are going to work. It is our privilege and of those assembled here to mark the transition in a particular way, in a way that will be remembered.

I began by saying that it is my proud privilege to be ordered to move this resolution. Now, Sir, may I say a few words about this particular Flag? It will be seen that there is a slight variation from the one many of us have used during these past years. The colours are the same, a deep saffron, a white and a dark green. In the white previously there was the charkha which symbolized the common man in India, which symbolized the masses of the people, which symbolized their industry and which came to us from the message which Mahatma Gandhi delivered. Now, this particular charkha symbol has been slightly varied in this Flag, not taken away at all. Why then has this been varied? Normally speaking, the symbol on one side of the Flag should be exactly the same as on the other side. Otherwise, there is a difficulty which goes against the rules. Now, the charkha, as it appeared previously on the Flag, had the wheel on one side and the spindle on the other. If you see the other side of the Flag, the spindle comes the other way and the wheel comes this way; if it does not do so, it is not proportionate, because the wheel must be towards the pole, not towards the end of the Flag. There was this practical difficulty. Therefore, after considerable thought we were of course convinced that this great symbol which had enthused people should continue but that it should continue in a slightly different form, that the wheel should be there, not the rest of the charkha, that is the spindle and the string which created this confusion, that the essential part of the charkha should be there, that is the wheel. So, the old tradition continues in regard to the charkha and the wheel. But what type of wheel should we have? Our minds went back to many wheels but notably one famous wheel, which had appeared in many places and which all of us have seen, the one at the top of the capital of the Asoka column and in many other places. That wheel is a symbol of India's ancient culture, it is a symbol of the many things that India had stood for through the ages. So we thought that this *chakra* emblem should be there and thus that wheel appears. For my part, I am exceedingly happy that in this sense indirectly we have associated with this Flag of ours not only this emblem but in a sense the name of Asoka, one of the most magnificent names not only in India's history but in world history. It is well that at this moment of strife, conflict and intolerance, our minds should go back towards what India stood for in the ancient days and what it has stood for, I hope and believe, essentially throughout the ages in spite of mistakes and errors and degradations from time to time. For, if India had not stood for something very great, I do not think that India could have survived and carried on its cultural traditions in a more or less continuous manner through these vast ages. It carried on its cultural tradition, not unchanging, not rigid, but always keeping its essence, always adapting itself to new developments, to new influences. That has been the tradition of India, always to put out fresh blooms and flowers, always receptive to the good things that it received, sometimes receptive to bad things also, but always true to her ancient culture. All manner of new influences through thousands of years have influenced us, while we influenced them tremendously also, for you will remember that India has not been in the past a tight little narrow country, disdaining other countries. India throughout the long ages of her history has been connected with other countries, not only connected with other countries, but has been an international centre, sending out her people abroad to far off countries carrying her message and receiving the message of other countries in exchange, but India was strong enough to remain embedded on the foundations on which she was built, although changes, many changes, have taken place. The strength of India, it has been said, consists in this strong foundation. It consists also in its amazing capacity to receive, to adapt what it wants to adapt, not to reject because something is outside its scope, but to accept and receive everything. It is folly for any nation or race to think that it can only give to and not receive from the rest of the world. Once a nation or a race begins to think like that, it becomes rigid, it becomes ungrowing; it grows backwards and decays. In fact, if India's history can be traced, India's periods of decay are those when it closed herself up into a shell and refused to receive or to look at the outside world. India's greatest periods are those when she stretched her hands to others in far off countries, sent her emissaries, ambassadors, her trade agents and merchants to these countries and received ambassadors and emissaries from abroad.

Now because I have mentioned the name of Asoka I should like you to think that the Asokan period in Indian history was essentially an international period of Indian history. It was not a narrowly national period. It was a period when India's ambassadors went abroad to far countries and went abroad not in the way of an empire and imperialism but as ambassadors of peace and culture and goodwill.

Therefore this Flag that I have the honour to present to you is not, I hope and trust, a Flag of empire, a Flag of imperialism, a Flag of domination over anybody, but a Flag of freedom not only for ourselves, but a symbol of freedom to all people who may see it. And wherever it may go—and I hope it will go far—not only where Indians dwell as our ambassadors and ministers but across the far seas where it may be carried by Indian ships, wherever it may go it will bring a message, I hope, of freedom to those people, a message of comradeship, a message that India wants to be friends with every country of the world and India wants to help any people who seek freedom. That I hope will be the message of this Flag everywhere and I hope that in the freedom that is coming to us, we will not do what many other people or some other people have unfortunately done, that is, in a new found strength suddenly to expand and become imperialistic in design. If that happened that would be a terrible ending to our struggle for freedom. But there is that danger and, therefore, I venture to remind this House of it—although this House needs no reminder—there is this danger in a country suddenly unshackled in stretching out its arms and legs and trying to hit out at other people. And if we do that we become just like other nations who seem to live in a kind of succession of conflicts and preparation for conflict. That is the world today unfortunately.

In some degree I have been responsible for the foreign policy during the past few months and always the question is asked here or elsewhere: 'What is your foreign policy? To what group do you adhere to in this warring world?' Right at the beginning I venture to say that we propose to belong to no power group. We propose to function as far as we can as peace-makers and peace-bringers because today we are not strong enough to be able to have our way. But at any rate we propose to avoid all entanglements with power politics in the world. It is not completely possible to do that in this complicated world of ours, but certainly we are going to do our utmost to that end.

It is stated in this resolution that the ratio of the width to the length of the Flag shall ordinarily be 2:3. Now you will notice the word 'ordinarily'. There is no absolute standard about the ratio because the same Flag on a particular occasion may have a certain ratio that might be more suitable or on any other occasion in another place the ratio might differ slightly. So there is no compulsion about this ratio. But generally speaking, the ratio of 2:3 is a proper ratio. Sometimes the ratio 2:1 may be suitable for a flag flying on a building. Whatever the ratio may be, the point is not so much the relative length and breadth, but the essential design.

So, Sir, now I would present to you not only the resolution but the Flag itself.

There are two of these National Flags before you. One is on silk—the one I am holding—and the other on the other side is of cotton khadi.

I beg to move this resolution.

INDIA BECOMES A REPUBLIC[1]

Since I first unfurled the National Flag on the Red Fort, two years have been added to India's long history which began thousands of years ago. During these two years, we have seen achievements and failures, we have experienced joy and sorrow. The good work we have done will remain even though we pass away. So will India, though generations come and go.

Great questions face us and our task will not be over till we have answered them. Our objective is to make it possible for the millions of India to lead contented and purposeful lives. We cannot do that till we have solved, to a large extent, the problems that face us.

On a day like this we should try to detach ourselves from the problems of the moment and see from a distance, as it were, what is happening in our country and in the world. It is right that we forget our little troubles for a while and think of the major currents that are flowing in our country.

Thirty years ago there appeared on the Indian scene a mighty man of destiny who lighted our path. That light illumined our minds and hearts and large numbers of our people, who, forgetting their own troubles and domestic difficulties, their property and family, responded to his call. It was not for personal gain of any kind. Among these there existed a friendly competition as to who could serve the motherland better and more effectively. Our consuming obsession was the liberation of our country.

The star of a free India beckoned us forward. We dreamt of freedom from poverty and distress. We gained our political freedom at last but the other freedom

[1] Translated from speech in Hindi delivered at the Red Fort, Delhi, 15 August 1949, *Jawaharlal Nehru: Selected Speeches*, vol. 2, 1949–53, pp. 3–6.

still remains for us to achieve. Before we could do much to achieve it, new problems came in our way. Sixty lakhs of people migrated to India as refugees. We faced this problem as we had faced others. I suppose we made some mistakes but no one reviewing these two years will fail to appreciate our forward march in the face of all kinds of difficulties.

Unarmed and peaceful, we faced a proud empire, not looking for aid to any other country and relying only on ourselves. We had faith in our leader, our country and in ourselves. This gave us the strength that sustained us during our struggle for independence. If we had faith and self-confidence when to outward seeming we were powerless, then surely we are much better off today when we are a free people with the strength of a great country behind us. Why then should our faith and our confidence in ourselves weaken? It is true that we have tremendous economic and other difficulties to face; it is also true that while we have rehabilitated lakhs of refugees, large numbers still remain to be helped and rehabilitated. But we have faced even bigger problems in the past. Why should we not face these in the same way also? We must not let our minds get entangled in petty questions and difficulties and forget the main issues.

We belong to a great country, a country that is not only great physically but in things far more important. If we are to be worthy of our country, we must have big minds and big hearts, for small men cannot face big issues or accomplish big tasks. Let each one of us do his duty to his country and to his people and not dwell too much on the duty of others. Some people get into the habit of criticizing others without doing anything themselves. Nothing good can come out of that type of criticism. So, wherever you may be, whether you are in the Army or the Air Force or the Navy or in the civil employ of the Government, each one of you must do your duty efficiently and in a spirit of service to the nation. If the vast number of our countrymen apply themselves to their tasks in their innumerable capacities and co-operate with others, forgetting the petty things that divide them, we shall marvel at the speed with which India will progress.

I want you to think for a moment of the days when we fought the battle of India's freedom without arms and without much by way of resources. We had a great leader who inspired us. We had other leaders, too, but it was the masses of this country who bore the brunt of the struggle. They had faith in their country and their leaders and they relied upon themselves. Today, we have more strength than we ever had. It is, therefore, surprising that some people should feel dejected, have no confidence in themselves and complain all the time.

Let us get back the purposefulness, the enthusiasm, the self-confidence and the faith which moved us at the time of our struggle for freedom. Let us put aside our petty quarrels and factions and think only of the great objective before us.

In our foreign policy, we have proclaimed that we shall join no power bloc and endeavour to co-operate and be friendly with all countries. Our position in the world ultimately depends on the unity and strength of the country, on how far we proceed in the solution of our economic and other problems and on how much we can raise the depressed masses of India. We may not be able to complete that task, for it is colossal. Even so, if we make some headway it will be easier for others to complete the task.

A nation's work never ends. Men may come and go, generations may pass but the life of a nation goes on. We must remember the basic fact that we can achieve little unless there is peace in the country, no matter what policy we pursue. There are some misguided people who indulge in violence and try to create disorder. I wonder how anybody with the least intelligence can think in terms of such anti-national activities. Bomb throwing, for instance, can do the country no good. On the contrary, it further aggravates our economic situation, which is a source of great anxiety to us. Therefore, it is the duty of everyone, no matter what his politics, to help in the maintenance of peace in the country.

The people have every right to change laws and even to change governments and they can exercise that right in a peaceful and democratic manner. But those who choose the path of violence have no faith in democracy. If their way were to prevail, there would be complete chaos in the country and the condition of the people would deteriorate even more. All progress would cease and the next few generations would have to carry a heavy burden.

I am still more distressed by those who, while condemning violence, join hands with those who indulge in violence. They think only in terms of winning an election and forget that the cause of the country and of the people is bigger than any party. If we forget India and her people while pursuing our smaller objectives, then we are indeed guilty of betraying our country. I wish to emphasize that all of us must understand that our most important objective is the safety and security of India and the prosperity and advancement of her people. That can only be achieved effectively if we stop quarrelling amongst ourselves and try to solve the great problems that confront us by democratic and peaceful methods.

We must look at our problems in a proper perspective. If we are preoccupied with petty problems, we shall fail to solve the larger and more important ones.

We must learn to depend on ourselves and not look to others for help every time we are in trouble. Certainly we want to make friends with the rest of the world.

We also seek the goodwill and co-operation of all those who reside in this country, whatever their race or nationality. We welcome help and co-operation from every quarter but we must depend primarily on our own resources. We should not forget that those who lean too much on others tend to become weak and helpless themselves. A country's freedom can be preserved only by her own strength and self-reliance.

We are not hostile to any country and we do not want to meddle in other people's affairs. Every nation should be free to choose the path it considers best. We do not wish to interfere with the freedom of other nations and we expect them to feel the same about our freedom. That is why we have decided not to join any of the power blocs in the world. We will remain aloof and try to be friendly to all. We intend to progress according to our own ideas. We have decided to follow this policy, not only because it is essentially a sound one from our country's point of view but also because it seems to be the only way to serve the cause of world peace. Another world war will spell ruin and we shall not escape the general disaster. We are determined to make every possible effort in the cause of peace. That explains our present foreign policy.

Perhaps you know that I am shortly going to visit a country which is great and powerful. I propose to carry with me a message of friendship and assurances of co-operation from our people. Keeping our own freedom intact, we wish to befriend other nations. Our friendship with one country should not be interpreted as hostility to another.

Asia is passing through a great revolutionary phase and naturally India has also been affected. In other parts of Asia there is struggle and ferment. This morning's newspaper contained the news of trouble and upheaval in a small but important country of Western Asia. We do not know all the facts and in any event I do not wish to express an opinion. All I want to say is that the prevalence of violence and violent methods weaken a country and undermine her progress.

In Eastern Asia, a great and ancient country is experiencing revolutionary changes of tremendous significance. Whatever our individual reactions to these may be, our policy, namely, that we do not wish to interfere in any way with the internal affairs of other countries, is clear. Each country should have the freedom to go the way it chooses. It is for its people to decide their future. Any attempt at outside interference or compulsion must necessarily lead to evil results. No country can impose freedom on any other. That is a contradiction in terms. The world has a great deal of variety and it should be no one's business to suppress this variety or to impose ways of thinking and acting on others. We should, therefore, survey world events in a spirit of understanding and friendship to all.

Our Constituent Assembly is busy framing a new constitution for India and soon we shall adopt a republican form of government. However, laws and constitutions do not by themselves make a country great. It is the enthusiasm, energy and constant effort of a people that make it a great nation. Men of Law lay down constitutions but history is really made by great minds, large hearts and stout arms; by the sweat, tears and toil of a people.

Let us, therefore, learn to study our country's problems in the larger perspective of the world and let us not permit the minor questions of the day to overwhelm us. I have faith in India and her great destiny. A country must have military strength but armed power does not by itself constitute a country's real strength. Her real strength lies in the capacity of her people for disciplined work. Only hard work can produce wealth for us and rid us of our poverty. Each one of us, man or woman, young or old, must, therefore, toil and work. Rest is not for us. We did not win our freedom so that we might rest afterwards, but in order to work harder to hold and strengthen that freedom. There is a great difference between the voluntary labour of a free man for an objective of his choice and the drudgery of a slave. Our labours as free men and women will lay the foundations for a great future and our labour of love for the cause of India and her people will endure; so will the fact that we are building, brick by brick, the great mansion of free India. There is joy in such work and even when we have departed that work will be there for future generations to see.

One of our most important problems today is that of growing more food. We must avoid wasting food at all costs. We must conserve our present resources with great care. We have to tighten our belts. If the co-operation of the people is forthcoming, we shall solve not only this problem but many others. Our petty squabbles and party differences can wait. What is vital and important for us is to keep before us the picture of a great India. India is enduring and will continue to be there long after we are gone.

Free India in the World Order

INDIA AND THE COMMONWEALTH[1]

THE HONOURABLE SHRI JAWAHARLAL NEHRU (United Provinces: General): Mr President, Sir, I have the honour to move the following motion:

'Resolved, that this Assembly do hereby ratify the declaration, agreed to by the Prime Minister of India, on the continued membership of India in the Commonwealth of Nations, as set out in the official statement issued at the conclusion of the Conference of the Commonwealth Prime Ministers in London on 27 April 1949.'

All honourable Members have been supplied with copies of this Declaration[2] and so I have not read it over again. I shall merely point out very briefly some salient features of this Declaration. It is a short and simple document in four

---

[1] 16 May 1949, *Constituent Assembly Debates: Official Report*, vol. 8, pp. 2–11, 65–71.

[2] The Governments of the United Kingdom, Canada, Australia, New Zealand, South Africa, India, Pakistan and Ceylon, whose countries are united as Members of the British Commonwealth of Nations and owe a common allegiance to the Crown, which is also the symbol of their free association, have considered the impending constitutional changes in India.

The Government of India have informed the other Governments of the Commonwealth of the intention of the Indian people that under the new constitution which is about to be adopted India shall become a sovereign independent Republic. The Government of India have however declared and affirmed India's desire to continue her full membership of the Commonwealth of Nations and her acceptance of the King as the symbol of the free association of its independent member nations and as such as the Head of the Commonwealth.

The Governments of the other countries of the Commonwealth, the basis of whose membership of the Commonwealth is not hereby changed, accept and recognise India's continuing membership in accordance with the terms of this Declaration.

paragraphs. The first paragraph, it will be noticed, deals with the present position in law. It refers to the British Commonwealth of Nations and to the fact that the people in this Commonwealth owe a common allegiance to the Crown. That in law is the present position.

The next paragraph of this Declaration states that the Government of India has informed the Governments of the other Commonwealth countries that India is soon going to be a sovereign independent Republic, further that it is desired that she continue her full membership of the Commonwealth of Nations, accepting the King as a symbol of the free association.

The third paragraph says that the other Commonwealth countries accept this and the fourth paragraph ends by saying that all these countries remain united as free and equal members of the Commonwealth of Nations. You will notice that while in the first paragraph that is referred to as the British Commonwealth of Nations, in the subsequent paragraphs that is referred to only as the Commonwealth of Nations. Further you will notice that while in the first paragraph there is the question of allegiance to the Crown which exists at present, later of course this question does not arise because India becoming a Republic goes outside the Crown area completely. There is reference, in connection with the Commonwealth, to the King as the symbol of that association. Observe that the reference is to the King and not to the Crown. It is a small matter but it has certain small significance. But the point is this, that so far as the Republic of India is concerned, her constitution and her working are concerned, she has nothing to do with any external authority, with any King, and none of her subjects owe any allegiance to the King or any other external authority. That Republic may however agree to associate itself with certain other countries that happen to be monarchies or whatever they choose to be. This Declaration therefore states that this new Republic of India, completely sovereign and owing no allegiance to the King, as the other Commonwealth countries do owe, will nevertheless be a full member of this Commonwealth and it agrees that as a symbol of this free partnership or association rather, the King will be recognized as such.

Now, I am placing this Declaration before this honourable House for their approval. Beyond this approval, there is no question of any law being framed in accordance with it. There is no law beyond the Commonwealth. It has not even

---

Accordingly the United Kingdom, Canada, Australia, New Zealand, South Africa, India, Pakistan and Ceylon hereby declare that they remain united as free and equal members of the Commonwealth of Nations, freely co-operating in the pursuit of peace, liberty and progress.

the formality which normally accompanies treaties. It is an agreement by free will, to be terminated by free will. Therefore there will be no further legislation or law if this House approves of this. In this particular Declaration nothing very much is said about the position of the King except that he will be a symbol, but it has been made perfectly clear—it was made perfectly clear—that the king has no functions at all. He has a certain status. The Commonwealth itself, as such, is nobody, if I may say so; it has no organization to function and the King also can have no functions.

Now, some consequences flow from this. Apart from certain friendly approaches to each other, apart from a desire to co-operate, which will always be conditioned by each party deciding on the measure of co-operation and following its own policy, there is no obligation. There is hardly any obligation in the nature of commitments that flow. But an attempt has been made to produce something which is entirely novel, and I can very well understand lawyers on the one hand feeling somewhat uncomfortable at a thing for which they can find no precedent or parallel. There may also be others feeling that behind this there might be something which they cannot quite understand, something risky, something dangerous, because the thing is so simple on the face of it. That kind of difficulty may arise in people's minds. What I have stated elsewhere I should like to repeat that there is absolutely nothing behind this except what is placed before this House.

One or two matters I may clear up, which are not mentioned in this Declaration. One of these, as I have said, is that the King has no functions at all. This was cleared up in the course of our proceedings; it has no doubt been recorded in the minutes of the Conference in London. Another point was that one of the objects of this kind of Commonwealth association is now to create a status which is something between being completely foreign and being of one nationality. Obviously the Commonwealth countries belong to different nations. There are different nationalities. Normally either you have a common nationality or you are foreign. There is no intermediate state. Up till now in this Commonwealth or the British Commonwealth of Nations, there was a binding link, which was allegiance to the King. With that link, therefore, in a sense there was common nationality in a broad way. That snaps, that ends when we become a Republic, and if we should desire to give a certain preference or a certain privilege to any one of these countries, we would normally be precluded from doing so because of what is called the 'most favoured nation clause' that every country would be as much foreign as any other country. Now, we want to take away that foreignness, keeping in our own hands what, if any, privileges or preference we can give to another country. That is a matter entirely for two countries to decide by treaty or arrangement, so that we create a new state of affairs—or we try to create it—that the other countries, although in a sense foreign, are nevertheless not completely foreign. I do not quite know how we shall proceed to deal with this matter at a later stage. That is for the House to decide—that is to say, to take the right, only the right, to deal with Commonwealth countries, should we so choose, in regard to certain preferences or privileges. What they are to be, all that, of course, we shall in each case be the judge ourselves. Apart form these facts there has nothing been decided in secret or otherwise which has not been put before the public.

The House will remember that there was some talk at one stage of a Commonwealth citizenship. Now it was difficult to understand what the contents of a Commonwealth citizenship might be, except that it meant that they were not completely foreign to one another. That un-foreignness remains, but I think it is as well that we left off talking about something vague, which could not be surely defined, but the other fact remains, as I have just stated: the fact that we should take the right to ourselves, if we so chose to exercise it at any time, to enter into treaties or arrangements with Commonwealth countries assuring certain mutual privileges and preferences.

I have briefly placed before this House this document. It is a simple document and yet the House is fully aware that it is a highly important document or rather what it contains is of great and historical significance. I went some weeks ago as the representative of India to this Conference. I had consulted my colleagues here, of course previously, because it was a great responsibility and no man is big enough to shoulder that responsibility by himself when the future of India is at stake. During the past many months we had often consulted each other, consulted great and representative organizations, consulted many Members of this House. Nevertheless when I went, I carried this great responsibility and I felt the burden of it. I had able colleagues to advise me, but I was the sole representative of India and in a sense that future of India for the moment was in my keeping. I was alone in that sense and yet not quite alone because, as I travelled through the air and as I sat there at that Conference table, the ghosts of many yesterdays of my life surrounded me and brought up picture after picture before me, sentinels and guardians keeping watch over me, telling me perhaps not to trip and not to forget them. I remembered, as many honourable Members might remember, that day nineteen years ago when we took a pledge on the bank of the River Ravi, at the midnight hour, and I remembered the 26th of January the first time and that oft-repeated Pledge year after year in spite of difficulty and obstruction, and finally, I remembered that day when standing at this very place, I placed a resolution before this House. That was one of the earliest resolutions placed before this honourable House, a Resolution that is known as the Objectives Resolution. Two years and five months have elapsed since that happened. In that Resolution we defined more or less the type of free Government or Republic that we were going to have. Later in another place and on a famous occasion, this subject also came up, that was at the Jaipur Session of the Congress, because not only my mind, but many minds were struggling with this problem, trying to find a way out that was in keeping with the honour and dignity and independence of India, and yet also in keeping with the changing world and with the facts as they were, something that would advance the cause of India, would help us, something that would advance the cause of peace in the world, and yet something which would be strictly and absolutely true to every single pledge that we have taken. It was clear to me that whatever the advantages might be of any association with the Commonwealth or with any other group, no single advantage, however great, could be purchased by a single iota of our pledges being given up, because no country can make progress by playing fast and loose with the principles which it has declared. So, during these months we have thought and we had discussed amongst ourselves and I carried all this advice with me. May I read to you, perhaps just to refresh your minds the Resolution passed at the Jaipur Session of the Congress? It might be of interest to you and I would beg of you to consider the very wording of this Resolution:

'In view of the attainment of complete independence and the establishment of the Republic of India which will symbolize with Independence and give to India the status among the nations of the world that is her rightful due, her present association with the United Kingdom and the Commonwealth of Nations will necessarily have to change. India, however desires to maintain all such links with other countries as do not come in the way of her freedom of action and independence and the Congress would welcome her free association with the independent nations of the Commonwealth for their common wealth and the promotion of world peace.'

You will observe that the last few lines of this Resolution are almost identical with the lines of the Declaration of London.

I went there guided and controlled by all our past pledges, ultimately guided and controlled by the Resolution of this honourable House, by the Objectives Resolution and all that has subsequently happened; also by the mandate given to me by the All-India Congress Committee in that Resolution, and I stand before you to say with all humility that I have fulfilled that mandate to the letter (*Loud Cheers*). All of us have been during these past many years through the valley of the Shadow; we have passed our lives in opposition, in struggle and sometimes in failure and sometimes success and most of us are haunted by those dreams and visions of old days and these hopes that filled us and the frustrations that often followed those hopes; yet we have seen that even out of that prickly thorn of frustration and despair, we have been able to pick out the rose of fulfilment.

Let us not be led away by considering the situation in terms of events which are no longer here. You will see in the resolution of the Congress that I have read out, it says that necessarily because India becomes a Republic, the association of India with the Commonwealth must change. Of course. Further it says that free association may continue subject only to our complete freedom being assured. Now, that is exactly what has been tried to be done in this Declaration of London. I ask you or any honourable Member to point out in what way the freedom, the independence of India has been limited in the slightest. I do not think it has been. In fact, the greatest stress has been laid not only on the independence of India, but on the independence of each individual nation in the Commonwealth.

I am asked often how can you join a Commonwealth in which there is racial discrimination, in which there are other things happening to which we object? That, I think, is a fair question and it is a matter which necessarily must cause us some trouble in our thinking. Nevertheless it is a question which does not really arise. That is to say, when we have entered into an alliance with a nation or a group of nations, it does not mean that we accept their other policies, etc.; it does not mean that we commit ourselves in any way to something that they may do. In fact, this House knows that we are carrying on at the present moment a struggle, or our countrymen are carrying on a struggle in regard to racial discrimination in various parts of the world.

This House knows that in the last few years one of the major questions before the United Nations, at the instance of India, has been the position of Indians in South Africa. May I, if the House will permit me, for a moment refer to an event which took place yesterday, that is, the passing of the resolution at the General Assembly of the United Nations, and express my appreciation and my Government's appreciation of the way our delegation have functioned in this matter and our appreciation of all those nations of the United Nations, almost all, in fact, all barring South Africa, which finally supported this attitude of India? One of the pillars of our foreign policy, repeatedly stated, is to fight against racial discrimination, is to fight for the freedom of suppressed nationalities. Are you compromising on that issue by remaining in the Commonwealth? We have been fighting on the South African Indian issue and on other issues even though we have been thus far a dominion of the Commonwealth. It was a dangerous thing for us to bring that matter within the purview of the Commonwealth. Because, then, that very thing to which you and I object might have taken place. That is, the Commonwealth might have been considered as some kind of a superior body which sometimes acts as a tribunal or judges, or in a sense supervises the activities of its member nations. That certainly would have meant a diminution in our independence and sovereignty, if we had once accepted that principle. Therefore we were not prepared and we are not prepared to treat the Commonwealth as such or even to bring disputes between member nations of the Commonwealth before the Commonwealth body. We may, of course, in a friendly way discuss this matter; that is a different matter. We are anxious to maintain the position of our countrymen in other countries in the Commonwealth. So far as we are concerned, we could not bring their domestic policies in dispute there; nor can we say in regard to any country that we are not going to associate ourselves with that country because we disapprove of certain policies of that country.

I am afraid if we adopted that attitude, then, there would be hardly any association for us with any country, because we have disapproved of something or other that that country does. Sometimes, it so happens that the difference is so great that you cut off relations with that country or there is a big conflict. Some years ago, the United Nations General Assembly decided to recommend to its member States to withdraw diplomatic representatives from Spain because Spain was supposed to be a Fascist country. I am not going into the merits of the question. Sometimes, the question comes up in that way. The question has come up again and they have reversed that decision and left it to each member State to do as it likes. If you proceed in this way, take any great country or a small country; you do not agree with everything that the Soviet Union does; therefore, why should we have representation there or why should we have a treaty of alliance in regard to commercial or trade matters with them? You may not agree with some policies of the United States of America; therefore, you cannot have a treaty with them. That is not the way nations carry on their foreign work or any work. The first thing to realize I think in this world is that there are different ways of thinking, different ways of living and different approaches to life in different parts of the world. Most of our troubles arise by one country imposing its will and its way of living on other countries. It is true that each country cannot live in isolation, because, the world as constituted today is progressively becoming an organic whole. If one country living in isolation does something which is dangerous to the other countries, the other countries have to intervene. To give a rather obvious example, if one country allows itself to become the breeding ground of all kinds of dangerous diseases, the world will have to come in and clear it up because it cannot afford to allow this disease to spread all over the world. The only safe principle to follow is that, subject to certain limitations, each country should be allowed to live its own life in its own way.

There are at present in the world several ideologies and major conflicts flowing from these ideologies. What is right or what is wrong, we can consider at a later stage, or may be something else is right. Either you want a major conflict, a great war which might result in the victory for this nation or that, or else you allow them to live at peace in their respective territories and to carry on their way of thinking, way of life, their structure of State, etc., allowing the facts to prove which is right ultimately. I have no doubt at all that ultimately, it will be the system that delivers the goods—the goods being the advancement and the betterment of the human race or the people of the individual countries—that will survive and no amount of theorizing and no amount of warfare can make the system that does not deliver the goods survive. I refer to this because of the argument that was raised that India cannot join the Commonwealth because it disapproves of certain policies of certain Commonwealth nations. I think we should keep these two matters completely apart.

We join the Commonwealth obviously because we think it is beneficial to us and to certain causes in the world that we wish to advance. The other countries of the Commonwealth want us to remain there because they think it is beneficial to them. It is mutually understood that it is to the advantage of the nations in the Commonwealth and therefore they join. At the same time, it is made perfectly clear that each country is completely free to go its own way; it may be that they may go, sometimes go so far as to break away from the Commonwealth. In the world today where there are so many disruptive forces at work, where we are often at the verge of war, I think it is not a safe thing to encourage to break up any association that one has. Break up the evil parts of this; break up anything that may come in the way of your growth, because nobody dare agree to anything which comes in the way of a nation's growth. Otherwise, apart from breaking the evil parts of the association, it is better to keep a co-operative association going which may do good in this world rather than break it.

Now this Declaration that is placed before you is not a new move and yet it is a complete reorientation of something that has existed in an entirely different way. Suppose we had been cut off from England completely and we had then desired to join the Commonwealth of Nations, it would have been a new move. Suppose a new group of nations wanted us to join them and we joined them in this way, that would have been a new move from which various consequences would have flown. In the present instance what is happening is that a certain association has been existing for a considerable time past. A very great change came in the way of that association about a year and eight or nine months ago, from 15 August 1947. Now another major change is contemplated. Gradually the conception is changing. Yet that certain link remains in a different form. Now politically we are completely independent. Economically we are as independent as independent nations can be. Nobody can be 100 per cent independent in the sense of absolute lack of inter- dependence, but nevertheless India has to depend on the rest of the world for her trade, for her commerce and for many supplies that she needs, today for her food unfortunately, and so many other things. We cannot be absolutely cut off from the world. Now the House knows that inevitably during the past century and more all kinds of contacts have arisen between England and this country, many of them were bad, very bad and we have struggled throughout our lives to put an end to them. Many of them were not so bad, many of them may be good and many of them good or bad whatever they may be, are there. Here I am, the patent example of these contacts, speaking in this honourable House in the English language. No doubt we are going to change that language for our use but the fact remains that I am doing so and the fact remains that most other Members who will speak will also do so. The fact remains that we are functioning here under certain rules and regulations for which the model has been the British Constitution. Those laws existing today have been largely forged by them. Therefore we have developed these things inevitably. Gradually, laws which are good we will keep and those that are bad we will throw away. Any marked change in this without something to follow creates a hiatus which may be harmful. Largely our educational apparatus has been influenced. Largely our military apparatus has been influenced by these considerations and we have grown up naturally as something rather like the British Army. I am placing before the House certain entirely practical considerations. If we break away completely, the result is that without making sufficient provision for carrying on in a different way we have a gap period; of course if we have to pay a price, we may choose to do so. If we do not want to pay the price, we should not pay it and face the consequences.

But in the present instance we have to consider not only these minor gains which I have mentioned to you, to us and to others but if I may say so, the larger approach to world problems. I felt as I was conferring there in London with the representatives of other Governments that I had necessarily to stick completely and absolutely to the sovereignty and independence of the Indian Republic. I could not possibly compromise on any allegiance to any foreign authority. I did that. I also felt that in the state of the world today and in the state of India and Asia, it would be a good thing if we approached this question in a friendly spirit there which would solve the problems in Asia and elsewhere. I am afraid I am a bad bargainer. I am not used to the ways of the market place. I hope I am a good fighter and I hope I am a good friend. I am not anything in between and so when you have to bargain hard for anything, do not send me. When you want to fight, I hope I shall fight and then when you are decided about a certain thing, then you must hold to it and hold to it to the death, but about other minor things I think it is far better to gain the goodwill of the other party. It is far more precious to come to a decision in friendship and goodwill than to gain a word here and there at the cost of ill-will. So I approached this problem and may I say how I felt about others. I would like to pay a tribute to the Prime Minister of the United Kingdom and to others also there because they approached this in that spirit also, not so much to get some debating point or a change of a word here and there in this Declaration. It was possible that if I had tried my hardest I might have got a word here and there changed in this Declaration but the essence could not have been changed because there was nothing more for us to get out of that Declaration. I preferred not to do so because I preferred creating an impression, and I hope a right impression, that the approach of India to these and the other problems of the world was not a narrow-minded approach. It was an approach based on faith and confidence in her own strength and in her own future and therefore it was not afraid of any country coming in the way of that faith, it was not afraid of any word or phrase in any document but it was based essentially on this that if you approach another country in a friendly way, with goodwill and generosity, you will be paid back in the same coin and probably the payment will be in even larger measure. I am quite convinced that in treatment of nations to one another, as in the case of individuals, only out of goodwill will you get goodwill and no amount of intrigues and cleverness will get you good results out of evil ways. Therefore, I thought that that was an occasion not only to impress England but others also, in fact to some extent the world, because this matter that was being discussed at No. 10 Downing Street in London was something that drew the attention of the entire world. It drew the attention of the world, partly because India is a very important country, potentially so, and actually so too. And the world was interested to see how this very complicated and difficult problem which appeared insoluble, could be solved. It could not be solved if we had left it to eminent lawyers. Lawyers have their use in life; but they should not be spread out everywhere. It could not have been solved by these extreme, narrow-minded nationalists who cannot see to the right or to the left, but live in a narrow sphere of their own, and therefore forget that the world is going ahead. It could not be solved by people who live in the past and cannot realize that the present is different from the past and that the future is going to be still more different. It could not be solved by any person who lacked faith in India and in India's destiny.

I wanted the world to see that India does not lack faith in herself, and that India is prepared to co-operate even with those with whom she had been fighting in the past; provided the basis of co-operation today is honourable that it is a free basis, a basis which would lead to the good not only of ourselves, but of the world also. That is to say, we would not deny that co-operation simply because in the past we have had a fight, and thus carry on the trail of our past 'karma' along with us. We have to wash out the past with all its evil. I wanted, if I may say so in all humility, to help in letting the world look at things in a slightly different perspective, or rather try to see now vital questions can be approached and dealt with. We have seen too often in the arguments that go on in the assemblies of the world, this bitter approach, this cursing of each other, this desire not, in the least, to understand the other, but deliberately to misunderstand the other, and to make clever points about it. Now, it may be a satisfying performance for any of us, on occasions to make clever points and be applauded by our people or by some other people. But in the state of the world today, it is a poor thing for any responsible person to do, when we live on the verge of catastrophic wars, when national passions are roused, and when even a casually spoken word might make all the difference.

Some people have thought that by our joining or continuing to remain in the Commonwealth of Nations we are drifting away from our neighbours in Asia, or that it has become more difficult for us to co-operate with other countries, great countries in the world. But I think it is easier for us to develop closer relations with other countries while we are in the Commonwealth than it might have been otherwise. That is rather a peculiar thing to say. Nevertheless I say it, and I have given a great deal of thought to this matter. The Commonwealth does not come in the way of our co-operation and friendship with other countries. Ultimately we shall have to decide, and the decision will depend on our own strength. If we completely dissociate from the Commonwealth, we are, for the moment completely isolated. We cannot remain completely isolated, and so inevitably by stress of circumstances, we have to incline in some direction or other. But that inclination in some direction or other will necessarily be a give-and-take affair. It may be in the nature of alliances, you give something yourself and get something in return. In other words, it may involve commitments, far more than at present. There are no commitments today. In that sense, I say we are freer today to come to friendly understandings with other countries and to play the part, if you like, of a bridge for mutual understanding between other countries. I do not wish to place this too high; nevertheless, it is no good placing it too low either. I should like you to look round at the world today and look more especially during the last two years or so, at the relative position of India and the rest of the world. I think you will find that during this period of two years or even slightly less, India has gone up in the scale of nations in its influence and in its prestige. It is a little difficult for me to tell you exactly what India had done or had not done. It would be absurd for anyone to expect that India can become the crusader for all causes in the world and bring forth results. Even in cases that have borne fruit, it is not a thing to be proclaimed from the housetops. But something which does not require any proclamation is the fact of India's present prestige and influence in world affairs. Considering that she came on the scene as an independent nation only a year and a half or a little more ago, it is astonishing—the part that India has played today.

One thing I should like to say, and it is this. Obviously a declaration of this type, or the Resolution that I have placed before the House is not capable of amendment. It is either accepted or rejected. I am surprised to see that some honourable Members have sent notices of amendments. Any treaty with any foreign power can be accepted or rejected. It is a joint Declaration of eight, or is it nine, countries—and it cannot be amended in this House or in any House. It can be accepted or rejected. I would, therefore, beg of you to consider this business in all its aspects. First of all, make sure that it is in conformity with our old pledges, that it does violence to none. If it is proved to me that it does violence to any pledge that we have undertaken, that it limits India's freedom in any way, then I certainly shall be no party to it. Second, you should see whether it does good to ourselves and to the rest of the world. I think there can be little doubt that it does us good, that this continuing association at the present moment is beneficial for us, and it is beneficial in the larger sense, to certain world causes that we represent. And last, if I may put it in a negative way, not to have had this agreement would certainly have been detrimental to those world causes as well as to ourselves.

And finally, about the value I should like this House to attach to this Declaration and to the whole business of those talks resulting in this Declaration. It is a method, a desirable method, and a method which brings a touch of healing with it. In this world which is today sick and which has not recovered from so many wounds during the last decade or more, it is necessary that we touch upon the world problems, not with passion and prejudice and with too much repetition of what has ceased to be, but in a friendly way and with a touch of healing, and I think the chief value of this Declaration and of what preceded it was that it did bring a touch of healing in our relations with certain countries. We are in no way subordinate to them, and they are in no way subordinate to us. We shall go our way and they shall go their way. But our ways, unless something happens, will be friendly ways; at any rate, attempts will be made to understand each other, to be friends with each other and to co-operate with each other. And the fact that we have begun this new type of association with a touch of healing will be good for us, good for them, and I think, good for the world (*Cheers*).

PROF. SHIBBAN LAL SAKSENA (United Provinces: General): Sir, I beg to move the following amendment to the motion:

1. That in the motion, for the words 'do hereby ratify' the words 'has carefully considered' be substituted:
2. That the following be added at the end of the motion:

and is of opinion that membership of the Commonwealth is incompatible with India's new status of a Sovereign Independent Republic. Besides, the terms of membership are derogatory to India's dignity and her new status, and as such are bound to circumscribe and limit her freedom of action in international affairs and tie her down to the chariot-wheel of Anglo-American power bloc. India with a population of 350 millions out of a total population of about 500 millions of the whole of the Commonwealth cannot accept the King of England as the Head of the Commonwealth in any shape or form. Also, India cannot become the member of a Commonwealth, many members of which still regard Indians as an inferior race and enforce a colour bar against them and deny them even the most elementary rights of citizenship. The recent anti-India riots in South Africa, the assertion of the all-White policy in Australia and the execution of Ganapathy and the refusal to commute the death sentence on Sambasivan in Malaya in spite of the representations of the Indian Government clearly show that India cannot derive any advantage from the membership of the Commonwealth and the Britain and the other members of the Commonwealth cannot give up their Imperialist and racial policies.

Considering all these facts, and also considering the fact that the Congress Party, which is in an absolute majority in the Constituent Assembly and in other provincial legislatures in the country, has had the complete independence of India with the severance of the British connection as its declared goal at the time of the last general elections, any new relationship in contravention of that policy with the British Commonwealth can only be properly decided by the new Parliament of the Indian Republic, which will be elected under the new constitution on the basis of adult suffrage.

This Assembly therefore resolves that the question of India's membership of the Commonwealth be deferred until the new Parliament is elected and the wishes of the people of the country clearly ascertained. The Assembly calls upon the Prime Minister of India to inform the Prime Minister of Great Britain and other members of the Commonwealth accordingly.

Sir, I have heard with great attention the historic speech of my Leader, the Prime Minister. He himself said that this is a historic occasion and the Declaration he has asked us to ratify is also a historic Declaration. In the recent past there have not been many such occasions when we have been called upon to decide issues of such great moment; perhaps the most recent occasion comparable to it was that when the country was called upon to decide the issue of India's partition. That issue was not discussed by this House but was decided by the All-India Congress Committee. We know the fruits of the decision that was taken on that occasion have not been very good. I was one of the most bitter opponents of the partition plan. Today also

I have to voice my disagreement with my Leader on this London Declaration to which he has agreed already and which he wants us to ratify.

PANDIT BALKRISHNA SHARMA (United Provinces: General): Sir, on a point of order. I should like to know whether in view of the almost negative character of the amendment it is in order.

MR PRESIDENT: The honourable Member himself said that it is 'almost a negative' and not 'a negative'; so I have therefore allowed it.

THE HONOURABLE SHRI JAWAHARLAL NEHRU: Sir, I should like to have your ruling regarding international treaties and whether such an amendment would be in order when a treaty of this type by the Government of the day has been concluded. I do not know: a treaty can be accepted or rejected; amendment cannot be made to a treaty.

MR PRESIDENT: Here we go by the rules and I have to see whether under the rules the amendment is in order. What the effect of that on the treaty will be I do not know but I think under the rules the amendment is in order matters may not get worse. From my own experience, I believe—I may be wrong—ultimately we will only be able to resolve the South African question according to the measures of our own strength. And that is why I say that our policy must be broad-based, and that India's strength should be built up most rapidly. It may take us five years; it may take us ten years. But any realist, any sober person must realize that in the world we are living in today, in the final analysis, one's strength is measured exactly by one's military might, and that is why I feel that ultimately will only be able to resolve the South African-Indian question when we are in a position to be able to demonstrate militarily—as the Japanese did—at Durban. But that is, as I have said, no reason for leaving the Commonwealth, because it may consist of one or two blacklegs or renegades.

And, finally, Sir, I want to end with this note. As I said, it is fortunate that India has today leaders of the present stature—persons who have been able to rise, as Prof. Shah has not been able to rise, above bitterness and irony of recent political events; that while the dust and din of political battle and political struggle have not subsided, they have the vision to see without that vision being blurred, to be able to judge without their judgment being clouded, where India's best interests lie. Sir, can any one say to this House that anyone in this country has discharged his duties to the people more selflessly than the Prime Minister? And, if we answer that question, as we are bound to answer it, then whatever decision he has taken has been taken against the background of his knowledge, which is perhaps much greater than the knowledge of anyone of us, in the sole interest of India. What then can any Indian do but whole-heartedly to endorse the resolution which has been moved in this House.

THE HONOURABLE SHRI SATYANARAYAN SINHA (Bihar: General): Sir, I move that the question be now put,

MR PRESIDENT: The question is:
    That the question be put.
    I think the majority is in favour of closure.

THE HONOURABLE SHRI JAWAHARLAL NEHRU (United Provinces: General): Mr President, Sir, we have had a fairly full debate since yesterday and many honourable Members have spoken in approval of this motion. In fact, if I may say so, some of them have even gone a little further than I might perhaps have gone. They have drawn some consequences and pointed out some implications which for my part I would not have approved or accepted. However, it is open to all of us and to each one of us to see the further in a particular way.

So far as this resolution of mine and the Declaration of London are concerned, what we have got to see are these: number one, that it fulfils, or at any rate it does not go against any pledges of ours; that is to say, that it takes India forward, or does not come in the way of India going forward to her natural destination of a Sovereign Independent Republic. Secondly, that it helps India, or does not hinder India in making rapid progress in the other domains in the course of the next few years. We have, in a sense, solved the political problem, but the political problem is intimately connected with the economic condition of the country. We are being faced by many economic difficulties. They are our domestic concern, no doubt, but obviously the world can help or hinder any policy that we might adopt. Now, does this proposal which is contained in this Declaration help our speedy progress economically and otherwise or not? That is another test. I am prepared to admit that even without external help, we will go ahead. But obviously it will be a far more difficult task and it will take a much longer time. It is not an easy matter to do that.

The third test is whether in the world, as it is today, it helps in the promotion of peace and the avoidance of war. Some people talk about encouraging this particular group or that, this bloc or that. We are all, I am afraid, in the habit of considering ourselves or our friends as angels and others the reverse of angels. We are all apt to think that we stand for the forces of progress and democracy and others do not. I must confess that in spite of my own pride in India and her people, I have grown more humble about talking in terms of our being in the vanguard of progress or democracy.

In the last two or three years we have passed through difficult times, humiliating times. We have lived through them. That has been something in our favour. We have survived them. But I hope we have learned out lesson from them. For my part I am a little chary now of condemning this or that person or this or that nation, because the hands of no individual or nation are clean in such matters. And there is far too much of the habit of condemning other nations as being the wrong-doers or the war-mongers, and yet doing exactly the same thing oneself.

If one looks round the world—of course one favours certain policies—one is against some things and thinks that those are dangerous and might lead to war, but others are not. But the most amazing thing that strikes me is this: if you look back during the last thirty years or more which have comprised two wars and the period between these wars, you will find the same cries, changing slightly with the changed situation of course, but nevertheless the same cries, the same approaches, the same fears and suspicions and the same arming on all sides and war coming. The same talk of this being the last war, the fight for democracy and all the rest of it is heard on every slide. And then the war ends, but the same conflicts continue and again the same preparation for war. Then another war comes. Now that is a very extraordinary thing, because I am convinced that hardly anybody in this wide world wants war, barring a few persons or groups who make profit by war. Nobody and no country wants war. As war becomes more and more terrible they want it still less. Yet some past evil or karma or some destiny goes on pushing people in a particular direction, towards the abyss and they go through the same arguments and they perform the same gestures like automatons.

Now, are we fated to do that? I do not know, but anyhow I want to fight against that tendency of talking about war and preparation for war. Obviously no country and no Government of any country dare allow its country to be unprepared for contingencies. We have to prepare ourselves unfortunately, unless we are brave enough to follow the policy the Mahatmaji laid down. If we are brave enough, well and good, we take the chance. I do believe that if we are brave enough that policy would be the right policy. But it is not so much a question of my being brave or your being brave, but of the country being brave enough to follow and understand that policy. I do not think we have been brought up to that level of understanding and behaviour. Indeed when we talk about that great level, I should say that in the last year and a half we have sunk to the lowest depths of behaviour in this country. So let us not take the name of the Mahatma in vain in this country. Anyhow we cannot, no Government can, say that it stands for peace and do nothing at all. We have to take precautions and prepare ourselves to the best of our ability. We cannot blame any other Government which does that, because that is an inevitable precaution that one has to take. But apart from that, it seems to me that some Governments or many Governments, go much further. They talk all the time of war. They blame the other party all the time. They try to make out that the other party is completely wrong or is a war-monger and so on and so forth. In fact they create the very conditions which lead to war. In talking of peace and our love of peace we or they create the conditions that in the past have invariably led to war. The conditions that ultimately generally lead to war are economic conflicts and this and that. But I do not think today it is economic conflict or even political conflict that is going to lead to war, but rather the overmastering fear, the fear that the other party will certainly overwhelm one, the feat that the other party is increasing its strength gradually and would become so strong as to be unassailable and so each party goes on arming and arming with the deadliest weapons. I am sorry I have drifted off in this direction.

How are we to meet this major evil of the day? Some people say, 'join up with this group which stands for peace', while others say 'join up with the other group' which, according to them, stands for some other kind of peace or progress. But I am quite convinced in my own mind that by joining up in this way, I do not help the cause of peace. That, in fact, only intensifies the atmosphere of fear. Then what am I to do? I do not believe in sitting inactively or practising the policy of escapism. You cannot escape. You have to face the problem and try to beat it and overcome it. Therefore the people who think that our policy is a kind of passive negation or is an inane policy, are mistaken. That has not been ever my idea on this subject. I think it is and it ought to be our policy, a positive policy, a definite policy, to strive to overcome the general trend towards war in people's minds.

I know that in this huge problem before the world India may not be a strong enough factor. She may be a feeble factor to change it or alter it. That may be so. I cannot claim any necessary results. But nevertheless I say that the only policy that India should pursue in this matter is a positive, definite policy of avoiding this drift to war by other countries also and of avoiding this atmosphere becoming so charged with fear and suspicion, etc., and of not acclaiming this country or that, even though they may claim to make the world rational, but rather laying stress on those qualities of those countries which are good, which are acceptable and drawing out the best from them and thereby, in so far as it may be possible, to work to lessen the tensions and work for peace. Whether we succeed or not is another thing. But it is in our hands now to work with might and main in the direction we consider right, not because we are afraid or fear has overwhelmed us. We have gone through many frightful things and I do not think anything is going to happen in India or the world that is going to frighten us any more. Nevertheless we do not want this world to suffer or go through another world disaster from which you and I cannot escape and our country cannot escape. No policy can make us escape from that. Even if war does not spread to this country, even so if the war comes from abroad it will engulf the world and India. We have to face this problem.

This is more a psychological problem than a practical one, although it has practical applications. I think that in a sense India is partly suited to do it, partly suited because in spite of our being feeble and rather unworthy followers of Gandhiji, nevertheless we have imbibed to some small extent what he told us. Secondly, in these world conflicts, you will see there is a succession of one action following another; inevitably one leading to another and so the chain of evils spreads; war comes and the evils that follow wars come after that and they themselves lead to another war and that chain of events goes on and each country is caught within this cycle of karma or evil or whatever you call it. Now, so far these evils have brought about wars in the West because in a sense these evils were concentrated in the Western powers; I do not by any means say that the Eastern powers are virtuous. So far the West or Europe has been the centre of political activity, has dominated the politics of the world. Therefore their disputes and their quarrels and their wars have dominated the world.

Now, fortunately we in India are not inheritors of these hatreds of Europe. We may like a person or dislike something or an idea, but we have not got that past inheritance on our backs. Therefore it may be slightly easier for us in facing these problems, whether in international assemblies or elsewhere, to deal with them not only objectively and dispassionately but also with the goodwill of others who may not suspect us of any fund of ill-will derived from the past. It may be that a country can only function effectively if it has a certain strength behind it. I am not for the moment thinking of material or war strength—that of course counts—but the general strength behind it. A feeble country which cannot look after itself, how is it to look after the World and others? All these considerations I should like this House to have before it and then to decide on this relatively minor question which I have placed before the House, because I had all those considerations and I felt first of all that it was my duty to see that Indian freedom and independence was in no way touched.

It was obvious that the Republic that we have decided on will come into existence. I think we have achieved that. We would have achieved that, of course, in any event, but we have achieved that with the goodwill of many others. That, I think, is some additional achievement. To achieve it with the goodwill of those who perhaps are hit by it is some achievement. It shows that the manner of doing things—the manner which does not leave any trace of hatred or ill-will behind it, starts a fund of goodwill—is important. Goodwill is always precious from any quarter. Therefore I had had a feeling when I was considering this matter in London and later, in a small measure perhaps, I had done something that would have met with the approval of Gandhiji. The manner of it I am thinking of, more than the thing itself. I thought that this in itself would raise a fund of goodwill in this world—goodwill which in a smaller sense is to our advantage certainly, and to the advantage of England, but also in a larger sense to the advantage of the world in these psychological conflicts which people try to resolve by blaming each other, by cursing each other and saying that the others are to blame. May be somebody is to blame; may be some politicians or big men are to blame, but nobody can blame those millions of men who will die in these catastrophic wars. In every country the vast masses of human beings do not want wars. They are frightened of wars. Sometimes this very fright is exploited to revive wars because it can always be said that the other party is coming to attack you.

Therefore I want this House to consider not only that we have achieved something politically—that we would have achieved in any event, nobody would have been able to prevent us—but what has a certain relevancy and importance is that we have achieved it in a way that helps us and helps others, in a way which does not leave evil consequences behind when we think that we have profited at somebody else's expense and that somebody thinks of that always and wants to take revenge later on. That is the way and if the world functions in that way, problems will be solved far more easily and wars and the consequences of wars will perhaps be fewer. They would be no more. It is easy to talk about the faults of the British or of the imperialism and the colonialism of other countries. Perfectly true. You can make out a list of the good qualities and the bad qualities of every nation today, including certainly India. Even if you made that list, the question still remains how anyone is going to draw the good from the other parties and yourself and to lay the foundations for good in the future.

I have come to the conclusion that it does not help us very much either in the government plane or in the national plane to lay stress on the evil in the other party. We must not ignore it; we have to fight it occasionally. We should be prepared for that, but with all that, I do not think this business of maintaining our own virtues and blaming the other party is going to help us in understanding our real problem. It no doubt gives an inner satisfaction that we are virtuous while others are sinners. I am talking in religious phraseology which does not suit me, but the fact is that I do wish to bring this slightly moral aspect of this question before this honourable House. I would not dare to do any injury to the cause of India and then justify it on some high moral ground. No government can do that. But if you can do a profitable business and at the same time it is good on moral grounds, then obviously it is worthy of our understanding and appreciation. I do submit that what we have done in no way, negatively speaking, injures us or can inure us. Positively, we have achieved politically what we wanted to achieve and we are likely to progress, to have more opportunities of progress, in this way than we would otherwise have in the next few years.

Finally, in the world context, it is something that encourages and helps peace, to what extent I do not know; and lastly, of course, it is a thing which in no way binds this country down to any country. It is open to this House or Parliament at any time to break this link, if they so choose, not that I want that link broken. But I am merely pointing out that we have not bound the future down in the slightest. The future is as free as air and this country can go any way it chooses. If it finds this way is a good way, it will stick to it; if not, it will go some otherway and we have not bound it down. I do submit that this resolution that I have placed before this House embodying approval of the Declaration, the decision at the Conference in London, is a motion which deserves the support and approval of this House, not merely, if I may say so, a passive approval and support, but the active appreciation of all that lies behind it and all that it may mean for the future of India that is gradually unrolling before our very eyes. Indeed all of us have hitched our wagons to the Star of India long ago. Our future, our individual future depends on the future of India; and we have thought and dreamt of the future for a long time. Now we have arrived at a stage when we have to mould by our decisions and activities this future at every step. It is no longer good enough for us to talk of that future in terms merely of resolutions, merely in terms of denunciations of others and criticism of others; it is we who have to make it for good or ill; sometimes some of us are too fond of thinking of that future only in negative terms of denouncing others. Some Members of this House who have opposed this motion and some others who are not in this House, who have opposed this motion, I have felt, have been totally unable to come out of that cage of the past in which we all of us have lived, even though the door was open for them to come mentally out. They have reminded us and some of our friends have been good enough to quote my speeches, which I delivered fifteen and twenty years ago. Well if they attach so much value to my speeches, they might listen to my present speech a little more carefully. The world has changed. Evil still remains evil, and good is good; I do not mean to say that it is not; and I think imperialism is an evil thing, and wherever it remains it has to be rooted out and colonialism is an evil thing and wherever it remains, it has to be rooted out, and racialism is an evil and has to be fought. All that is true. Nevertheless the world has changed; England has changed; Europe has changed; India has changed;

everything has changed and is changing; and look at it now. Look at Europe which for the last three hundred years has a period of magnificent achievement in the arts and sciences and it has built up a new civilization all over the world. It is really a magnificent period of which Europe or some countries of Europe can be greatly proud, but Europe also during those three hundred years or more had gradually spread out its domination over Asia and Africa, has been an Imperialist power and exploited the rest of the world and in a sense dominated the political scene of the world. Well, Europe has still, I believe, a great many fine qualities and those people there who have fine qualities will make good, but Europe can no longer be the centre of the world politically speaking, or exercise that influence over other parts of the world, which it had done in the past. From that point of view, Europe belongs to the past and the centre of world history, of political and other activities, shifts elsewhere. I do not mean to say that any other continent becomes a dominating force, dominates the rest—not in that way. However, we are looking at it in an entirely changed scene. If you talk of British Imperialism and the rest of it, I would say that there is no capacity for imperialism even if the will was there; it cannot be done. The French are imperialistically, in parts of Asia. But the fact remains that capacity for doing it is past. They may carry on for a year or two years, but it just cannot be done. The Dutch may do it elsewhere and if you look at it in the historical perspective all these things are hangovers of something past and the thing cannot be done. There may be strength behind today; it may last even a few years and therefore, we have to fight it and therefore, we have to be vigilant—I do not deny that—but let us not think as if Europe or England was the same as it was fifteen or twenty years ago. It is not.

I was saying about our friends who have criticized us and taken this rather negative and passive view. I mentioned at another place that their view was static. I said that, in this particular context, it was rather reactionary and I am sorry I used that word because I do not wish to use words that hurt and I do not wish to hurt people in this way; I have certainly the capacity to use language, clever language to hurt people, and dialectical language, but I do not wish to use it, because we are up against great problems, and it is poor satisfaction just to say a word against an opponent in an argument and defeat him by a word, and not reach heart or mind, and I want to reach the hearts and minds of our people (*loud cheers*) and I feel that whatever our domestic differences might be—let there be differences honestly felt— we do not want a cold regimentation of this country (*Cheers*).

So far as foreign affairs are concerned, there may also be differences, I do not deny that, but the fundamental things before any man who is—whatever else he may be—an Indian patriot, who wants India to progress and the world also to progress, must be necessarily Indian freedom, that is, complete freedom, India's progress, economically and the rest, India playing a part in this freedom of the world and the preservation of peace, etc., in the world. These are the fundamental things: India must progress. India must progress internally. We can play no part unless we are strong in our country economically and otherwise. How we should do so internally may be a matter of difference of opinion. Now I think it should be possible for people who differ considerably in regard to our internal policy, it should be possible for us to have more or less a unified foreign policy in which they agree or mostly agree. May I make myself clear? I do not wish in the slightest to stop argument or comment or criticism; not that; and I want that; it is a sign of a healthy nation, but I do wish that argument to be the argument just of a friend and not of an opponent who sometimes uses that argument, not for argument's sake, but just to injure the opposite party, which often is done in the game of politics. I do not see any major difference for any person. I do see a major difference between those individuals or groups who think in terms of other countries and not of India at all as the primary thing. That is a basic difference and with them it is exceedingly difficult to have any common approach about anything; but where people think in terms of India's independence and progress in the near future and in the distant future and who want peace in the world, of course, there will be no great difference in our foreign policy. And I do not think there is, in fact, although it may be expressed differently. Although a Government can only speak in the language of a Government, others speak a language which we all used to speak, of opposition and agitation. So I would beg this House, and if I may say so, the country to look upon this problem not in any party spirit, not in the sense of bargaining over this little matter or that.

We have to be careful in any business deal not to lose a thing which is advantageous to the nation. At the same time, we have to look at this problem in a big way. We are big nation. If we are a nation big in size, that will not bring bigness to us unless we are big in mind, big in heart, big in understanding and big in action also. You may lose perhaps a little here or there with your bargainers and hagglers in the market place. If you act in a big way, the response to you is very big in a world and their reaction is also big. Because, good always brings good and draws good from others and a big action which shows generosity of spirit brings generosity from the other side.

Therefore, may I finish by commending this resolution to you and trusting that the House will not only accept it, but accept it as something, as a harbinger of good relations, or our acting in a generous way towards other countries, towards the world, and thus strengthening ourselves and strengthening the cause of peace.

Mr President: The House will recollect that there are two amendments to the motion. I would put the motion of Prof. Shibban Lal Saksena; if it is carried, it will obviate the necessity of putting the other amendment to vote.

Shri Lakshminarayan Sahu (Orissa: General): [Mr President, I beg leave of the House to withdraw my amendment.]

Mr President: Mr Lakshminarayan Sahu wants to withdraw his amendment. Does the House permit him to do that?

The amendment was, by leave of the Assembly, withdrawn.

Mr President: Mr Shibban Lal Saksena's amendment alone now remains. I now put Mr Shibban Lal's amendment to vote.

The question is:

That in the motion, for the words 'do hereby ratify' the words 'has carefully considered' be substituted, and

That the following be added at the end of the motion:

and is of opinion that membership of the Commonwealth is incompatible with India's new status of a Sovereign Independent Republic. Besides, the terms of membership are derogatory to India's dignity and her new status, and as such are bound to circumscribe and limit her freedom of action in international affairs and tie her down to the chariot-wheel of Anglo-American power bloc. India with a population of 350 millions out of a total population of about 500 millions of the whole of the Commonwealth cannot accept the King of England as the Head of the Commonwealth in any shape or form. Also, India cannot become the member of a Commonwealth, many members of which still regard Indians as an inferior race and enforce a colour bar against them and deny them even the most elementary rights of citizenship. The recent anti-Indian riots in South Africa, the assertion of the all-White policy in Australia and the execution of Ganapathy and the refusal to commute the death sentence of Sambasivam in Malaya in spite of the representations of the Indian Government clearly show that India cannot derive any advantage from the membership of the Commonwealth and that Britain and the other members of the Commonwealth cannot give up their Imperialist and racial policies.

Considering all these facts, and also considering the fact that the Congress Party which is in an absolute majority in the Constituent Assembly and in other provincial legislatures in the country, has had the Complete Independence of India with the severance of the British connection as its declared goal at the time of the last general elections, any new relationship in contravention of that policy with the British Commonwealth can only be properly decided by the new Parliament of the Indian Republic, which will be elected under the new Constitution on the basis of adult suffrage.

INTERNATIONAL AFFAIRS

Now to come to the issues of foreign policy[1]. It is clear that there has been very little criticism of our foreign policy except in so far as it applied to Pakistan. I would like to say that the record of our foreign policy, in the two and a half years since we attained independence, is a very satisfactory one, judged by the status of the nation in international affairs. There is no doubt that, for a variety of reasons, India's reputation in international affairs is high. We have adopted, as the House knows, a policy which has been described as one of neutrality or non-alignment. I dislike the word 'neutrality' because there is a certain passivity about it and our policy is not passive. Why we are criticized as sitting on the fence or as siding with this or that group, I do not quite understand. A country's foreign policy ultimately emerges from its own traditions, urges, objectives and, more particularly, from its recent past. India is being powerfully affected by her recent past. We were laying down the basic of our foreign policy even when we were opposing the British Government during the last twenty or thirty years. I submit that within the limits of a changing situation, we have tried to follow that policy. It seems to me extraordinarily presumptuous on anybody's part to ask me to join or that bloc. Is my country so small, so insignificant, so lacking in worth or strength, that it cannot say what it wants to say, that it must say ditto to this or that? Why should my policy be the policy of this country or that country? It is going to be my policy, the Indian policy and my country's policy.

It is true that no policy can be viewed in isolation. We co-operate with other countries and we seek the co-operation of others. We have our likes and dislikes. In

[1] Reply to debate on the President's address in Parliament, 3 February 1950, *Jawaharlal Nehru: Selected Speeches*, vol. 2, 1949–53, pp. 127–34.

regard to our likes, they help us to co-operate; but in regard to our dislikes, they come in the way. Indeed, we tone down our dislikes deliberately because we want to be friendly with other countries.

We see that the world today is blinded by fear and hatred. It is an extraordinary situation and it is becoming more and more difficult for countries to take an objective view of any subject or problem. This enveloping fear and hatred lead them to violence and war. What it will ultimately lead to, I cannot say. I still think it possible that grave disasters and catastrophes might be avoided for the world, not by the efforts of India alone but also by enlisting the aid of earnest people of goodwill in other parts of the world, who think likewise.

Whatever the consequences of another war may be, it is dead certain—and it is terrible to contemplate—that in every country and in every part of the world most things that we value in life will vanish. Whether you call yourself a communist, a socialist or any others 'ist,' you cannot let the very basis of progress and civilized existence be destroyed for a whole generation or more. Of course, some third or fourth generation may be able to arise from the ashes of that war but any person who thinks at all earnestly must come to the conclusion that every effort must be made to prevent this great catastrophe overwhelming the world.

I am not so vain as to imagine that any efforts on the part of our Government will make a great difference to world affairs. Yet, every little effort counts and, in any event, I do not see why our efforts should not be in that direction and why we should take for granted that war is inevitable and give up all attempts to prevent it. This, therefore, is the aim of our foreign policy.

Some honourable Members criticized our association with the Commonwealth of Nations. May I beg the House or those Members who object to it to dissociate this question from past sentiment? I do feel that it is the past sentiment that governs them more than the present situation. Presumably, some people imagine that our association with the Commonwealth imposes some kind of restricting or limiting factor upon our activities, be they political, economic, foreign, domestic or anything else. That impression is completely unfounded. In the case of the United Nations or the International Monetary Fund, some limiting factors certainly come in, as they must, if we join an international organization of that type; but in our association with the Commonwealth, there is not the least vestige of such a limiting factor.

As the House well knows, this is not a constitutional issue; it is in the nature of a gentleman's agreement between the countries of the Commonwealth which we entered into deliberately and after serious thought because we felt that this relationship was to our advantage.

I think an honourable Member said something about devaluation. Whether devaluation was good or bad has nothing to do with our membership of the Commonwealth. We may carry out any policy we like regardless of whether we are in the Commonwealth or not. When people think of the Commonwealth influencing us in our policies, may I suggest to them the possibility that we may also greatly influence others in the right direction?

Then, a reference was made to countries like South Africa whose policy brings them into conflict with us in the various phases of our activities. Questions are often asked of me: 'Did you consider the South African issue or the Pakistan issue at the Colombo Conference and elsewhere?' My answer invariably is that we did not, because we do not deliberately want to make the Commonwealth Conference a kind of tribunal or a kind of superior body to decide our issues. We are all independent countries dealing directly with one another. The House knows that our membership of the Commonwealth has made no difference whatever to our dealing with the South African issue. If we go out of the Commonwealth, it will not make much difference to our policy, except, perhaps, that it might, in some ways, become slightly easier for us to deal with each country in the Commonwealth on a reciprocal basis.

Apart from the general reason, namely, that there is absolutely no object in our breaking an association which might help and certainly cannot hinder and which helps in the larger context of world affairs, there is one major reason for our remaining in the Commonwealth and that is that a very large number of Indians live abroad in what are called British colonies or dependencies. I am not talking about the self-governing or independent countries of the Commonwealth but about other places. By our remaining in the Commonwealth, these Indians are in a better position than they would be otherwise. In the latter case, they would have to make a sudden choice and break with India or with the country where they reside. Had we left the Commonwealth it would have put millions of our people in a very difficult position, quite unnecessarily.

Coming to our relations with Pakistan, many honourable Members have expressed the opinion that we have been too gentle, that we have been indulging in appeasement or that we have not been firm enough and so on. Well, to discuss specific matters and give an answer is also not easy, because in the very delicate state of relations between India and Pakistan during the last two and a half years, everything that has happened does not see the light of day. We don't shout from the house-tops about what we do and, therefore, all the facts are sometimes not before the public. I do not, however, wish to take shelter behind that plea. Most of the facts are before the public and before this House. I should like the House and honourable Members—if not now, at a later stage—to tell me what they think should or should not be done about any specific matter. The vague idea of 'being firm' does not help.

The partition of India was, from every point of view, a very unnatural thing. Well, we accepted it, we continue to accept it and we will act accordingly. But as the President said in his Address, it inflicted such wounds on the vast masses of people in India and Pakistan as would take some time to heal.

Some honourable Members have often pointed out that Pakistan employs wrong methods and does not follow a straight policy. I agree. But would honourable Members suggest to this Government that it should also not follow a straight policy in regard to Pakistan? I want that question to be considered and answered, because I am quite convinced in my mind that whatever policy Pakistan may follow, we should not follow a crooked policy. I say that, not merely on grounds of high principles but from the point of view of sheer opportunism. If I have gained any experience in the last thirty or forty years of my public life or if I have learnt any lesson from the Great Master who taught us many things, it is this, that a crooked policy does not pay in the end. It may pay temporarily.

I do not mean—how could I—that any Member is suggesting such a policy but there are people and organizations outside the House who do suggest it and that is why I referred to it. Some of the things suggested by bodies like the Hindu Mahasabha seem to me the stupidest of things. But there is a market for stupidity and cupidity in this country. Suggestions, which according to me are crooked suggestions and come out of crooked minds, will not be accepted by us, whatever the consequences. It is not so much to this House that I am addressing myself as to the people outside who irresponsibly say things which affect our foreign policy and which give cause to the people on the other side of the frontier to create more trouble.

We are a great country and this House has great authority over matters of State, both domestic and foreign. What this House says or what an honourable Member in this House may say is carried to far countries and this is how other people judge our country. Therefore, we must speak with a great deal of responsibility. Our lightest utterance may have a special meaning for other countries. I try, in spite of the failing on my part not to talk rashly at times, to restrain myself. I have tried to speak with as much moderation as I can on matters concerning Pakistan and other countries. I am convinced that we must be strong and firm in our policies and preparation, be they military or other; we must not give in on any point we consider wrong, whatever happens; but our attitude should, at the same time, be restrained, moderate and friendly. Whether it is possible to combine the two or not, it is difficult to say.

Anyhow, that is my training and that was the training we received even when we were fighting a powerful imperialism and risking everything in that fight: not to bow down to evil but to be firm with it, not to compromise with it or stoop to its own level but to prepare to meet it on every front and, at the same time, be gentle in our conduct and moderate in our language. Perhaps, some honourable Member may sometimes mistake our soft language or our moderate approach for lack of firmness. Why not examine our actions—whether they are in the plains or in the mountains of Kashmir—and study them?

May I beg of you to consider here that we are facing a new situation, at any rate, a new development, to which an honourable Member drew attention yesterday? The exodus from East to West Bengal is increasing. I agree that is a bad thing and everything should be done to check it and to help those who come over. But behind it lies something much bigger. If this kind of thing goes on, obviously it may lead to disastrous consequences. Should we, in a moment of anger, say or do things which precipitate further crises and further disasters? I submit to this honourable House that a responsible government should not do that. It should, of course, take every effective step. But shouting aggressively is not such a 'step'. Unfortunately, the old traditions of diplomacy have been forgotten in the modern world. Diplomacy in the olden days may have been good or bad but people at least did not curse one another in public. The new tradition today is to carry on publicly a verbal warfare in the strongest language. Perhaps, that is better than actual fighting but it leads to fighting or rather may lead to fighting.

I, therefore, submit that, in our relations with Pakistan, we have first of all to follow a policy of firmness and adequate preparation but always to maintain a friendly approach. Again, there can be no doubt that India and Pakistan, situated as they are geographically and otherwise and with their historical background, cannot carry on for ever as enemies. If they do, catastrophe after catastrophe will follow; either they will wipe each other out or one will wipe the other out and suffer the consequences, which is unthinkable. We are passing through trouble and crisis, largely due, in my opinion, to a certain fund of hatred and violence accumulated during the days before Partition. We have inherited this legacy and we must face it. Let us forget the Governments—our Government and the Government of Pakistan—and think of the millions of people who live next door to one another. At some time or other, those millions will have to come together, will have to co-operate, will have to be friends. There is no doubt about it. Let us think of that future which may not be very distant and let us not do things today which may lead to generations of rivalry and conflict.

We have, as the House knows, offered to make a joint declaration with the Government of Pakistan for the avoidance of war. Some honourable Members may think that it is a gesture of weakness. Well, I am sorry if they think so, because it is in fact a gesture of strength. We know exactly to what limit we are going to permit things to go. We have made that offer, because we are convinced that, if it was agreed to, it would lay the foundations for a gradual, if not sudden, improvement and for the settlement of various questions. I do not want honourable Members to think lightly of a question which they want solved by war. I can understand war in the context of defence. I don't wish to think of war in the context of aggression and I want to make this point perfectly clear on behalf of myself and my Government.

We have, indeed, fallen far below what might be called the Gandhian ideology but it still influences us to some extent. And, anyway, it is not a question of ideologies at all; it is a question of looking at the world today with clear eyes. As the House remembers, Mahatma Gandhi once spoke warningly of the countries of the world looking at one another with bloodshot eyes. There is something fateful about that sentence. He said, 'keep your eyes clear.' So, I try as far as I can, to keep my eyes clear when I look at the scene, whether it is India or the world scene or the relations between India and Pakistan; for bloodshot eyes bode nothing good, no clear thinking and no clear action. An honourable Member implied that people grow weak because they don't have bloodshot eyes or because they don't urge one another on to war all the time. That is not only a wrong policy but a policy of despair.

If we can maintain a certain state of mental preparedness only by strong drinks and intoxicating words, we must obviously succumb when we do not have them. Therefore, it is well to be prepared for all contingencies, whether military or any other. It is well to be firm and not bow down to evil. But it is also well always to be conciliatory and always to stretch out your hand to those who will grasp it; because, though their Government may not do so, the people will always grasp an outstretched hand, not only the people of a particular country but the people of all the countries of the world.

FIVE POWER RESOLUTION[2]

Mr President, two or three days ago, I presented on behalf of Ghana, the United Arab Republic, Indonesia, Yugoslavia and India, a resolution to the General Assembly. That resolution is a simple one and requires little argument to support

[2] Speech in the U.N. General Assembly, New York, 3 October 1960, *Jawaharlal Nehru: Selected Speeches*, 1957–63, vol. 4, 1996.

it. It does not seek to pre-judge any issue, or to bring pressure to bear on any country or individual. There is no cynicism in it. The main purpose of the resolution is to help avoid a deadlock in the international situation. Every delegate present here knows how unsatisfactory that situation is today, and how gradually every door and window for a discussion of vital issues is being closed and bolted. As the resolution says, we are deeply concerned with the recent deterioration in international relations which threatens the world with grave consequences.

There can be no doubt that people everywhere in the world look to this Assembly to take some step to help ease this situation and lessen world tension. If this Assembly is unable to take that step, there will be utter disappointment everywhere. Not only will the deadlock continue, but there will be a drift in a direction from which it will become increasingly difficult to turn back. This Assembly cannot allow itself to be paralysed in a matter of such vital importance. Responsibility for this deadlock has to be shared by all of us. But, in the circumstances as they exist today, a great deal depends upon two mighty nations, the Untied States of America and the Soviet Union, and if even a small step can be taken by them, the world will heave a sigh of relief.

We do not expect that some solution is likely to emerge from a renewal of contacts between these two countries. We do not underrate the difficulties. Realizing all these and after giving a great deal of thought to these matters, we decided to share our apprehensions with this Assembly, and to suggest a step which will undoubtedly help to ease the tension. The resolution has been placed before this Assembly not to add to the controversies already existing or to embarrass anyone, but solely with the desire, which is anxiously felt, that something must be done. We cannot meet here in this Assembly and sit helplessly watching the world drift in a direction which can only end in a catastrophe.

Last night I received a letter from the President of the United States in which he was good enough to deal with this resolution. I presume that the other sponsors of the resolution have also received a similar reply. I am grateful to the President for writing to us in reply immediately after receiving our communication. Although the letter does not indicate that any contacts such as we had recommended are likely to take place in the near future, the President has not wholly rejected the idea. The door is still open for consideration of the idea. The President has expressed his deep anxiety to help in a lessening of international tensions. He has pointed out that 'the chief problems in the world today are not due to differences between the Soviet Union and the United States alone and, therefore, are not possible of solution on a bilateral basis. The questions which are disrupting the world at the present time are of immediate and vital concern to other nations as well.'

May I express respectfully my complete agreement with what the President has said? We are convinced that these great questions cannot be dealt with on a bilateral basis or even by a group of countries. They are of intimate and vital concern to the entire world and to all those who have gathered here from the four corners of the earth. It was because of this feeling that some of us ventured to put the resolution before this Assembly. If the matter is of concern only to the two countries, perhaps no necessity would have arisen for us to raise it here. Nor did we think that a renewal of contacts would lead to some magical solution. A solution will come after long and arduous labour in which many countries participate. But we did think that in the present situation of dangerous drift, even a small approach on behalf of the two great countries would make a difference and might mark a turn of the tide.

Oppressed by the growing anger and bitterness in international relations, we wanted to find some way out so that further consideration might be given to these problems. We have suggested no remedy nor any particular solution in the resolution. But we did and still feel that the General Assembly should consider this problem and try its utmost to find a way to remove the new barriers that have arisen.

As the President of the United States has rightly stated, the importance of these matters is such as goes beyond the personal or official relations between any two individuals. We are dealing with the future of humanity and no effort which might perhaps improve the situation should be left out. It is with this intention that we put forward the resolution as a part of the efforts which should be made to open the door for future consultations.

I earnestly trust, and appeal to the Assembly to adopt this resolution unanimously at an early date. Enveloped and bedevilled by the cold war and all its progeny, the world is faced with problems awaiting urgent solution, and I have ventured to add my voice in appeal.

I should like, right at the beginning,[3] to say that I welcome the amendment which was proposed to the draft resolution by the Foreign Minister of the United Arab Republic. The amendment makes no effective change, but I think it is a happier way of putting forward the idea contained in the resolution.

When I had the privilege to put forward the resolution from five nations before this Assembly, I expressed the hope that it would be accepted unanimously. It did

---

[3] Speech in the U.N. General Assembly on the amendment proposed by Australia to the five-nation draft resolution, New York, 5 October 1960.

not seem to me reasonably possible that any member of this Assembly could object to the resolution. It was straightforward. It contained nothing in it against any individual or this group or that group. But it did represent a strong and passionate desire that things should get moving, and that this Assembly should not sit paralysed, as if it could not act. Therefore, it was with considerable surprise that I received the paper containing an amendment on behalf of Australia.

I read it with care. I found some difficulty in understanding it. And the more I read it the more surprised I was that any member of this Assembly should have put this forward as an amendment. I venture to place before this Assembly my reasons for this.

First of all, it seemed to me, quite patently, that it had nothing to do by way of amending the proposition which we had put forward. It is not an amendment. I do not perhaps know the rules of this Assembly, but it is not an amendment. It may be, of course, a separate resolution in some form or another, and might have been brought forward and considered, by this House, If it was so considered, I would have had much to say about it and against it. The Prime Minister of Australia in his speech made it quite clear that it was not an amendment, although he might call it so. Therefore, I could not quite understand what meaning lay behind this amendment.

I have the greatest respect for the Prime Minister of Australia, more especially for his keen mind and ability. I wondered if that keen mind and ability had not tried to cover up, with a jumble of words, something which had no meaning at all—or the wrong meaning. I was particularly keen and anxious to listen to the Prime Minister of Australia in the hope that he might throw some light on this aspect of the question which I had failed to understand. I listened to him with great care. The more I listened, the more confused I grew and the more I realized that there was no substantive idea in this motion, but just a dislike of what the five-nation resolution had suggested.

He stated clearly that he dissented from the last paragraph of the resolution—a very innocuous one, nevertheless with very considerable meaning. In fact, the whole resolution led upto this paragraph, the rest being a preamble. Therefore, he dissented from the very basis of the resolution. Coming forward with his amendment, he said that the effect of the resolution, if carried, would be undesirable. I wondered if I had understood him correctly or if I had made some mistake in regard to what he said. Why, I ask the Prime Minister, from any point of view, or from any approach, could the passage of the resolution possibly be undesirable? I have given thought to this matter, but I am quite unable to understand his reasoning. Therefore, it must be undesirable from some point of view of which

I am not aware and which has nothing to do with the resolution. That is the conclusion I arrived at.

I would put it to this distinguished Assembly, with respect and without meaning offence, that this a rather trivial way of dealing with this not only important question but vital question which is shaking the world—the question of the world conflict and how to avoid it—by calling it an amendment of the resolution. I submit that we are discussing very important matters, affecting this Assembly and the world.

The Prime Minister, in his argument, talked about a conference. Why does the resolution suggest a meeting or a conference? I would beg him to read the resolution again, because he has failed to understand it. It does not necessarily suggest a conference or a meeting. It suggests a renewal of contacts.

Again, he asked, 'Why should two people meet? Why should not four meet? Why dismiss the United Kingdom and France? Why omit them from summit talks?' These are quotations which I took down when he was speaking. 'Why all this?' he asked. Well, simply because there is no 'Why?' about it, because nobody is dismissing or pushing out anybody, or suggesting it. He has missed the point of the draft resolution and has considered, possibly, that there is some kind of a secret motive behind this. I really regret that any such idea should have gone aboard.

The draft resolution was put forward in all good faith for the purposes named in it, and to suspect it of some secret device to push out somebody or not to pay adequate respect to some country is not fair on the part of the honourable gentleman. Indeed, I greatly regret to say that the Prime Minister of Australia has done very little justice to himself in proposing this amendment or in making the speech which he did. I am sure that this Assembly will not take at this matter from the superficial point of view which the Prime Minister put forward, but will consider it from the basic point of view which is of the highest importance to this Assembly and to the world.

Let us look at this amendment. The wording in interesting. In the second paragraph it says:

'Recalling that a conference between the President of the United States of America, the Chairman of the Council of Ministers of the Union of Soviet Socialist Republics, the President of the French Republic and the Prime Minister of the United Kingdom of Great Britain and Northern Ireland was arranged to take place in Paris on 17th May 1960,'—

now note the words—

'in order that these four leaders should examine matters of particular and major concern for their four nations.'

It is a private matter between the four nations, according to the Prime Minister of Australia. What has this Assembly to do with it? Then, later, this amendment says:

'Believing that much benefit for the world could arise from a co-operative meeting of the heads of Government of these four nations in relation to those problems which particularly concern them...'

This is a very extraordinary idea to put before this Assembly—that is, these so-called summit meetings and the rest are private concerns of the four eminent dignitaries, heads of States or Prime Ministers of these four countries. Where does this Assembly come in? Where do all of us who happen to be in the outer darkness come in?

The Prime Minister of Australia then said that we, the sponsors of the draft resolution, had fallen into some communist trap which was aimed at describing the world as being divided up, or as dealing with two great protagonists and ignoring the world.

What the communist technique may be in regard to this matter, I am not aware. There may or may not be one; I am not particularly concerned with such techniques. But it seems to me that the Australian Prime Minister's technique is obvious. It is: 'There are these four powers'—whom, of course, we respect and honour—'so leave it to them. What business has this Assembly to deal with these matters?' This is obvious and the amendment says so. Now, surely, this kind of idea or approach cannot, should not and must not be accepted.

When we suggested that the distinguished heads of the two great States should renew contacts, it was not with an idea that they should discuss the affairs of the world and finalize them. I personally would not agree to a finalization of these matters between two powers or four powers or ten powers. Only this Assembly should finalize them. But it is true that while dealing with these tremendous questions it is convenient and desirable for matters to be discussed in small groups and—more particularly for a question such as disarmament—by some of the countries which have most to disarm. Most of the people sitting here have practically nothing to disarm although we are greatly interested in the disarmament of others so that war may not break out and destroy the world.

Therefore, it is right that two powers or four powers or ten committees or commissions may consider these matters quietly, and from a constructive point of view. That is all right. But, in a matter of this magnitude, no group of powers, however big, can dispose of the density of the world. However, that appears to be the idea behind the mind of the Prime Minister of Australia. Because he has that idea, he was somewhat irritated that only two powers should do so. It is not my intention that any two powers, or four or six or more, should do so. Therefore, I should like to disabuse his mind of the wrong opinion which he has.

My difficulty in dealing with this amendment is that it proceeds, I imagine, from some kind of a basic suspicion that there is a trick in the draft resolution. The Prime Minister is not able to put his finger on it, but he thinks that there must be a trick because the idea contained in the resolution has not come from him or his group. Personally I am rather innocent of the working of this Assembly. But certainly I can assure the Prime Minister with all earnestness that there is no trickery in the draft resolution. However, there is something which I would like him to appreciate, and that is that there is a passion in this draft resolution. It is not a question of words. The Prime Minister said that he prayed daily for the avoidance of armed conflict. I was happy to hear that. I earnestly hope that his prayers as well as the prayers of all of us will have effect. Even prayers require some action. We meet here not merely to pray but to initiate action and to give a lead to the world by inducing, urging and sometimes pushing people to act in a particular way.

The draft resolution that we ventured to put before this Assembly represented that passion and conviction that something or the beginning of something must be initiated which may take effect later on. Above all, it seemed to us that for this great organization to meet, with members coming from the four corners of the earth, and to avoid discussing this matter was a confession of helplessness and of paralysis. I submit that it would be an intolerable position that this great Assembly could not deal with these matters because some people were angry with each other. Anger may be justified but should not override the consideration of major issues which we have to deal with. We realize that the resolution which we put before this Assembly cannot lead to the path of a solution or even to a basic consideration of these problems. But what we were concerned with was the hope that this glacier that had come to surround us, as it were, might be pushed a little or might be made to melt here and there, so that in the future discussions could take place at suitable times. At the present moment they cannot. The United States of America is engaged in the great election and I quite realize that it is not convenient for it to enter into these basic talks. But if nothing is done to arrest the process of deterioration in international relations, it can become even more difficult at a later stage to have these talks. That is a fact which is to be borne in mind. Therefore, we suggested that this small but highly important step might be taken as an urgent step towards the renewal of contacts.

We think we were perfectly right. On the other hand, let us consider what the effect would be if the advice of the Prime Minister of Australia were to be followed. It would mean—it says so quite clearly—that this renewal of contacts would not take place, that the negative view prevails and that we should wait for some future occasion for some kind of summit conference to be held. I am all in favour of a summit conference, but I realize and this Assembly realizes that it cannot be held in the next few months. Therefore, we should have to wait and spend our time, presumably in daily prayer that this might take place and that war might be avoided.

I submit that this position is not only a completely untenable position, but it verges on absurdity. I am surprised that a man of the high ability of the Prime Minister of Australia should put this idea forward. I regret to say that this amendment does have a tinge of the cold war approach. It is obvious that if we are to seek solutions for these mighty problems it cannot be through such approaches. We have had plenty of charges and counter-charges, accusations and counter-accusations and perhaps we shall continue to have these. But the fact remains that if we are to deal with serious questions the approach has to be different. We have to recognize facts as they are and deal with the problems as they are.

I am anxious, therefore, that the resolution which has been sponsored by the five nations should be passed unanimously, or, if not unanimously, nearly unanimously. Not to pass it would be a dangerous thing from this point of view of the objectives for which the United Nations stands, and from the point of view of creating some kind of a disengagement, the beginnings of a *detente* indicating some movement in the right direction. It would be dangerous, harmful and wholly unjustifiable not to pass it. Therefore, the resolution should be passed. I hope that the Prime Minister of Australia will realize that his amendment is not what he apparently imagined it to be and that it is harmful. The amendment would mean that we should let months pass and that subsequently these four great countries can meet together and possibly renew their charges and counter-charges. That position is not good enough. Even we of the humbler countries, without vast armies and nuclear weapons, may sometimes unburden our hearts; if we cannot unburden our hearts and our minds in this Assembly, what are we to do? Are we to be shepherded into this group or that group, and not allowed to express even our innermost feelings? I do submit that this kind of approach would not be right.

Therefore, I beg again to press for the passage of this draft resolution, if not Unanimously, nearly unanimously.

Mr President[4], you were good enough to allow the sponsors of the draft resolution an opportunity to consult amongst themselves on the position that has been created

---

[4] Speech in the U.N. General Assembly while announcing the withdrawal of the draft resolution, New York, 5 October 1960.

because of certain changes which have been made in the draft. We have consulted amongst ourselves and with many others who have supported the resolution. We feel that the changes made are of such a character as to make a difference to the purpose of the draft resolution. These, according to our thinking, not only make a part of the resolution contrary to fact, but also make an essential change which takes away from the main purpose underlying the draft resolution.

The resolution was drafted under great stress of feeling, almost of oppression, at what it described as 'the recent deterioration in international relations'. All over the world people will be looking to this august Assembly to indicate some step to prepare the way for an easing of world tension. Therefore, the resolution referred to 'the grave and urgent responsibility that rests on the United Nations to initiate helpful efforts'. As the draft resolution has now been changed, it seems to us that that essential urgency has gone, and the passionate feeling that something should be done has faded away in the wording of the resolution as it is. Further, something is being said in it which is not true to fact, that is, that these two great countries, the United States of America and the Soviet Union, should renew their contacts. There has in fact been no break in those contacts politically, diplomatically or otherwise. Therefore, it is not a correct statement. It does not seem proper that this Assembly should be responsible for a statement which is so patently incorrect. At any rate, the sponsors of the draft resolution do not wish to associate themselves with such a statement. This is a relatively minor matter. The major point is that the resolution as it stands now lacks that sense of passion and energy and dynamism which we thought the situation required.

We have had considerable discussion over procedural matters. As has become evident during these discussions, high questions of policy lay behind those procedural matters. We held certain opinions about the procedural matters also, but I shall not refer to them. It transpired throughout this late hour in the evening that there were differences of opinion on basic matters and those differences were sought to be brought about in these changes which now form part of the draft resolution. Therefore, according to us, the purpose for which the sponsors had submitted the resolution is not being served. The resolution, which has now been changed, may indeed create an impression of these matters being taken up by this Assembly without that sense of urgency which we thought was necessary.

From another point of view, all this discussion has seemed to us to raise major moral issues. I shall not go into them in any detail, but we do consider that the resolution did involve a moral issue and that the way it has been changed has deprived it of that moral approach.

Because of all these reasons, the sponsors of the resolution feel that they cannot, after these changes, associate themselves any longer with the resolution as it is now. Its sponsors are unable to support it and, therefore, I would like to withdraw the resolution.

An Extraordinary Approach[5]

The Kashmir Question has been brought up before the Security Council as a matter of urgent importance. For six or seven years it had not been there, and suddenly it cropped up and it was said to be very urgent. Why? Because it was stated that India was on the point of marching on Pakistan or on that portion of Kashmir occupied by Pakistan. The leaders of Pakistan knew very well that nothing of this kind was going to happen. They have the habit of making statements which have no foundation whatsoever.

It is absurd to imagine that India is going to march an army over that part of Kashmir which Pakistan occupies. However, the leaders of Pakistan made this a matter of great urgency. We had no particular objection to it, except that we saw no benefit arising out of a debate in the Security Council. It was only likely that the speeches would embitter our relations still further. That is why we were against a debate.

After a tremendous plea of hurry lest something should happen, a date was ultimately fixed a few days ago. Mr Zafrullah Khan delivered an address which he did not finish that day. The next day for him to continue that address fell a week later. Suddenly the element of hurry was absent. This postponement of the address by a week upset our programme or rather the programme of our Defence Minister who had to speak on our behalf. He had gone there for three or four days to answer the charge and come back. But when he arrived at the Security Council, he was told that he had to stay there a week to listen to the concluding part of Mr Zafrullah Khan's speech. He naturally said that it was very awkward for him. He had important work here and with great difficulty he got the date advanced by one day. Thereupon, Mr Zafrullah Khan said that he had not been given enough time to prepare his case.

This is very extraordinary. Here is a matter pending for several years. Mr Zafrullah Khan has been preparing his case and wanting a debate urgently. Then because the date was fixed a day earlier than he wanted, he said he was not prepared to put forward his case.

[5] From reply to debate in Rajya Sabha on the President's Address, 3 May 1962, *Jawaharlal Nehru: Selected Speeches*, 1957–63, (Second Series), vol. 4, 1996, pp. 501–2.

In the course of his speech in the Security Council Mr Zafrullah Khan said, among other things, that a second tribal invasion of Kashmir would take place if the Council failed to find a suitable solution.

We have got definite information that for some months past the Pakistan authorities have been registering names of tribesmen for 'khasedars' on a monthly salary of Rs 54. Nearly 5,000 men have offered their services, but actual recruitment has not taken place yet. These figures are for one small bazaar area only. Probably it is taking place elsewhere too. These tribals we invited first to a function as 'khasedars', which is the name used for the local levies who have functioned in those areas from the British times. They asked these 'khasedars' to serve in their own areas and they agreed to that on salary. When they were told that they had to go to Kashmir they were not at all anxious to do so, perhaps because they were likely to meet the Indian Army there. Many therefore withdrew their names. But Pakistan leaders go to the Security Council with threats of tribal invasion and of war. I would beg the House to consider the extent to which the Pakistan Government's whole attitude is unrealistic, because they know that if any such thing happens, there will be war, an all-out war. Unfortunately, all their strength consists in the military aid which they have got from the United States. If they had not got that aid, they would probably talk in a much lower key. And by their threats they seek to get more aid from the United States. I should like the United States Government, which I respect greatly, more especially under the present leadership, to consider the effect of their aid, and how they counter-balance their own policy by the military aid which they give to Pakistan.

A New Era in Asian Fellowship[6]

There is struggle and turmoil in various parts of Asia today and yet behind it all there is a new vitality. Asia, the mother of continents, is waking up from her old slumber. There is something of the turbulence of youth about her today and there is also something of the sparkle of youth in her eyes. An age is coming to an end and a new era is beginning for the countries of Asia. It is fitting that on the eve of this historic change India should play hostess to the representatives of the other countries of this continent with whom she has had close and intimate relations for

[6] Message, 3 March 1947, printed in the Inter-Asian Conference Special Number of the *National Herald*, 23 March 1947.

243 delegates from 28 Asian countries attended the Conference held at New Delhi from 23 March to 2 April 1947.

ages past. Those relations and contacts were cut off when India became a subject country. Her land frontiers became an effective barrier to such contacts and practically the only window she had to the outside world looked at Europe, and more particularly England.

Now again after these centuries she is opening her doors and windows to all her neighbours and old friends and inviting them to meet together on her ancient soil which is so full of memories of the great deeds and great men and women. It is a high privilege for India to inaugurate in this way this new era of Asian fellowship and comradeship in the cause of peace, freedom and progress.

Many eminent men and women are coming to our country inspired by this common desire for the peoples of Asia to co-operate together in common tasks. Long and bitter experience has taught them that no country in the world today can isolate itself or even retain its freedom without co-operating with others. And so we meet together and for a moment the past two centuries fade away from our minds and we think again of earlier times when we used to function as free nations. And yet it is not of the past that we are going to think but rather of the future that is taking shape before our eyes and in the making of which all of us are taking part. That future, we hope, will be even greater than the past. It will not be a future for Asia alone but for the world, for we do not meet to form a new Asian bloc of nations against others but rather to co-operate with all the nations of the world to help in furthering the cause of peace and freedom.

Not even in the long and chequered history of Asia has there been such a gathering of representatives from the many countries of Asia as we are having in Delhi. The occasion is unique and full of historic significance. May it be the harbinger of a closer fellowship in the works of peace and progress and may it light a flame which will burn brightly in every country of Asia and bring light in the darkness that envelops world affairs today.

NEED FOR A TEMPER OF PEACE[7]

Friends,

It is always a pleasure for me to come to England. I have many friends here, and the memory of my earlier days surrounds me. I welcome, therefore, this opportunity to come here again, but the pleasure that this would have brought me has been marred somewhat by the crisis which confronts the world, and the burdens which each one of us has to bear. This makes me somewhat hesitant to talk to you. It

---

[7] Broadcast from the B.B.C., London, 12 January 1951.

would serve little purpose for me to repeat platitudes. To refer frankly to the matters of grave import which oppress us today is not easy for me in my present position. It would ill become of me to say anything which embarrasses friends here, and yet, this very consciousness of pervasive friendliness in England emboldens me to talk to you in a manner of friends who have a common purpose in view and who wish to co-operate in achieving it.

What is that purpose? Surely today it is the avoidance of war and the maintenance of peace. Of my generation many have lived the greater part of our lives and only a few years remain to us. It matters little what happens to our generation; but it does matter a great deal what happens to hundreds of millions of others, and to the world at large. Today these hundreds of millions all over the world live under some kind of suspended sentence of death, and from day to day an atmosphere is created in people's minds of the inevitability of war. Helplessly we seem to be driven towards the abyss. More and more people in responsible positions talk in terms of passion, revenge and retaliation. They talk of security, and behave in a way which is likely to put an end to all security. They talk of peace, and think and act in terms of war.

Are we so helpless that we cannot stop this drift towards catastrophe? I am sure that we can, because vast masses of people in every country want peace. Why, then, should they be driven by forces apparently beyond their control in a contrary direction? Politicians and statesmen strive for peace through the technique of politics which consists in devising carefully worded formulae. During the last ten days the Commonwealth Prime Ministers have wrestled with this problem of world peace. All of us earnestly seek peace. I hope that our labours will help in producing the desired result. But something more is necessary than mere formulae. It is a passion for peace and for civilized behaviour in international affairs that is necessary. It is the temper of peace and not the temper of war, even though peace is casually mentioned.

It is to this temper of peace that I want especially to direct my mind and your mind. We are in the midst of an international crisis, and perhaps an even greater crisis that confronts us today is the crisis in the spirit of man. We have built up a great civilization whose achievements are remarkable and which holds the promise of even greater achievement in the future. But while these material achievements are very great, somehow we appear to be slipping away from the very essence of civilization. Ultimately, culture and civilization rest in the mind and behaviour of man and not in the material evidence of it that we see around us. During war the civilising process stops and we go back to some barbarous phase of the human mind. Are we speeding back to this barbarism of the mind?

If we desire peace, we must develop the temper of peace and try to win even those who may be suspicious of us or who we think are against us. We have to try to understand others just as we expect them to understand us. We cannot seek peace in the language of war or of threats. You will all remember the magnificent example of which both England and India have reason to be proud. Both of us, in spite of long continued struggle, approached our problems with this basic temper of peace, and we not only resolved them, but produced at the same time an abiding understanding and friendship for each other. That is a great example which we might well bear in mind whenever any other crisis in the relations of nations confronts us. That is the civilized approach to problems which leaves no ill will or bitterness behind.

I am not a pacifist. Unhappily the world of today finds that it cannot do without force. We have to protect ourselves and to prepare ourselves for any contingency. We have to meet aggression or any other kinds of evil. To surrender to evil is always bad. But in resisting evil we must not allow ourselves to be swept away by our own passions and fears and act in a manner which is itself evil. Even in resisting evil and aggression, we have always to maintain the temper of peace and hold out the hand of friendship to those who, through fear or for other reasons, may be opposed to us. That is the lesson that our great leader Mahatma Gandhi taught us and, imperfect as we are, we draw inspiration from that great teaching.

In Asia, as you know, great changes have taken place. I fear that most of us, and perhaps more particularly you of the West, do not realize the vastness of these changes. We are living through a great historic process which has created a ferment in the minds of hundreds of millions of people and which can be seen at work in political and economic changes. Asia has a very long history behind it and for long ages it played an outstanding part in the world. During the last two or three hundred years it suffered eclipse. Now it is emerging from colonial status. Inevitably this is making a great difference to the balance of forces in the world. The old equilibrium has been upset and can never come back again. That is a basic fact to remember. Asia is essentially peaceful, but it is also proud and sensitive and very conscious of its newly-won freedom. In its exuberance it may go wrong occasionally. It has mighty problems of its own and wishes to live at peace with the rest of the world, but it is no longer prepared to tolerate any domination or threat of domination, or any behaviour after the old pattern of colonialism. It demands recognition of its new position in the world. Therefore I would like you to look with understanding and sympathy on these historic changes which are taking place in Asia, for it is of the utmost importance that Europe, America and Asia as well as other parts of the world should understand each other. Nor should we forget the millions of people who are still under colonial status in Africa and elsewhere. Outworn formulae of a past age will not help. A new approach and understanding are needed, and if these are forthcoming I feel sure that Asia will respond with all friendship. The countries of Asia need and seek friendship and co-operation, for they have tremendous problems to solve. These problems are concerned with the primary needs of their peoples—food, clothing, housing and the other necessities of life. They are too busy with these problems to desire to be entangled in international conflicts. But against their will they are dragged into them.

Great nations have arisen in Asia with long memories of the past they have lived through, and with their eyes fixed on a future of promise. India, Pakistan, Burma, Ceylon and Indonesia have recently acquired their freedom. China has taken a new shape and a new form. But, whether we like that shape and form or not, we have to recognize that a great nation has been reborn and is conscious of her new strength. China in her new-found strength has acted sometimes in a manner which I deeply regret. But we have to remember the background of China, as of other Asian countries—the long period of struggle and frustration, the insolent treatment that they have received from imperialist Powers, and the latter's refusal to deal with them in terms of equality. It is neither right nor practical to ignore the feelings of hundreds of millions of people. It is no longer safe to do so. We in India have two thousand years of friendship with China. We have differences of opinion and even small conflicts, but that long past comes up before us and something of the wisdom of that past also helps us to understand each other. And so we endeavour to maintain friendly relations with this great neighbour of ours, for the peace of Asia depends upon these relations.

The immediate problem of today is the problem of the Far East. If that is not solved satisfactorily, trouble will spread to Europe and to the rest of the world. And perhaps Europe, with her magnificent record of progress, not only in material achievements but also in the culture of the mind and spirit, will suffer most if war comes. Therefore we must come to grips with this Far Eastern problem with the firm determination to solve it. We can only do so with the temper and approach of peace and friendliness, and not by threats. The time when threats were effective is long past. No question of saving face or prestige should come in the way of this human and civilized approach to the problems of our age.

Our task is the preservation of peace and indeed of our civilization. To this task let us bend our energies and find fellowship and strength in each other.

IN THE CAUSE OF PEACE[1]

I have come to you not so much in my capacity as Prime Minister of a great country or a politician but rather as a humble seeker after truth and as one who has continuously struggled to find the way, not always with success, to fit action to the objectives and ideals that he has held. The process is always difficult but it becomes increasingly so in this world of conflict and passion. Politicians have to deal with day to day problems and they seek immediate remedies. Philosophers think of ultimate objectives and are apt to lose touch with the day to day world and its problems. Neither approach appears to be adequate by itself. Is it possible to combine those two approaches and function after the manner of Plato's philosopher-kings? You, Sir, who have had the experience of the role of a great man of action and also that of a philosopher as head of this university, should be able to help us to answer this question.

In this world of incessant and feverish activity, men have little time to think, much less to consider ideals and objectives. Yet, how are we to act, even in the present, unless we know which way we are going and what our objectives are? It is only in the peaceful atmosphere of a university that these basic problems can be adequately considered. It is only when the young men and women, who are in the university today and on whom the burden of life's problems will fall tomorrow, learn to have clear objectives and standards of values that there is hope for the next generation. The past generation produced some great men but as a generation it

[1] Address on the occasion of the conferment of the degree of Doctor of Laws at Columbia University, New York, 17 October 1949, *Jawaharlal Nehru: Selected Speeches*, vol. 2, 1949–53, pp. 391–8.

led the world repeatedly to disaster. Two world wars are the price that has been paid for the lack of wisdom on man's part in this generation. It is a terrible price and the tragedy of it is that, even after the price has been paid, we have not purchased real peace or a cessation of conflict and an even deeper tragedy is that mankind does not profit by its experience and continues to go the same way that led previously to disaster.

We have had wars and we have had victory and we have celebrated that victory; yet, what is victory and how do we measure it? A war is fought presumably to gain certain objectives. The defeat of the enemy is not by itself an objective but rather the removal of an obstruction towards the attainment of the objective. If that objective is not attained, then that victory over the enemy brings only negative relief and indeed is not a real victory. We have seen, however, that the aim in wars is almost entirely to defeat the enemy and the other and real objectives are often forgotten. The result has been that the victory attained by defeating the enemy has only been a very partial one and has not solved the real problem; if it has solved the immediate problem, it has, at the same time, given rise to many other and sometimes worse problems. Therefore, it becomes necessary to have the real objective clear in our minds at all times whether in war or in peace and always to aim at achieving the objective.

I think also that there is always a close and intimate relationship between the end we aim at and the means adopted to attain it. Even if the end is right but the means are wrong, it will vitiate the end or divert us in a wrong direction. Means and ends are thus intimately and inextricably connected and cannot be separated. That, indeed, has been the lesson of old taught us by many great men in the past but unfortunately it is seldom remembered.

I am venturing to place some of these ideas before you, not because they are novel but because they have impressed themselves upon me in the course of my life which has been spent in alternating periods of incessant activity and conflict and enforced leisure. The great leader of my country, Mahatma Gandhi, under whose inspiration and sheltering care I grew up, always laid stress on moral values and warned us never to subordinate means to ends. We were not worthy of him and yet, to the best of our ability, we tried to follow his teaching. Even the limited extent to which we could follow his teaching yielded rich results. After a generation of intense struggle with a great and powerful nation, we achieved success and, perhaps, the most significant part of it, for which credit is due to both parties, was the manner of its achievement. History hardly affords a parallel to the solution of such a conflict in a peaceful way, followed by friendly and co-operative relations. It is astonishing how rapidly bitterness and ill will between the two nations have faded away, giving place to co-operation. And we in India have decided of our own free will to continue this co-operation as an independent nation.

I would not presume to offer advice to other and more experienced nations in any way. But may I suggest for your consideration that there is some lesson in India's peaceful revolution which might be applied to the larger problems before the world today? That revolution demonstrated to us that physical force need not necessarily be the arbiter of man's destiny and that the method of waging a struggle and the way of its termination are of paramount importance. Past history shows us the important part that physical force has played. But it also shows us that no such force can ultimately ignore the moral forces of the world; and if it attempts to do so, it does so at its peril. Today, this problem faces us in all its intensity, because the weapons that physical force has at its disposal are terrible to contemplate. Must the twentieth century differ from primitive barbarism only in the destructive efficacy of the weapons that man's ingenuity has invented for man's destruction? I do believe, in accordance with my master's teaching, that there is another way to meet this situation and solve the problem that faces us.

I realize that a statesman or a man who has to deal with public affairs cannot ignore realities and cannot act in terms of abstract truth. His activity is always limited by the degree of receptivity of the truth by his fellow-men. Nevertheless, the basic truth remains truth and is always to be kept in view and, as far as possible, it should guide our actions. Otherwise we get caught up in a vicious circle of evil when one evil action leads to another.

India is a very old country with a great past. But she is a new country also with new urges and desires. Since August 1947, she has been in a position to pursue a foreign policy of her own. She was limited by the realities of the situation which we could not ignore or overcome. But even so, she could not forget the lesson of her great leader. She has tried to adapt, however imperfectly, theory to reality in so far as she could. In the family of nations she was a newcomer and could not influence them greatly to begin with. But she had a certain advantage. She had great potential resources that could, no doubt, increase her power and influence. A greater advantage lay in the fact that she was not fettered by the past, by old enmities or old ties, by historic claims or traditional rivalries. Even against her former rulers there was no bitterness left. Thus, India came into the family of nations with no prejudices or enmities, ready to welcome and be welcomed. Inevitably, she had to consider her foreign policy in terms of enlightened self-interest but at the same time she brought to it a touch of her idealism. Thus, she has tried to combine idealism with national interest. The main objectives of that policy are: the pursuit of peace, not through alignment with any major power or group of powers but through an independent approach to each controversial or disputed issue, the liberation of subject peoples, the maintenance of freedom, both national and individual, the elimination of racial discrimination and the elimination of want, disease and ignorance which afflict the greater part of the world's population. I am asked frequently why India does not align herself with a particular nation or a group of nations and told that because we have refrained from doing so we are sitting on the fence. The question and the comment are easily understood, because in times of crisis it is not unnatural for those who are involved in it deeply to regard calm objectivity in others as irrational, short-sighted, negative, unreal or even unmanly. But I should like to make it clear that the policy India has sought to pursue is not a negative and neutral policy. It is a positive and a vital policy that flows from our struggle for freedom and from the teachings of Mahatma Gandhi. Peace is not only an absolute necessity for us in India in order to progress and develop but is also of paramount importance to the world. How can that peace be preserved? Not by surrendering to aggression, not by compromising with evil or injustice but also not by talking and preparing for war! Aggression has to be met, for it endangers peace. At the same time, the lesson of the last two wars has to be remembered and it seems to me astonishing that, in spite of that lesson, we go the same way. The very process of marshalling the world into two hostile camps precipitates the conflict which it has sought to avoid. It produces a sense of terrible fear, and that fear darkens men's minds and leads them into wrong courses. There is perhaps nothing so bad and so dangerous in life as fear. As a great President of the United States said, there is nothing really to fear except fear itself.

Our problem, therefore, becomes one of lessening and ultimately putting an end to this fear. That will not happen if all the world takes sides and talks of war. War becomes almost certain then.

We are a member of the family of nations and we have no wish to shirk any of the obligations and burdens of that membership. We have accepted fully the obligations of membership in the United Nations and intend to abide by them. We wish to make our full contribution to the common store and to render our full measure of service. But that can only be done effectively in our own way and of our own choice. We believe passionately in the democratic method and we seek to enlarge the bounds of democracy both on the political and the economical plane, for no democracy can exist for long in the midst of want and poverty and inequality. Our immediate needs are economic betterment and raising the standards of our people. The more we succeed in this, the more we can serve the cause of peace in the world. We are fully aware of our weaknesses and failings and claim no superior virtue; but we do not wish to forfeit the advantage that our present detachment gives us. We believe that the maintenance of that detachment is not only in our interest but also in the interest of world peace and freedom. That the detachment is neither isolationism nor indifference nor neutrality when peace or freedom is threatened. When man's liberty or peace is in danger we cannot and shall not be neutral; neutrality then would be a betrayal of what we have fought for and stand for.

If we seek to ensure peace we must attack the root causes of war and not merely the symptoms. What are the underlying causes of war in the modern world?

One of the basic causes is the domination of one country by another or an attempt to dominate. Large parts of Asia were ruled till recently by foreign and chiefly European Powers. We ourselves were part of the British Empire, as were also Pakistan, Ceylon and Burma; France, Holland and Portugal still have territories over which they rule. But the rising tide of nationalism and the love of independence have submerged most of the Western Empires in Asia. In Indonesia, I hope that there will soon be an independent Sovereign State. We hope also that French Indo-China will achieve freedom and peace before long under a government of its own choice. Much of Africa, however, is subject to Foreign Powers, some of whom still attempt to enlarge their dominions. It is clear that all remaining vestiges of imperialism and colonialism will have to disappear.

Secondly, there is the problem of racial relations. The progress of some races in knowledge or in invention, their success in war and conquest, has tempted them to believe that they are racially superior and has led them to treat other nations with contempt. A recent example of this was the horrible attempt, so largely successful, to exterminate the Jews. In Asia and Africa, racial superiority has been most widely and most insolently exhibited. It is forgotten that nearly all the great religions of mankind arose in the East and that wonderful civilizations grew up there when Europe and America were still unknown to history. The west has too often despised the Asian and the African and still, in many places, denies them not only equality of rights but even common humanity and kindliness. This is one of the great danger points of our modern world; and now that Asia and Africa are shaking off their torpor and arousing themselves, out of this evil may come a conflagration of which no man can see the range of consequences. One of your greatest men said that this country cannot exist half slave and half free. The world cannot long maintain peace if half of it is enslaved and despised. The problem is not always simple nor can it be solved by a resolution or a decree. Unless there is a firm and sincere determination to solve it, there will be no peace.

The third reason for war and revolution is the misery and want of millions of people in many countries and, in particular, in Asia and Africa. In the West, though the war has brought much misery and many difficulties, the common man generally lives in some measure of comfort—he has food, clothing and shelter to some extent. The basic problem of the East, therefore, is to obtain these necessities of life. If they are lacking, then there is the apathy of despair or the destructive rage of the revolutionary. Political subjection, racial inequality, economic inequality and misery—these are the evils that we have to remove if we would ensure peace. If we can offer no remedy, then no other cries and slogans will make an appeal to the minds of the people.

Many of the countries of Asia have entered the family of nations; others we hope will soon find a place in this circle. We have the same hopes for the countries of Africa. This process should proceed rapidly and America and Europe should use their great influence and power to facilitate it. We see before us vast changes taking place, not only in the political and economic spheres but even more so in the minds of men. Asia is becoming dynamic again and is passionately eager to progress and raise the economic standards of her vast masses. This awakening of a giant continent is of the greatest importance to the future of mankind and requires imaginative statesmanship of a high order. The problems of this awakening will not be solved by looking at it with fear or in a spirit of isolationism by any of us. It requires a friendly and understanding approach, clear objectives and a common effort to realize them. The colossal expenditure of energy and resources on armaments is an outstanding feature of many national budgets today but that does not solve the problem of world peace. Perhaps, even a fraction of that outlay, utilized in other ways and for other purposes, will provide a more enduring basis for peace and happiness.

That is India's view, offered in all friendliness to all thinking men and women, to all persons of goodwill in the name of our common humanity. That view is not based on wishful thinking but on a deep consideration of the problems that afflict us all, and on its merits. I venture to place it before you.

I should like to add a few words, Sir. I have been deeply moved by what you have said, by what was said about me in the previous citation and I have felt very humble as I listened to these remarks.

The scene that I see here under your distinguished presidentship will long remain in my mind. Indeed, I do not think that I shall ever forget it. I shall remember the scene and above all I shall remember the great courtesy, kindliness and generosity with which you have received me here and made me one of yourselves.

I shall prize the honour of being a fellow member with you of this great university, above the other honours that have come my way. I shall prize it, not only in my individual capacity as I believe that this honour was, perhaps, meant for more than an individual and that, for the moment, you have treated me not as an individual but also as a symbol for and representative of India. And here, Sir, forgetting myself for a moment, I thank you on behalf of my country and my people.

We are living in a revolutionary age of transition. On the one hand, we see a divided and disintegrating world, a multitude of conflicts and an ever-present fear of world war. On the other hand, we see creative and co-operative impulses seeking a new integration and a new unity. New problems arise from day to day which, in their implications, concern all of us or many of us. The Americans have already recognized a certain community of interest and have created machinery for the protection and promotion of common interests. A similar movement is in progress in Europe. Is it not natural that the free countries of Asia should begin to think of some more permanent arrangement than this Conference for effective mutual consultation and concerted effort in the pursuit of common aims—not in a spirit of selfishness or hostility to any other nation or group of nations, but in order to strengthen and bring nearer fulfilment of the aims and ideals of the Charter of the United Nations? In this world of hatred, conflict and violence, let us endeavour to work jointly and in co-operation with others of goodwill to further the cause of peace and tolerance and freedom. We shall not succeed in our mission if we follow the path of violence or seek to divide the world further, but we may well make a difference to the world if we fashion ourselves in accordance with the old spirit of Asia and hold up the torch of truth and peace to a war-distracted world. May I, in all humility but also with pride, remind this Conference of the message of the Father of our Nation who led us through the long night of our subjection to the dawn of freedom? It was not through hatred or violence or intolerance of each other, he told us, that nations grow in stature or attain their freedom. It is by following his lead in some measure that we attained our independence through peaceful methods. The world has got caught in a vicious circle of fear, hatred and violence. It will never get out of that vicious circle unless it seeks other ways and practises other means. Therefore, let us adhere to the right means with the conviction that right means will inevitably lead to right ends. Thus, we shall help in the process of integration and synthesis which is so urgently needed in the world of today.

The Secular State

TRAVAILS OF PARTITION[1]

On the 15th and 16th of August, India celebrated the coming of independence; not only India but Indians wherever they happened to be in this wide world. I have received thousands of messages of greetings from abroad. They have come from representatives of great nations, from famous men and from Indians from every remote corner of the world. While I have been deeply moved by these messages from the leaders of other countries welcoming India into the fellowship of free nations, nothing has affected me more than the very touching messages from our countrymen overseas. Cut away from their Motherland they have hungered for India's freedom even more perhaps than we have, and the coming of this freedom has been a tremendous event in their lives. May the New India always remember her children abroad who look to her with such pride and affection and give them all the succour she can.

Nearly the whole of India celebrated the coming of independence, but not so the unhappy land of the five rivers. In the Punjab, in both the east and the west, there was disaster and sorrow. There was murder and arson and looting in many places and streams of refugees poured out from one place to another.

One of the first tasks of our Government was to think of the Punjab and so I hurried thither on the morning of the 17th, accompanied by my colleague, Sardar Baldev Singh, the Defence Minister, and Mr Liaquat Ali Khan, the Prime Minister of Pakistan, and some of his colleagues. I want to tell you what we found there and what we did there. There have been wild rumours enough and people's minds all over India are naturally agitated, because whatever happens, the people of the

[1] Broadcast from New Delhi, 19 August 1947, *Jawaharlal Nehru: Selected Speeches*, vol. 1, 1946–9, pp. 64–8.

Punjab, whether they live to the east or to the west, are our own kith and kin and anything that affects them affects us.

You must remember that till the 15th August there was a different regime in the Punjab as a whole. The province was governed under Section 93 of the Government of India Act. The change-over took place on the 15th and the new Provincial Governments thus are only four days old. So also are the new Central Governments. These Governments, Central or Provincial, are directly responsible only since the 15th August. The Provincial Governments of East and West Punjab had to face a terrible crisis in the very hour of their birth, even before they had settled down to work or had proper offices functioning.

The story of the disastrous happenings in the Punjab takes us back many months to March of this year. One disaster has followed another, each producing its reaction elsewhere. I am not going to narrate the story, nor am I going to apportion blame. There has been sufficient murder and arson and crime of all descriptions in many parts of the Punjab, and this fair province, so rich in promise, has suffered untold agony during these months. It would serve little purpose to go into this long story. We begin our new life from the 15th August.

Mr Liaquat Ali Khan, Sardar Baldev Singh and I went to Ambala first and held a conference there with Ministers of East and West Punjab and various civil and military officers. We met also the leaders of various communities, notably the Akali Sikh leaders, Master Tara Singh and Giani Kartar Singh. We went then to Lahore and had a first-hand account of occurrences there and then to Amritsar.

In both Amritsar and Lahore we heard a ghastly tale and we saw thousands of refugees, Hindu, Muslim and Sikh. There were some fires still burning in the cities and reports of recent outrages reached us. We were all unanimously of opinion that we must deal firmly with the situation as we found it and not enter into acrimonious debate about the past, and that the situation demanded that crime must be put an end to immediately at whatever cost.

The alternative was complete chaos and ruin for the land and for every community. Anti-social elements were abroad, defying all authority and destroying the very structure of society. Unless these elements were suppressed, to whatever community they belonged, there was no freedom or even security for any person; and so all of us who were present, whether we belonged to the two Central or the two Provincial Governments or whether we were leading members of the various communities, pledged ourselves to do our utmost to put an end to this orgy of murder and arson.

We have taken effective steps to this end, effective not only from the administrative and military point of view, but what is even more important, from the point of view of a popular approach to all our people. We have established high-level committees of the two Provincial Governments of the Punjab and liaison officers between the civil and the military authorities, so that there should be the fullest amount of co-operation between the two Provincial Governments and the military forces. We have pledged the Central Governments to help in this task. Popular leaders have assured us of their fullest co-operation.

I am convinced that we shall deal with this situation effectively and that fairly soon security will return to the Punjab, but that requires the utmost effort and constant vigilance from all concerned, whether they are Government officers or others. Each one of us who cares for his country must help in this business of restoring peace and security.

In the past we have unfortunately had communal troubles on a large scale. They are not going to be tolerated in the future. So far as the Government of India is concerned, it will deal with any communal outbreak with the greatest firmness. It will treat every Indian on an equal basis and try to secure for him all the rights which he shares with others.

Our State is not a communal state but a democratic state in which every citizen has equal rights. The Government is determined to protect these rights.

I have been assured by Mr Liaquat Ali Khan that this is also the policy of the Pakistan Government.

We have made arrangements for the transport of refugees from Lahore to Amritsar and Amritsar to Lahore. They will be carried by railway trains and motor lorries and we hope that very soon most of those who so want will be carried to their destinations. We are further making arrangements for their proper accommodation and food. The Government of India have sanctioned today a sum of Rs 5 lakhs to the East Punjab Government for the care of refugees. They have sanctioned a further sum of Rs 5 lakhs for the help of refugees who have come to Delhi and elsewhere. Our Refugees Commissioner, Mr Chandra, is proceeding immediately to Amritsar.

We are appointing a Deputy High Commissioner in Lahore to look after our interest there, and more especially to look after the refugees who wish to come to East Punjab. We hope to provide a number of tents to the East Punjab Government for accommodating the refugees. In every way that is possible to us we shall help the unfortunate sufferers in the Punjab. So far as Eastern Punjab is concerned, it is our direct responsibility and we shall act accordingly.

While we shall give every help to those who wish to come to East Punjab, we would not like to encourage mass migration of peoples across the new borders, for this will involve tremendous misery for all concerned. We hope that very soon peace and order will be established and people will have security to carry on their avocations.

While we have done all this, ultimately the future depends on the co-operation we receive from the people. It is with confident expectation of this co-operation that we are proceeding and declaring with conviction that we shall settle this Punjab problem soon. We can make no progress there or elsewhere in India if these horrible disturbances continue. I appeal, therefore, to all people concerned to face this task with firmness and courage and thus to demonstrate how Free India can handle a difficult situation.

The Punjab problem is one of first priority with us and I propose to go there again soon, or whenever needed. Because we seek the co-operation of the people, we must also take them into our confidence. I have, therefore, spoken to you today and I propose to do so again whenever necessity arises. Meanwhile, I hope that people will not give credence to wild rumours which spread so easily and influence people's opinions. The reality has been bad enough, but rumour makes it worse.

To those who have suffered during these dark days in the Punjab, our deepest sympathy goes out. Many have lost their lives, many others have lost everything else that they possessed. We cannot restore the dead, but those who are alive must certainly receive aid from the State now, which should later rehabilitate them.

DOING AWAY WITH
MINORITY RESERVATIONS[1]

...[A]s I have already said, we have set our sails in the right direction. As the Prime Minister said at a meeting the other day, at which I was present, in accepting the abolition of reservations and limiting it for a period of ten years, the majority community and above all the leaders have expressed faith in themselves, to achieve what they believe. It is an act of faith on their part. It was not inspired by any intention to do away with anything which the minorities wanted. It was an act of faith made by the majority community in agreement with the minority communities. I believe that India can achieve her full status only as a secular State. Any attempt to go back to the past, any attempt at revivalism must inevitably shrivel the potentialities and stunt the growth of this great country. And may I say this, that in our march towards the goal—it is still a goal—the minorities must be in the vanguard. Any minority which thinks that it can flourish on sectarianism is asking for ruin and death.

And, Sir, may I, before I end, refer in passing to another thing. Some people say, 'Oh, Anthony, in spite of your grandiose opinions, of your grandiose sentiments, if you feel so strongly, why don't you drop this prefix "Anglo"?' Well, I say 'The word "Anglo-Indian" may be good or bad but rightly or wrongly it connotes to me many things which I hold dear.' But I go further and say to the same friends of mine 'I will drop it readily, as soon as you drop your label of "Hindu"'. The day you drop the label of 'Hindu', the day you forget that you are a Hindu, that day— no, two days before that—I will drop by deed poll, by beat of drum if necessary the

<hr>

[1] 26 May 1949, *Constituent Assembly Debates: Official Report*, vol. 8, pp. 329–32.

prefix 'Anglo': because, believe me that when we all begin to drop these prefixes or labels, not only by paying lip-service to them, not only by making professions about them, but when we really feel them in our hearts, when we by our actions, not by our professions, equate these to our beliefs in a secular State, that day will be welcome first and foremost to the minorities of India, who by that time will have forgotten that they are minorities and that they are Indians first, last and always.

THE HONOURABLE SHRI JAWAHARLAL NEHRU (United Provinces: General): Sir, there has been such an abundance of goodwill shown towards this motion that it is hardly necessary for me to intervene in support of it. But I have felt the urge to do so because I wish to associate myself with this historic turn in our destiny: for, indeed, it is a historic motion that my colleague, the Deputy Prime Minister has put before this House. It is a motion which means not only discarding something that was evil, but turning back upon it and determining with all our strength that we shall pursue a path which we consider fundamentally good for every part of the nation.

Now, all of us here, I believe, are convinced that this business of separatism, whether it took the shape of separate electorates or other shapes, had done a tremendous amount of evil to our country and to our people. We came to the conclusion some time back that we must get rid of separate electorates. That was the major evil. Reluctantly we agreed to carry on with some measure of reservation. Reluctantly we did so for two reasons: Reason No. 1 was that we felt that we could not remove that without the goodwill of the minorities concerned. It was for them to take the lead or to say that they did not want it. For a majority to force that down their throats would not be fair to the various assurances that we had given in the past, and otherwise, too, it did not look the right thing to do. Secondly, because in our heart of hearts we were not sure about ourselves nor about our own people as to how they would function when all these reservations were removed, we agreed to that reservation, but always there was this doubt in our minds, namely, whether we had not shown weakness in dealing with a thing that was wrong. So when this matter came up in another context, and it was proposed that we do away with all reservations, except in the case of the Scheduled Castes, for my part I accepted that with alacrity and with a feeling of great relief, because I had been fighting in my own mind and heart against this business of keeping up some measure of separatism in our political domain: and the more I thought of it the more I felt that it was the right thing to do not only from the point of view of pure nationalism, which it is, but also from the separate and individual view-point of each group if you like, majority or minority.

We call ourselves nationalists, but perhaps in the mind of each, the colour, the texture of nationalism that is present is somewhat different from what it is in the mind of the other. We call ourselves nationalists—and rightly so—and yet few of us are free from those separatist tendencies—whether they are communal, whether they are provincial or other: yet, because we have those tendencies, it does not necessarily follow that we should surrender to them all the time. It does follow that we should not take the cloak of nationalism to cover those bad tendencies.

So I thought about this matter and I came to the conclusion that if at this stage of our nation's history, when we are formulating this Constitution, which may not be a very permanent one because the world changes, nevertheless which we wish to be a fairly solid and lasting one, if at this stage we put things into it which are obviously wrong, and which obviously make people look the wrong way, then it is an evil thing that we are doing to the nation. We decided some time ago in another connection that we should have no truck with communalism or separatism. It was rightly pointed out to us then that if that is so, why do you keep these reservations because this itself will make people think in terms of separate compartments in the political domain.

I would like you to consider this business, whether it is reservation or any other kind of safeguard for the minority, objectively. There is some point in having a safeguard of this type or any other type where there is autocratic rule or foreign rule. As soon as you get something that can be called political democracy, then this kind of reservation, instead of helping the party to be safeguarded and aided, is likely actually to turn against it. But where there is a third party, or where there is an autocratic monarch, or some other ruler, it is possible that these safeguards may be good. Perhaps the monarch may play one off against the other, or the foreign ruler. But where you are up against a full-blooded democracy, if you seek to give safeguards to a minority, and a relatively small minority, you isolate it. May be you protect it to a slight extent, but at what cost? At the cost of isolating it and keeping it away from the main current in which the majority is going,—I am talking on the political plane of course—at the cost of forfeiting that inner sympathy and fellow-feeling with the majority. Now, of course, if it is a democracy, in the long run or in the short run, it is the will of the majority that will prevail. Even if you are limited by various articles in the Constitution to protect the individual or the group, nevertheless, in the very nature of things, in a democracy the will of the majority will ultimately prevail. It is a bad thing for any small group or minority to make it appear to the world and to the majority that 'we wish to keep apart from you, that we do not trust you, that we look to ourselves and that therefore we want safeguards and other things'. The result is that they may get one anna in the rupee of protection at the cost of the remaining fifteen annas. That is not good enough looked at from the point of view of the majority either. It is all very well for the majority to feel that they are strong in numbers and in other ways and therefore they can afford to ride rough-shod over the wishes of the majority. If the majority feels that way, it is not only exceedingly mistaken, but it has not learnt any lesson from history, because, however big the majority, if injustice is done to minorities, it rankles and it is a running sore and the majority ultimately suffers from it. So, ultimately the only way to proceed about it—whether from the point of view of the minority or from the point of view of the majority—is to remove every barrier which separates them in the political domain so that they may develop and we may all work together. That does not mean, of course, and kind of regimented working. They may have many ways of thinking; they may form groups; they may form parties, but not on the majority or minority or religious or social plane, but on other planes which will be mixed planes, thus developing the habit of looking at things in mixed groups and not in separate groups. At any time that is obviously a desirable thing to do. In a democracy it becomes an essential thing to do, because if you do not do it, then trouble follows—trouble both for the minority and for the majority, but far more for the minority.

In the present state of affairs, whether you take India or whether you take a larger world group, the one thing we have to develop is to think as much as possible in larger terms; otherwise we get cut off from reality. If we do not appreciate what is happening, the vast and enormous changes happening elsewhere which really are changing the shape of things, and cut off our future almost completely from the past as we found it, if we stick to certain ideas and suspicions of the past, we shall never understand the present, much less the future that is taking shape. Many of our discussions here are inevitably derived from the past. We cannot get rid of them. None of us can, because we are part of the past. But we ought to try to get ourselves disconnected from the past if we are to mould the future gradually. Therefore from every point of view, whether it is theoretical or ideological or national or whether it is in the interests of the minority or of the majority or whether it is in order to come to grips with the realities of today and of tomorrow which is so different from yesterday, I welcome this proposal.

Frankly I would like this proposal to go further and put an end to such reservations as there still remain. But again, speaking frankly, I realize that in the present state of affairs in India that would not be a desirable thing to do, that is to say, in regard to the Scheduled Castes. I try to look upon the problem not in the sense of a religious minority, but rather in the sense of helping backward groups in the country. I do not look at it from the religious point of view or the caste point of view, but from the point of view that a backward group ought to be helped and I am glad that this reservation also will be limited to ten years.

Now I would like you to think for a moment in a particular way just to realize how the present is different from the past. Think of, let us say, five years ago which is not a long time. Think of the problems that you and I and the country had to face then. Make a list of them and then make a list of the various problems that this honourable House has to consider from day to day. If you do this you will see an enormous difference between the lists. The questions that are before us demanding answer, demanding solution show how we have changed for good or for evil. The world is changing; India is changing, not alone politically. The real test of all change is, what are the problems that face us at a particular moment. The problems today are entirely different from the problems that five years ago faced us in any domain, economic or in regard to the States. If that is so, we have to tackle problems in a different way, no doubt holding onto the basic ideals and the basic ideology that has moved us in the past, but nevertheless remembering that the other appurtenances of those ideologies of the past have perhaps no function today. One of the biggest things in regard to them is this one of separate electorates, reservation of seats and the rest. Therefore, I think that doing away with this reservation business is not only a good thing in itself—good for all concerned, and more especially for the minorities—but psychologically too it is a very good move for the nation and for the world. It shows that we are really sincere about this business of having a secular democracy. Now I use the words 'secular democracy' and many others use these words. But sometimes I have the feeling that these words are used today too much and by people who do not understand their significance. It is an ideal to be aimed at and every one of us whether we are Hindus or Muslims, Sikhs or Christians, whatever we are, none of us can say in his heart of hearts that he has no prejudice and no taint of communalism in his mind or heart. None or very few can say that, because we are all products of the past. I do not myself particularly enjoy any one of us trying to deliver sermons and homilies to the others as to how they should behave, or one group telling the other group whether of the majority or of the minority, how they should do this or that in order to earn goodwill. Of course something has to be done to gain goodwill. That is essential. But goodwill and all loyalty and all affection are hardly things which are obtained by sermonising. These develop because of certain circumstances, certain appeals of the mind and heart and a realization of what is really good for everyone in the long analysis.

So now let me take this decision—a major decision—of this honourable House which is going to affect our future greatly. Let us be clear in our own minds over this question, that in order to proceed further we have, each one of us whether we belong to the majority or to a minority, to try to function in a way to gain the goodwill of the other group of individual. It is a trite saying, still I would like to say it, because this conviction has grown in my mind that whether any individual belongs to this or that group, in national or international dealings, ultimately the thing that counts is the generosity, the goodwill and the affection with which you approach the other party. If that is lacking, then your advice becomes hollow. If there is, then it is bound to produce a like reaction on the other side. If there were something of that today in the international field, probably even the great international problems of today would be much easier of solution. If we in India approach our problems in that spirit, I am sure they will be far easier of solution. All of us have a blend of good and evil in us and it is so extremely easy for us to point to the evil in the other party. It is easy to do that, but it is not easy to pick out the evil in ourselves. Why not try this method of the great people, the great ones of the earth, who have always tried to lay emphasis on the good of the other and thereby draw it out? How did the Father of the Nation function? How did he draw unto himself every type, every group and every individual and got the best from him? He always laid stress on the good of the man, knowing perhaps the evil too. He laid stress on the good of the individual or group and made him function to the best of his ability. That I think is the only way how to behave. I am quite convinced that ultimately, this will be to our good. Nevertheless, as I said on another occasion. I would remind the House that this is an act of faith, an act of faith for all of us, an act of faith above all for the majority community because they will have to show after this that they can behave to others in a generous, fair and just way. Let us live up to that faith.

UNIVERSITIES STAND FOR TOLERANCE

I have come back after a long while to my home town of Allahabad[1] to which I have almost become a stranger. During these past fifteen months I have lived in New Delhi, next door to Old Delhi City. What do those two cities convey to us, what pictures and thoughts do they bring to our minds? When I think of them, the long vista of India's history stretches out before me, not so much the succession of kings and emperors, but rather that of the inner life of a nation, its cultural activities in many fields, its spiritual adventures and its voyages in the realms of thought and action. The life of a nation, and more especially of a nation like India, is lived principally in the villages. Nevertheless, it is the cities that represent the highest cultural achievements of the age, as they also do sometimes the more unpleasant aspects of human life. So these cities remind me of the cultural growth of India, of that inner strength and balance which come from long ages of civilization and culture. We have been very proud of this inheritance of ours in India, and rightly so. And yet, where do we stand today?

It is well that we put this question to ourselves in this ancient city of Allahabad and in this seat of learning. The universities have much to teach in the modern world and their scope of activity ever enlarges. I am myself a devotee of science and believe that the world will ultimately be saved, if it is to be saved, by the method and approach of science. But whatever path of learning we may pursue, and however profitable it might seem to us, there is a certain basis and foundation without which the house of learning is built on shifting sands. It is for a university to realize and to lay stress on this essential basis and foundation, those standards of thought and

[1] Address to a special convocation of the University of Allahabad, 13 December 1947. *Jawaharlal Nehru: Selected Speeches*, vol. 1, 1946–9, pp. 329–38.

action which make an individual and a nation. Above all, this is necessary today, during this phase of extremely rapid transition, when old values have almost left us and we have adopted no new ones. Freedom came to us, our long-sought freedom, and it came with a minimum of violence. But immediately after, we had to wade through oceans of blood and tears. Worse than the blood and tears was the shame and disgrace that accompanied them. Where were our values and standards then, where was our old culture, our humanism and spirituality and all that India has stood for in the past? Suddenly darkness descended upon this land and madness seized the people. Fear and hatred blinded our minds and all the restraints which civilization imposes were swept away. Horror piled on horror and a sudden emptiness seized us at the brute savagery of human beings. The lights seemed all to go out; not all, for a few still flickered in the raging tempest. We sorrowed for the dead and the dying and for those whose suffering was greater than death. We sorrowed even more for India, our common mother, for whose freedom we had laboured these long years.

The lights seemed to go out. But one bright flame continued to burn and shed its light on the surrounding gloom. And looking at the pure flame, strength and hope returned to us and we felt that whatever momentary disaster might overwhelm our people, there was the spirit of India, strong and unsullied, rising above the turmoil of the present and not caring for the petty exigencies of the day. How many of you realize what it has meant to India to have the presence of Mahatma Gandhi during these months? We all know of his magnificent services to India and to freedom during the past half century and more. But no service could have been greater than the one he has performed during the past four months when in a dissolving world he has been like a rock of purpose and a lighthouse of truth, and his firm, low voice has risen above the clamours of the multitude, pointing to the path of rightful endeavour.

And because of this bright flame we could not lose faith in India and her people. And yet the surrounding gloom was in itself a menace. Why should we relapse into this gloom when the sun of freedom had arisen? It is necessary for all of us, and more especially for young men and young women in the universities to pause and think for a while on these basic matters, for the future of India in taking shape in the present, and the future is going to be what millions of young men and women want it to be. There is today a narrowness and intolerance and insensitiveness and lack of awareness which rather frighten me. We have recently passed through a great world war. That war has not brought peace and freedom, but it should teach us many lessons. It brought the downfall of what had been called Fascism and Nazism. Both of these creeds were narrow and overbearing and based on hatred and violence. I watched their growth in their respective countries as well as elsewhere. They brought a certain prestige to their people for a while, but they also killed the spirit and destroyed all values and standards of thought and behaviour. They ended by ruining the nations they sought to exalt.

I see something very similar to that flourishing in India today. It talks in the name of nationalism, sometimes of religion and culture, and yet it is the very opposite of nationalism, of true morality and of real culture. If there was any doubt of this, the past few months have shown us the real picture. For some years we have had to contend against the policy of hatred and violence and narrow communalism on the part of a section of the community. Now, that section has succeeded in forming a state carved out of certain parts of India. Muslim communalism, which had been such a danger and obstruction to Indian freedom, now calls itself a State. It has ceased to be a living force in India proper today, because its strength is concentrated in other parts. But it has resulted in degrading other sections of the community who seek to copy it and sometimes even to improve upon it. We have now to face this reaction in India and the cry is raised for a communal State, even though the words used may be different. And not only a communal State is demanded, but in all fields of political and cultural activity the same narrowing and strangling demand is put forward.

If we look back at India's long history we find that our forefathers made wonderful progress whenever they looked out on the world with clear and fearless eyes and kept the windows of their minds open to give and to receive. And, in later periods, when they grew narrow in outlook and shrank from outside influences, India suffered a setback politically and culturally. What a magnificent inheritance we have, though we have abused it often enough! India has been and is a vital nation, in spite of all the misery and suffering she has experienced. That vitality in the realm of constructive and creative effort spread to many parts of the Asian world and elsewhere and brought splendid conquests in its train. Those conquests were not so much of the sword, but of the mind and heart which bring healing and which endure when the men of the sword and their work are forgotten. But that very vitality, if not rightly and creatively directed, may turn inward and destroy and degrade.

Even during the brief span of our lives we have seen these two forces at play in India and the world at large—the forces of constructive and creative effort and the forces of destruction. Which will triumph in the end? And on which side do we stand? That is a vital question for each one of us and more especially, for those from whom the leaders of the nation will be drawn, and on whom the burden of tomorrow will fall. We dare not sit on the fence and refuse to face the issue. We dare not allow our minds to be befuddled by passion and hatred when clear thought and effective action are necessary.

What kind of India are we working for, and what kind of world? Are hatred and violence and fear and communalism and narrow provincialism to mould our future? Surely not, if there has been any truth in us and in our professions. Here in this city of Allahabad, dear to me not only because of my close association with it, but also because of its part in India's history, my boyhood and youth were spent in dreaming dreams and seeing visions of India's future. Was there any real substance in those dreams or were they merely the fancies of a fevered brain? Some small part of those dreams has come true, but not in the manner I had imagined, and so much still remains. Instead of a feeling of triumph at achievement, there is an emptiness and distress at the sorrow that surrounds us, and we have to wipe the tears from a million eyes.

A university stands for humanism, for tolerance, for reason, for progress, for the adventure of ideas and for the search for truth. It stands for the onward march of the human race towards even higher objectives. If the universities discharge their duty adequately, then it is well with the nation and the people. But if the temple of learning itself becomes a home of narrow bigotry and petty objectives, how then will the nation prosper or a people grow in stature?

A vast responsibility, therefore, rests on our universities and educational institutions and those who guide their destinies. They have to keep their lights burning and must not stray from the right path even when passion convulses the multitude and blinds many amongst those whose duty it is to set an example to others. We are not going to reach our goal through crookedness or flirting with evil in the hope that it may lead to good. The right end can never be fully achieved through wrong means.

Let us be clear about our national objective. We aim at a strong, free and democratic India where every citizen has an equal place and full opportunity of growth and service, where present-day inequalities in wealth and status have ceased to be, where our vital impulses are directed to creative and co-operative endeavour. In such an India communalism, separatism, isolation, untouchability, bigotry, and exploitation of man by man have no place, and while religion is free, it is not allowed to interfere with the political and economic aspects of a nation's life. If that is so, then all this business of Hindu and Muslim and Christian and Sikh must cease in so far as our political life is concerned and we must build a united but composite nation where both individual and national freedom are secure.

We have passed through grievous trials. We have survived them but at a terrible cost, and the legacy they have left in tortured minds and stunted souls will pursue us for a long time. Our trials are not over. Let us prepare ourselves for them in the spirit of free and disciplined men and women, stout of heart and purpose, who will not stray from the right path or forget our ideals and objectives. We have to start this work of healing and we have to build and create. The wounded body and spirit of India call upon all of us to dedicate ourselves to this great task. May we be worthy of the task and of India!

INDIA'S UNIFIED CULTURE[2]

I have come back to Aligarh and to this University after a long interval. We have been separated not only by a distance of time, but also by a distance of spirit and outlook. I do not quite know where you, or for the matter of that most of us, stand today, for we have gone through convulsions and heart-breaks which have no doubt created in many of us doubts and disillusionment. While the present is full of uncertainty, the future is even more shrouded and difficult to pierce. Nevertheless, we have to face this present and try to mould the future. We have to see, each one of us, where we stand and what we stand for. Without a stout anchor of faith in the future we will drift in the present and life itself would have no objective worth striving for.

I have accepted the invitation of your Vice-Chancellor with pleasure, for I wanted to meet all of you and to probe somewhat into your minds and to let you have a glimpse of my own mind. We have to understand one another, and if we cannot agree about everything, we must at least agree to differ and know where we agree and where we differ.

For every sensitive human being in India the last six months have brought pain and sorrow, and what is worst of all, a humiliation of the spirit. It has been bad enough for those who are old in years and experienced, but I often wonder how the young feel who, at the threshold of their lives, have seen and experienced catastrophe and disaster. They will, no doubt, survive it, for youth is resilient; but it may well be that they will carry the mark of it for the rest of their days. Perhaps if we are wise and strong enough to think and act rightly even now, we may succeed in erasing that mark.

For my part I wish to say that, in spite of everything, I have a firm faith in India's future. Indeed, if I did not have it, it would not have been possible for me to work effectively. Although many of my old dreams have been shattered by recent

[2] Address to the annual convocation of the Muslim University of Aligarh, 24 January 1948.

events, yet the basic objective still holds and I see no reason to change it. That objective is to build up a free India of high ideals and noble endeavour where there is equality of opportunity for all and where many variegated streams of thought and culture meet together to form a mighty river of progress and advancement for her people.

I am proud of India, not only because of her ancient, magnificent heritage, but also because of her remarkable capacity to add to it by keeping the doors and windows of her mind and spirit open to fresh and invigorating winds from distant lands. India's strength has been twofold; her own innate culture which flowered through the ages, and her capacity to draw from other sources and thus add to her own. She was far too strong to be submerged by outside streams, and she was too wise to isolate herself from them, and so there is a continuing synthesis in India's real history and the many political changes which have taken place have had little effect on the growth of this variegated and yet essentially unified culture.

I have said that I am proud of our inheritance and our ancestors who gave an intellectual and cultural pre-eminence to India. How do you feel about this past? Do you feel that you are also sharers in it and inheritors of it and, therefore proud of something that belongs to you as much as to me? Or do you feel alien to it and pass it by without understanding it or feeling that strange thrill which comes from the realization that we are the trustees and inheritors of this vast treasure? I ask you these questions, because in recent years many forces have been at play diverting people's minds into wrong channels and trying to pervert the course of history. You are Muslims and I am a Hindu. We may adhere to different religious faiths or even to none; but that does not take away from that cultural inheritance that is yours as well as mine. The past holds us together; why should the present or the future divide us in spirit?

Political changes produce certain results, but the essential changes are in the spirit and outlook of a nation. What has troubled me very greatly during these past months and years is not the political changes, but rather the creeping sense of a change of spirit which has created enormous barriers between us. The attempt to change the spirit of India was a reversal of the historical process through which we had been passing for long ages past and it is because we tried to reverse the current of history that disaster overwhelmed us. We cannot easily play about with geography or with the powerful trends which make history. And it is infinitely worse if we make hatred and violence the springs of action.

Pakistan has come into being, rather unnaturally I think. Nevertheless, it represents the urges of a large number of persons. I believe that this development has been a throw-back but we accepted it in good faith. I want you to understand clearly what our present view is. We have been charged with desiring to strangle and crush Pakistan and to force it into a reunion with India. That charge, as many others, is based on fear and a complete misunderstanding of our attitude. I believe that, for a variety of reasons, it is inevitable that India and Pakistan should draw closer to each other, or else they will come into conflict. There is no middle way, for we have known each other too long to be indifferent neighbours. I believe indeed that in the present context of the world India must develop a closer union with many other neighbouring countries. But all this does not mean any desire to strangle or compel Pakistan. Compulsion there can never be, and an attempt to disrupt Pakistan would recoil to India's disadvantage. If we had wanted to break Pakistan, why did we agree to the partition? It was easier to prevent it then than to try to do so now after all that has happened. There is no going back in history. As a matter of fact it is to India's advantage that Pakistan should be a secure and prosperous State with which we can develop close and friendly relations. If today by any chance I were offered the reunion of India and Pakistan, I would decline it for obvious reasons. I do not want to carry the burden of Pakistan's great problems. I have enough of my own. Any closer association must come out of a normal process and in a friendly way which does not end Pakistan as a State, but makes it an equal part of a larger union in which several countries might be associated.

I have spoken of Pakistan because that subject must be in your minds and you would like to know what our attitude towards it is. Your minds are probably in a fluid state at present, not knowing which way to look and what to do. All of us have to be clear about our basic allegiance to certain ideas. Do we believe in a national State which includes people of all religions and shades of opinion and is essentially secular as a State, or do we believe in the religious, theocratic conception of a State which regards people of other faiths as somebody beyond the pale? That is an odd question to ask, for the idea of a religious or theocratic State was given up by the world some centuries ago and has no place in the mind of the modern man. And yet the question has to be put in India today, for many of us have tried to jump back to a past age. I have no doubt that whatever our individual answers may be, it is not possible for us to go back to a conception that the world has outlived and that is completely out of tune with modern conceptions. As far as India is concerned, I can speak with some certainty. We shall proceed on secular and national lines in keeping with the powerful trends towards internationalism. Whatever confusion the present may contain, in the future, India will be a land, as in the past, of many faiths equally honoured and respected, but of one national outlook, not, I hope, a narrow nationalism living in its own shell, but rather the tolerant creative nationalism which, believing in itself and the genius of its people, takes full part in the establishment of an international order. The only ultimate aim we can have is that of One World. That seems a far cry today with warring groups and preparations for and shouting of World War III. Yet, despite all this shouting, that is the only aim that we can keep in view, for the alternative to world co-operation is world disaster.

We must cultivate this broad outlook and not be led away by the narrowness of others into becoming narrow in spirit and outlook ourselves. We have had enough of what has been called communalism in this country and we have tasted of its bitter and poisonous fruit. It is time that we put an end to it. For my part I do not like the intrusion of this communal spirit anywhere, and least of all in educational institutions. Education is meant to free the spirit of man and not to imprison it in set frames. I do not like this university being called the Muslim University just as I do not like the Benares University to be called the Hindu University. This does not mean that a university should not specialize in particular cultural subjects and studies. I think it is right that this University should lay special stress on certain aspects of Islamic thought and culture.

I want you to think about those problems and come to your own conclusions. These conclusions cannot be forced upon you except to some extent, of course, by the compulsion of events which none of us can ignore. Do not think that you are outsiders here, for you are as much flesh and blood of India as anyone else, and you have every right to share in what India has to offer. But those who seek rights must share in the obligations also. Indeed, if the duties and obligations are accepted, then rights flow of themselves. I invite you as free citizens of free India to play your role in the building up of this great country and to be sharers, in common with others, in the triumphs and setbacks alike that may come our way. The present with all its unhappiness and misery will pass. It is the future that counts, more especially to the young, and it is that future that beckons to you. How will you answer that call?

TOLERANCE AND
COMMUNAL HARMONY[1]

Sir, before this debate proceeds any further I should like to indicate the attitude of the Government in regard to this resolution.[2] The Government would welcome this resolution and also desire to say that they wish to do everything in their power to achieve the objective which lies behind this resolution. After the eloquent speech of the Honourable Mover[3] I need not say much about the desirability of this resolution; as a matter of fact it is an inevitable policy which an independent country must adopt. There might have been in the past various reasons which came in the way of such policy being given effect to, although I think that even in the past those of us who accepted any measure of communalism erred and acted unwisely, and we have suffered greatly for our unwisdom. However, in the past conditions were different; but when a country is functioning independently there is no alternative except to follow this. The only alternative is civil conflict. We have seen as a matter of fact how far communalism in politics has led us; all of us remember the grave dangers through which we have passed and the terrible consequences we

[1] Speech in the Constituent Assembly on a resolution on elimination of communal organizations, 3 April 1948, *Constituent Assembly of India (Legislative) Debates, (Official Report)*, vol. IV, 1948, pp. 3116–23.

[2] M. Ananthasayanam Ayyangar's resolution pleaded for separation of religion from politics and for India becoming a secular state and demanded administrative and legislative measures to be taken to give effect to it.

[3] M. Ananthasayanam Ayyangar (1891–1978); took part in noncooperation movement, 1921–2; elected to Central Legislative Assembly, 1934; elected secretary. Congress Parliamentary Party, 1947; Deputy Speaker, Lower House, and first Lok Sabha, 1949 and 1952 respectively and Speaker, 1953–62; Governor of Bihar, 1962–7.

have seen. In any event, now there is no other alternative; and we must have it clearly in our minds and in the mind of the country that the alliance of religion and politics in the shape of communalism is a most dangerous alliance, and it yields the most abnormal kind of illegitimate brood. We have talked a great deal about politics being allied to ethics; that is something which I hope we shall always stand for. During the last quarter of a century or more Mahatma Gandhi taught us to place politics on an ethical level. How far we succeeded is for the world to judge and for future generations to decide. But it was something at least that we placed that great ideal before us and tried in our own weak and halting way to give effect to it. But the combination of politics and religion in the narrowest sense of the word, resulting in communal politics, is—there can be no doubt—a most dangerous combination and must be put an end to. It is clear, as has been pointed out by the Honourable Mover, that this combination is harmful to the country as a whole; it is harmful to the majority, but probably it is most harmful to any minority that seeks to have some advantage from it. I think even the past history of India will show that. But in any event a minority in an independent state which seeks to isolate and separate itself does some injury to the cause of the country, and most of all it injures its own interest, because inevitably it puts a barrier between itself and the others, a barrier not on the religious plane but on the political plane, sometimes even to some extent on the economic plane; and it can never really exercise the influence which it legitimately ought to aspire to exercise if it functions in that way.

Now the future constitution of India is being hammered out in the Constituent Assembly and no doubt it will give shape to it in the course of the next two or three months and finalize it, and any resolution that we may pass is not going to alter that constitution as it is finally adopted. But, after all, the constitution-making body is more or less this body; there is not much difference. And if this House thinks in terms of this resolution I have no doubt that the constitution-making body will also think in terms of this resolution. Further, from such evidence as we have got of the working of that constitution-making body, it has already gone a long way in terms of this resolution. It has put aside many of the dangerous features of our old constitution which led to communalism. Whether other features will remain or not I cannot obviously guarantee. But as far as I am concerned, I think the less we have of any form of communalism the better it is for our constitution and for the practical working of our Government.

Now, Sir, so far as this resolution is concerned, as I said, we warmly welcome the objective underlying it and the spirit behind it. But this resolution mentioned administrative and legislative measures to be taken to give effect to it. Exactly what those administrative and legislative measures might be, it is impossible to say straight off; it will require the closest scrutiny, certainly the legislative part of it. And presumably the right course for Government will be—if this resolution is passed, as I feel sure it will be—to consider this matter and see what administrative and—more specially—what legislative measures are necessary to gain this end; and then later, when this House meets again for another session, to consider any recommendations in that respect so far as legislative measures are concerned. Meanwhile, no doubt our new constitution will have taken shape also and it will help us then to consider those legislative measures in terms of that new constitution. But we need not wait till then. The point is so far as the Government is concerned that we should function as closely as possible in accordance with the spirit of this resolution. Further, the purpose of this resolution, I take it, is also to give a lead to the country in this matter, so that the country may realize as clearly as possible that the only right way for us to function is to do away with communalism in its political aspect in every shape and form. That we accept. Now there are at the present moment, as some members may later point out, in the Draft Constitution that has been proposed, certain definite communal elements. For instance, I believe that there is a proposal that although there should be joint and common electorate, still there might be some reservation of seats for minorities or for the scheduled castes on more or less, I take it, the population basis. Now what the final decision will be about that I cannot say. I hope personally that the less reservation there is the better, and I think that is so mostly even more from the point of view of the group or the minority that might have that reservation than from the point of view of any other group or majority.

There is another aspect of this matter which must be remembered. We talk about democracy and unity and all that and I hope we shall rapidly have more and more democracy and more and more unity in this country. Democracy is not purely a political affair. The nineteenth-century conception of democracy, that is, each person having a vote was a good enough conception in those days but it was incomplete and people think in terms of a larger and deeper democracy today. After all, there is no equality between the pauper who has a vote and the millionaire who has a vote. There are a hundred ways of exercising influence for the millionaire which the pauper has not got. After all, there is no equality between the person who has got tremendous educational advantages and the person who has had none. So educationally, economically and otherwise people differ greatly. People will, I suppose, differ to some extent. All human beings are not equal in the sense of ability or capacity. But the whole point is that people should have equality of opportunity and that they should be able to go as far as they can go.

Now it is patent in India today that there are huge differences between certain groups, classes and individuals. There is a big hiatus between those at the top and those at the bottom. If we are to have democracy it becomes necessary and essential for us to not merely bridge that gap but to lessen it very greatly; in fact to bring them closer together so far as opportunities are concerned, as far as ultimately general living conditions are concerned, and in so far as the necessities of life are concerned, leaving out for the moment luxuries and the rest, though ultimately there seems to me to be no particular reason why any particular group or class should be favoured even in regard to the luxuries of life. But that is perhaps a rather distant picture. Now, because there are such great differences in India, it becomes incumbent upon us, not only for humanitarian reasons but from the standpoint of the fulfilment of democracy, to raise up those people who are low down in the social, economic and other levels and to bring to them every opportunity of growth and progress, national and otherwise. That has been the general accepted policy of this country and it is the accepted policy of this Government. Now in pursuance of that policy, certain reservation of seats was granted, for instance to the scheduled castes, and various scholarships and educational amenities, etc., have been granted and no doubt will be granted still more, not only to the scheduled castes but there may also be other backward groups in the country. There are tribal people and others who require every help. It is no good for us to say that we have given a vote to the member of a tribal folk and we have done our duty to him; having for hundreds and thousands of years not done our duty to him, by giving him a vote we consider ourselves absolved of all further duty. Therefore, we have to think always in terms of raising the level of all those who have been denied opportunities in the past. I do not personally think myself that the best way to do that on the political plane is reservation of seats and the rest. I think the best way, and the more basic and fundamental way, is to advance them rapidly in the economic and educational spheres and then they will stand on their own feet.

There is a great danger, whether you deal with an individual, group or community, of giving a certain prop to that community which gives it a false sense of strength which does not belong to it, which does not come out of its own strength, but which is external to it and which when removed suddenly makes it weak. A nation ultimately ought to stand on its own feet. So long as it relies on some external prop it is not strong. It is weak. So these external props, as I might call them—that is reservation of seats and the rest—may occasionally be helpful possibly in the case of the backward groups, but they produce a false sense of political relations, a false sense of strength, and ultimately therefore they are not so nearly as important as real educational, cultural and economic advance, which gives them inner strength to face any difficulty or any opponent. However, I can conceive that in the present context of affairs in regard to these unfortunate countrymen of ours, who have not had these opportunities in the past, special attempts should be made of course in the educational and economic field and even in the political field to see that they have a proper place till they find their own legs to stand upon without any external aid.

So I accept this resolution on behalf of Government, but in accepting it I should like to make it perfectly clear again that so far as the implementation of it is concerned, more especially in regard to the legislative aspect of it, will have to be very carefully considered and will ultimately have to come before this House.

I have no objection on behalf of Government to accept the addition of the words 'social and educational' which are mentioned in one of the amendments to this resolution. It would read: '... should be permitted to engage in any activities other than those essential for the *bona fide* religious, cultural, social and educational needs of the community....'

COMMUNALISM, A BADGE OF BACKWARDNESS[4]

The strength of India will increase in the measure we can march together. Communalism is the badge of a backward nation, not of the modern age. People have their religion and they have a right to hold firmly to it, but to import religion into politics and to break up the country is something which was done in Europe 300 or 400 years back. We in India have to get rid of it.

We have declared that we will fight communal organizations in every way, whether they are Muslim organizations or Hindu organizations or Sikh or any other. Nationalism cannot exist together with communalism. Nationalism does not mean Hindu nationalism, Muslim nationalism or Sikh nationalism. As soon as you speak of Hindu, Sikh or Muslim, you do not speak for India. Each person has to ask himself the question: What do I want to make of India, one country, one nation or 10, 20 or 25 nations, a fragmented and divided nation without any strength or endurance, ready to break to pieces at the slightest shock? Each person has to answer this question. Separateness has always been the weakness of India. Fissiparous tendencies, whether they belong to Hindus, Muslims, Sikhs, Christians or others, are very dangerous and wrong tendencies. They belong to petty and backward minds. No one who understands the spirit of the times can think in terms of communalism.

[4] From speech in Hindi at Srinagar, 19 July 1961.

We have big problems in India. We have undertaken a great task and have achieved success to some extent. We are confident of success, but success will come only through toil and hard work and through subordinating our petty interests to the bigger interests of India.

SOCIETY AND COMMUNALISM[1]

...[W]hen the immediate danger seemed to have passed, when there was no actual fighting going on, many of our people relapsed into complacency and started forgetting the menace and the dangers, although they were still there. They lost themselves in mutual squabbles, complaints, slogans and the like. That shows that although we are basically united and there is something in us which makes us rise when danger threatens us, we soften and go back to our petty thoughts and conflicts when the threat does not appear to be so obvious.

We have the Chinese menace before us. Even before this menace occurred, we had, and continue to have, the real menace of poverty. We have to fight that as stoutly and as bravely as we fight any enemy who invades our country. We can build our nation only when we build our people and make them happy and contented.

Therefore, this habit of ours to slacken when no immediate danger threatens us, is bad. We must get over it. We talk of solidarity and unity, and yet we know that in our country, behind this certain feeling of solidarity and unity, there are many forces which are fissiparous and which interested people use for separating us. It is unfortunate that some people forget the essential unity of the country by encouraging these forces.

Sometimes religion is employed in this behalf; sometimes caste, sometimes language; sometimes there is conflict between States and so on.

We are a great country, a country with enormous variety, a variety that is good. There is no reason why we should be regimented and be made to look like one

[1] *Jawaharlal Nehru: Selected Speeches*, vol. V, 1963–4, New Delhi: Publication Division, Ministry of Information and Broadcasting, Government of India, 1996.

person. We should keep the variety, but that variety is only good when we are united and there is an essential unity behind it.

I am not asking you to forget this rich variety, but I am asking you to remember that this variety itself, along with everything that we value, will go if we do not remember that unity is essential. That unity is not a superficial unity on the map or of some Constitution, but the unity of heart and mind, which makes us feel like a large family, which has to be defended, which has to be worked for and which will lead us to co-operate with one another.

You know that we have stood for peace in the past, and we became known all over the world as a nation pledged to peace. We still have not given up our ideal of peace and we want peaceful settlement of disputes.

We should like peaceful settlement even of the dispute with China, provided it is in consonance with our integrity and honour, because if we forget our freedom and our integrity and our honour, then, indeed, it will not become a settlement; it would be a shameful and disgraceful surrender, which can bring no good to the country.

So, while we stand for peace as we have done, we also prepare for any challenge to us, to meet it adequately, to preserve our freedom and the integrity of our country.

Therefore, I hope that tomorrow we shall take this resolve firmly and we shall remember that this means not merely bravery on the battlefield, but the courage to do the right thing in our homes, in our towns and in our relations with one another. We have to show that we are full of the spirit of co-operation and solidarity and that we belong to a country which will not tolerate any disorder. We have to stand up to resist any invader who challenges us.

It is that spirit which must be with us always and if we possess that spirit, we shall not only become strong but we shall also become prosperous. Out of this co-operation will grow much that will benefit our country and our people.

Communal Goodwill and Harmony[2]

We have many difficult problems to face. There is the menace of China and Pakistan. There is the tremendous influx of refugees from East Pakistan and the duty to look after them and rehabilitate them. There is the problem of rising prices which affects all our people.

But I am speaking to you today about something which is more important than anything else. This is the communal disharmony which has resulted in many

---

[2] Broadcast to the nation, New Delhi, 26 March 1964.

deaths in East Pakistan and in India and has created bitterness and fear amongst various communities. This feeling is fatal for all of us and, unless stopped completely, will lead to most dangerous consequences.

This communal trouble is entirely opposed to our policy and to our future, and I do appeal to you to fight it and to put an end to it.

India is a country of many communities and unless we can live in harmony with each other, respecting each other's beliefs and habits, we cannot build up a great and united nation.

Ever since the distant past, it has been the proud privilege of the people of India to live in harmony with one another. That has been the basis of India's culture. Long ago, the Buddha taught us this lesson. From the days of Asoka, 2,300 years ago, this aspect of our thought has been repeatedly declared and practised. In our own day, Mahatma Gandhi laid great stress on it and indeed lost his life because he laid great stress on communal goodwill and harmony. We have, therefore, a precious heritage to keep up, and we cannot allow ourselves to act contrary to it.

Pakistan came into existence on the basis of hatred and intolerance. We must not allow ourselves to react to this in the same way. That surely will be a defeat for us. We have to live up to our immemorial culture and try to win over those who are opposed to us. To compete with each other in hatred and barbarity is to sink below the human level and tarnish the name of our country and our people. One evil deed leads to another. Thus evil grows. That is not the way to stop these inhuman deeds. If we can behave with tolerance and friendship to each other, that surely will have its effect elsewhere. If not, this vicious circle will go on bringing sorrow and disaster to all of us and to others.

It is, therefore, of the utmost importance that we should realize our duty to all our countrymen, whoever they might be. We must always remember that every Indian, to whatever religion he might belong, is a brother and must be treated as such.

A few days ago, I wrote to President Ayub Khan of Pakistan appealing to him against these inhumanities that were taking place and suggesting that our Home Ministers might meet soon to curb these. Today, I received a reply from President Ayub Khan in which he has entirely agreed with my proposal. I hope that soon a meeting of the Home Ministers will take place, probably in Delhi, to consider this vital problem and what steps we should take to meet it. I hope that that will have a salutary effect on our people.

But it is not so much Home Ministers and others in authority who can put an end to this unhappy business. It is the people themselves who have to act rightly and speedily and thus promote an atmosphere of friendship and harmony between different religious groups and not allow their anger and bitterness to grow. I appeal, therefore, to all my countrymen to put an end to this inhuman behaviour. I would specially appeal to our friends and countrymen, the Adivasis in Bihar and Orissa, who have been agitated greatly by the stories they have heard. I hope that they will check themselves and try to create an atmosphere of goodwill and friendship for those of our countrymen who are Muslims. Our great public enterprises are suffering because of this communal trouble, and the whole of India's future is bound up with this.

I earnestly trust that our efforts will be directed towards creating communal harmony and that all our people and especially our newspapers will appreciate the grave dangers that are caused by communal conflict and disharmony. Let us all be careful in what we say or write lest it might create fear and conflict. Let us put ourselves together and create an atmosphere of co-operation and work for the advancement of India and of all those who live here as her sons. Thus only can we serve our motherland and help in making her great, united and strong.

The Nation's Vision

THE NEW TASKS BEFORE THE NATION[1]

Fellow countrymen,

It has been my privilege to serve India and the cause of India's freedom for many years. Today I address you for the first time officially as the first servant of the Indian people, pledged to their service and their betterment. I am here because you willed it so and I remain here so long as you choose to honour me with your confidence. We are a free and sovereign people today and we have rid ourselves of the burden of the past. We look at the world with clear and friendly eyes and at the future with faith and confidence. The burden of foreign domination is done away with, but freedom brings its own responsibilities and burdens and they can only be shouldered in the spirit of a free people, self-disciplined and determined to preserve and enlarge that freedom. We have achieved much, we have to achieve much more. Let us then address ourselves to our new tasks with the determination and adherence to high principles which our great leader has taught us.

Mahatma Gandhi is fortunately with us to guide and inspire and ever to point out to us the path of high endeavour. He taught us long ago that ideals and objectives can never be divorced from the methods adopted to realize them, that worthy ends can only be achieved through worthy means. If we aim at the big things of life, if we dream of India as a great nation giving her age-old message of peace and freedom to others, then we have to be big ourselves and worthy children of mother India. The eyes of the world are upon us, watching this birth of freedom in the East and wondering what it means.

Our first and immediate objective must be to put an end to all internal strife and violence which disfigure and degrade us and injure the cause of freedom. They

[1] Broadcast to the nation, New Delhi, 15 August 1947.

come in the way of consideration of the great economic problems of the masses of the people which so urgently demand attention. Our long subjection and the World War and its aftermath have made us inherit an accumulation of vital problems; and today our people lack food and clothing and other necessaries and we are caught in a spiral of inflation and rising prices. We cannot solve these problems suddenly but we cannot also delay their solution. So we must plan wisely so that the burdens on the masses may grow less, and their standards of living go up. We wish ill to none. But it must be clearly understood that the interests of our long-suffering masses must come first and every entrenched interest that comes in their way must yield to them. We have to change rapidly our antiquated land tenure system and we have also to promote industrialization on a large and balanced scale so as to add to the wealth of the country and thus to the national dividend which can be equitably distributed.

Production today is the first priority and every attempt to hamper or lessen production is injuring the nation and is more especially harmful to our labouring masses. But production by itself is not enough, for this may lead to an even greater concentration of wealth in a few hands, which comes in the way of progress and which, in the context of today, produces instability and conflict. Therefore, fair and equitable distribution is essential for any solution of the problem.

The Government of India has in hand at present several vast schemes for developing river valleys by controlling the flow of rivers, building dams and reservoirs and irrigation works and developing hydro-electric power. These will lead to greater food production and to the growth of industry and to all-round development. These schemes are thus basic to all planning and we intend to complete them as rapidly as possible so that the masses may profit. All this requires peaceful conditions and the cooperation of all concerned, and hard and continuous work. Let us then address ourselves to these great and worthy tasks, and forget our mutual wrangling and conflicts. There is a time for quarrelling, and there is a time for co-operative endeavour, there is a time for work and there is a time for play. Today there is no time for quarrelling or overmuch play, unless we prove false to our country and our people. Today we must cooperate with each other, and work together and work with right goodwill.

I should like to address a few words to our services, civil and military. The old distinctions and differences are gone, and today we are all free sons and daughters of India, proud of our country's freedom and joining together in our service to her. Our common allegiance is to India. In the difficult days ahead our services and our experts have a vital role to fulfil and we invite them to do so as comrades in the service of India.

Jai Hind!

A NATIONAL VISION[1]

INTO THE SECOND HALF OF THE TWENTIETH CENTURY[2]

Friends and Comrades,

Within a few hours from now, this year will pass away, and the half century will also end. We stand, as it were, on the edge of the line that divides the first half of the twentieth century from the second. This first half has been full of wars and tumults and of vast changes—political, scientific, cultural, social and economic. We have seen great revolutions which have changed the face of many countries. The world is a very different place today, even from what it was in my early boyhood days. This half century is over, but it has brought no peace to us or promise even of future peace, and as we stand on this New Year's eve, on the sword's edge of the present, darkness seems to envelop the future.

I am addressing you after a long interval and much has happened since I spoke to you last on the radio.[3] Many calamities have befallen us, bringing distress to our people. But the greatest of these calamities and sorrows has been the passing away from amongst us of a giant among men.[4] Sardar Vallabhbhai Patel was a dear and valued comrade in the brave days of our struggle for freedom, full of wisdom and determination, a rock of patient strength, to whom instinctively all of us went for guidance. Later, when we occupied the seats of government, inevitably some of

---

[1] *Selected Works of Jawaharlal Nehru* (Second Series), vol. 15 (part II), 1993, pp. 14–17.

[2] Broadcast to the nation from All India Radio, Delhi, 31 December 1950. From AIR tapes, NMML.

[3] On 9 September 1950. See *Selected Works* (Second Series), vol. 15 (Part I), pp. 166–70.

[4] Vallabhbhai Patel died on 15 December 1950 in Bombay.

the heaviest burdens fell on him and history will record how he discharged that duty. His name will always be remembered, not only as that of a great leader in the fight for freedom, but also as a great builder, unifier and consolidator of new India. That is a proud title to fame which he well deserved. For him it is well for his life's duty was well performed and is done, but for us it is not well, for we miss that strength and that wisdom and we can no longer go to him for counsel and advice. That burden which his broad shoulders carried so lightly has now to be shared by all of us.

Tomorrow morning, as the sun of the New Year comes out, I shall leave Delhi on my way to the West. I shall pay a brief visit to Bangalore to open the Science Congress there,[5] and then proceed to Bombay and England, where the Commonwealth Prime Ministers are going to meet in conference. I am leaving India reluctantly, for I want to face our problems here, and to give all my strength and energy in search of their solution. I do not wish to escape even for a while from the burden and the responsibility that Fate has cast upon me, but after full consideration I have decided to attend this conference in London. Big issues are at stake in the world today and, indeed, the fate of humanity itself hangs in the balance. I do not suggest that the London Conference will decide any of these issues or will finally avert the grave danger of war that confronts us. But it is possible that this Conference may help in lessening the gloom somewhat and in showing a way which might lead to peace. In this grave emergency, therefore, I have thought it necessary to travel to London and to take counsel there with others, who have also to shoulder heavy burdens, and who are trying to find some light in the prevailing darkness. If we take even a small step in the right direction, then the Conference will have done well.

You know how India has laboured with all earnestness of purpose in the cause of peace. We have sometimes been misunderstood by our friends, but I think it is widely realized now that the dominant urge that governs our actions is the desire to help in the maintenance of peace in this world. Everybody knows that large-scale war today is horrible beyond words and that its consequences will be appalling. It may even bring about the ruin of the proud structure of modern civilization. The small war that has been going on in Korea has already devastated that unfortunate country and brought untold misery on its people. And yet people fight, they say, to bring freedom to the people of Korea.

Peace cannot be purchased by compromise with evil or by surrender to it. Nor can peace be maintained by methods that themselves are the negation of peace.

[5] See *post*, pp. 76–84.

During our long struggle for freedom, we never surrendered and we did not compromise at any time with what we considered evil. Yet under Gandhiji's guidance we tried to follow the method of peace and were friendly even to those who tried to crush us. That was the method of peaceful but unyielding approach. That was the temper of peace even in a struggle.

Today we talk of peace, but if we do so, sometimes people mistake it for appeasement of evil. That temper of peace is completely absent today and the only alternative to a surrender appears to many people to be war with all its terrible consequences. Surely, there are other alternatives which are far removed from surrender and yet lead to the objective aimed at. It is in this spirit that we have tried to approach the world's problems. We are not pacifist. We keep an army and a navy and an air force and if danger threatens us we shall use them. But we seek no dominion over other people. Our sole object is to be left in peace ourselves to solve our own problems, and where possible to help and co-operate with others. In doing so we try not to be swept away by passion and danger and to maintain that temper of peaceful approach. It is in this spirit and with all humility and carefulness that I have endeavoured to guide India's policy in the present juncture. I have done so in the belief that I have the trust and goodwill of my countrymen behind me. That has fortified me and given me strength, even when the outlook was very dark.

In our own country there is a multitude of problems. The first of these is that of food. You know that we have had an unparallelled series of natural disasters and calamities during the last six months. The fates have been most unkind to us. Perhaps they wanted to test us to the uttermost. We will survive that test, for something of the old courage and determination is in us still, and whether danger threatens us from within or without, we shall face it calmly and unflinchingly, remembering always the great Master who led us to freedom.

We are trying to get food from all over the world, wherever it may be available. We will make every possible effort to fight starvation and famine. If we cannot get enough food from abroad to meet all our needs, then the entire country and all the people must evenly face the problem of food shortage. We cannot tolerate that there should be an abundance in one part and starvation in another. If we spread out this burden and all of us share it, then we may well pass this critical period of the next few months. Therefore, let us come to grips with this problem in all earnestness and determination. Let there be no waste. Let there be no selfish hoarding. Let no man shift for himself at the cost of his neighbour. It is a common peril that faces us, and we can only meet it together as comrades helping each other and thus lightening each other's distress. We have a hard time ahead. We will not escape it by running away from it, or by blaming others or by futile argument.

Some people suggest to us to get rid of our commitments by putting an end to food rationing over large areas. That would be an easy way of escape for governments but that would also be a criminal escape from the duty and responsibility that we owe to our people. We do not like rationing and controls, and we should like to get rid of them as soon as possible. But at a time of great scarcity, we cannot afford to see our people starve and to make the excuse that we are not responsible. The only way to meet this is by a common sharing of what we have and a common lack of what we have not.

Both the international and national situation are a challenge to us and to our manhood. How are we going to stand up to this challenge? Not by slogan and resolution, not by mutual bickering, not by feeling despondent and helpless. but rather by putting aside our petty conflicts and differences and pulling together and pooling our resources and facing the world as a united nation, determined to overcome all obstacles that come in its way.

As Prime Minister, I am the servant of all our people and I can make no distinction. But I have another capacity also which I treasure. I am a Congressman, a member for the last thirty-eight years of a great organization, which fought a mighty empire and brought freedom to this country. During this long period of years, in common with innumerable countrymen of mine, it has been my proud privilege to work through this Congress organization for the freedom of India and the welfare of our people. With the coming of independence a great responsibility came to all Congressmen. That responsibility was not merely to occupy the seats of authority but rather to keep the old flame alive in ourselves and in our people, to continue to serve to the best of our capacity and to remember always the lessons that our Master taught us. How have we discharged that responsibility? I fear that we cannot claim great success. But this is no time for us to criticize and find fault with each other. We have to get back to our old moorings and put an end to all disruptive and fissiparous tendencies in the Congress and in the country. That was our aim and objective several decades ago. For that we laboured throughout this period and a large measure of success came to us. Today the same call comes to us, and we must listen to it and act in accordance with it. That means that we seek no power or profit for ourselves, but only endeavour to serve our people; that we seek the cooperation of all others and avoid everything that weakens and disrupts. If remembering the inspiration of our great Master we act on these lines then the fears that fill our minds and the difficulties that surround us will fade away.

So on this eve of the New Year, and a new half century, I make earnest appeal to you, men and women of India, let us make this new year a turning point in our national life; let us make a fresh start and light again that old flame in our hearts which warmed us when the struggle was the fiercest. Let us, above all, co-operate with each other in the service of India.

Friends and comrades, I ask you for your good wishes and blessings in this new lap of life's journey that begins with the New Year, in which we are all fellow-travellers marching to a common goal. *Jai Hind.*

GREATER PRODUCTION THE FIRST TASK[6]

... In the world of today, we must look more towards ourselves and less towards other countries. We want to have friendly relations with other countries. But if we cannot stand on our feet by our own efforts, hard work and labour, we cannot survive on others' help either. There is the question of food which is causing great hardship in the country. We have got large quantities of food from outside.[7] But ultimately if we are not able to produce enough food in the country, we will find ourselves in great difficulties. This problem has been discussed over and over again in the last two to three years. So, when I see a grand gathering like this one, I think how easy it would be for us if we once made up our minds to do something. But somehow we are forgetting the habit of working together. I remember a time when we used to come here to Sabarmati quite often, twenty-five, thirty years ago, to consult Mahatma Gandhi and to seek his advice and whenever we came here, the talk would be of big issues, of satyagraha and our course of action against the British Government or about some constructive programme. We did not indulge in futile talk or long lectures. The talks were business-like and then we would go out to work. Now the talk is less to do with work and more about quarrels and squabbles, for people think that it is the duty of the Government to do everything. So in a way, our habit of working together is growing less, and this weakens the nation a great deal because, after all, a country marches ahead only on the work done by its people.

We have achieved independence, political independence, but that has not solved our other problems. We want that there should be economic progress. We want many things to happen in the country but they cannot be done by the government alone. If we want to make economic progress, it means producing more wealth. Wealth can be produced by the work done by the people, the farmers,

[6] Speech at a public meeting, Ahmedabad, 30 January 1951. AIR tapes, NMML Original in Hindi. Extracts.

[7] In 1949, 3.7 million tons of food worth Rs 144.6 crores was imported and, in 1950, 2.1 million tons of food costing Rs 79.8 crores was imported.

the labourers and other artisans. What is produced by everyone working together constitutes the wealth of the country. The country can spend only as much as it produces. No law can increase the wealth of a country. Yes, you may borrow from other countries—that is a different matter. The United States is a rich country. Why is it rich? It is rich because the United States produces a tremendous amount of goods very rapidly. The more we produce in our country, the more wealthy we shall become. Then there is the problem of equitable distribution of the wealth among the people. It should not find its way into a few pockets. But, first of all, we have to produce wealth by hard work. If you take the rate of production anywhere in the world, whether in Egypt or China or any other country, ours is much lower. If we produced as much as China or Egypt produce from their land, our country's income would be doubled. Why is it that we are unable to produce more? It is not the fault of our farmers....

Now, as you know, there is yet another problem. With the gradual increase in production, our population is also increasing very rapidly.[8] The more we produce, the more mouths there are to feed. So the increase in production does not help very much. Either we have to increase the production a great deal more to feed the population or try to curb the growth in population. What is to be done? You may laugh, but this is no laughing matter. It is a very important matter. Every year our population is going up by millions. So our production is just able to keep pace with the increasing population. Nothing is left over. How are we to make progress? The rate of progress has to be so rapid that the growth in population should not make a difference. How is that to be done? Development can take place only on savings which we can invest in factories or plants or land or fertilizers or such things. But we need to save in order to undertake developmental activities. We cannot save anything in our country—a few individuals may be able to save, but I am talking about the country as a whole. So development gets retarded. How are the poor people to save when they do not have enough to make both ends meet, when they do not get enough for food or for clothes, housing, and such necessities? So the greatest problem in our country is that most people do not earn enough to be able to save and development is slow.

... So this is the situation in our country. If you look elsewhere, there is talk of war; and if there is war, we may be able to keep out of it—we shall make every effort to do so—but we will certainly be affected by it. We must be prepared for that eventuality—and not give in to panic or fear but face the consequences with

---

[8] The total population of India increased by 13.4 per cent during 1941–1951.

strength. Again we come back to the same point that in order to be strong we must be self-sufficient and produce whatever we need in the country and not depend on others for essential goods. That includes military hardware because if we are not able to produce what we need for our armed forces but have to import these goods from other countries, we may find ourselves stranded if they do not arrive in time. Our forces will be useless in that case.

... The most important problem is, I think, how to change the atmosphere in this country so that the common people are involved in the task of nation-building and all of us may be able to work together. There I sit in Delhi and of course there is a great deal of work, so much so that it becomes difficult to get out of Delhi. But the result of being stuck in Delhi is that my going out and meeting people is becoming less. My contacts are growing less which is a bad thing—it has harmed me and possibly others too because it is very essential to understand one another in this huge country and learn from one another too. If we put up these barriers, understanding becomes more difficult. So how are we, the citizens of India, going to produce an atmosphere in which to make rapid progress? Ultimately the matter is entirely in our hands. No resolutions in the AICC or agreements with foreign countries can achieve that, though they do have some effect. I want you to consider this and read the resolutions which are being passed by the AICC because they are fundamental resolutions and if we implement them, it will be well and if we do not, then we will have to look for other ways of running this country .... *Jai Hind.*

A National Vision[9]

Friends and Comrades,

Within a few hours, this year will come to an end and we shall all step into the New Year. I should like to wish all of you who listen to me tonight, as well as others, happiness, for the New Year, and work for the building up of our country. Happiness and work are really together for there can be no true happiness without a feeling of doing something worthwhile. What can be more worthwhile for any of us in this great land of India, than to participate in the building up a new, ancient and ever-young country.

Three days ago, I was in the southern-most State of India, Travancore-Cochin, amidst some of the loveliest scenery that India possesses. In this State live a gifted people with educational standards higher than in any other part of the country. It

---

[9] Broadcast to the Nation on New Year's eve, 31 December 1952, AIR tapes, NMML.

is a progressive State, and I was happy to perform two important functions there. One was to start the construction of a new railway link joining the north and the south of the State and the other was to inaugurate a factory for processing monazite. I spent two unusual days in seclusion in a game sanctuary where wild animals live, protected from civilized man.

From that southern tip of India my mind pictured this great country spread out before me right up to the Himalayas in the north, and thought of its long and chequered story. What a wonderful inheritance is ours and how shall we maintain it, how shall we serve our country, which has given so much to us, and make her great and strong in spirit, and in the material things of the world, and make her people happy and prosperous.

We look at the world around us, and there is much to give us hope, but there is also a great deal to fill us with dismay for there is fear, hatred, violence and talk of war, just when it would seem that the prize that the world has so long sought was almost within its grasp. We look at our own country and find both good and evil, powerful forces at work to build her, and also disruptive forces, which would disrupt, and disintegrate her. We cannot do much, to affect the destiny of this world as a whole, but surely we can make a brave attempt to mould the destiny of our 360 million people. What then are we to do? What should we aim at? And by what road we should travel? It is of the first importance, that we should not lose ourselves in the passion and the prejudice of the moment. If we are to aim high, we must keep to our moorings and adhere to the high principles which have always formed the background of Indian thought, from the days of the Buddha, to our own day when Gandhiji showed us the path to right action.

Greatness comes from vision, from the spirit of tolerance, compassion, and an even temper, which is not ruffled by ill fortune or good fortune. Not through hatred and violence or internal discord can we make real progress. As in the world today, so also in our own country, the philosophy of force, can no longer pay dividends, and our progress must be based on peaceful co-operation, and tolerance of each other. In India, the first essential is the maintenance of the unity of the country, not merely a political unity, but a unity of mind and heart, which discards the narrow urges that separate and disunite, and which breaks down the barriers, which are raised in the name of religion or between State and State, or in any other form. Our economy and social structure have outlived their day and it has become a matter of urgent necessity, that we should refashion them, so that they might promote the happiness of all our people both in the material things of the world, and in the domain of culture and the spirit.

We have to aim deliberately at a social philosophy, which seeks a fundamental transformation of the structure—a society which is not dominated by the urge of private profit, and individual greed, and where there is a distribution of political and economic power. We must aim at a classless society, based on co-operative effort, where there is opportunity for all. To realize this, we have to pursue peaceful methods in a democratic way....

I want to tell you about the Five Year Plan which after two and a half year's labour, and much consultation, our Planning Commission has produced. Parliament has put its seal on it and now the time has come to implement it with all our strength all over India. That Plan endeavours to embody the social philosophy to which, I have made reference. Democratic planning means the utilization of all our available resources, and in particular, the maximum quantity of labour, which is willingly given and rightly directed for the good of the community and the individual. I cannot tell you much about this Plan, within a few minutes and I should like you to study it or at least the summaries that have been available, because it affects each one of you, and in a democratic society every one should understand and help in fulfilling the task ahead.

The Plan embraces the entire country, and deals also separately with each part of it, the States, as well as the smaller local areas. It offers also opportunities for voluntary organizations and voluntary workers to fulfil a vital and increasing role in national development. It has a public sector and a private sector, though even the latter has necessarily to have a measure of control so as to fit into the Plan. It endeavours to integrate various activities, i.e., agriculture, industry and social services. Agriculture is bound to continue to be our principal activity. Therefore, the greatest stress is laid upon this, as it is only on the basis of prosperous agriculture that we can make industrial progress. But agriculture has to be fitted in to the larger economy of the nation.

The growth of industry, both big and small, is essential for any modern nation, indeed, without industrial development, there can be no higher standards for our people, no strength in the nation and perhaps not even our freedom can be preserved. For the progress of agriculture, as indeed, for any kind of national progress, a proper land policy is basic. We have gone some way towards this, by putting an end, in many States to the *Zamindari* and *Jagirdari* systems. We must complete this task, and eliminate all intermediaries in land, and put a ceiling on the holding of land.

We hope that the next step will be co-operative farming, which will take advantage of the latest techniques in agriculture. Greater production is essential, both through agriculture and industry, if we are to fight poverty and raise standards, as we must. We want to develop therefore, as far as possible, self-sufficiency in our country, and a balanced economy in various parts of it. We want to work more particularly for the expansion of the home market, so that standards may go up.

In this development of self-sufficiency, and in providing work and employment, village and cottage industries have a supreme importance. I shall mention a few of the targets that we have laid down, first and foremost, there is food. We must become self-sufficient in food so as not to have to go to other countries, for our most essential requirement. The Plan raises food production, by nearly eight million tons. It is intended to provide new irrigation, through major works, to more than eight million acres, and through minor works to eleven million acres. Further, it is proposed to reclaim and develop, more than seven million acres of land. You know about our great river valley schemes which, in addition to irrigation, will supply over a million kilowatts of power for industry. Power is the essential foundation of all development today. We have attached great importance to minor works of irrigation as they yield quicker and more widespread results all over the country. Cotton production will be raised by over twelve lakh bales, and jute by twenty lakh bales. It is proposed to increase handloom production from 800 to 1700 million yards. In steel and cement, there will be substantial increase in production. At Sindri, we have already a great fertilizer factory, and at Chittaranjan, a locomotive factory. We are setting up a new steel plant, a machine tool factory, and a plant for the manufacture of heavy electrical equipment. Air transport is being nationalized and modern ship-building industry developed.

You know, about the many community centres, that have been started, all over the country. We attach great importance to these, for here an attempt is made to train our men and women in rural areas, in co-operative effort, for the good of the community. Here, even more than elsewhere, there is room for voluntary effort.

We have high ideals, great objectives, and compared to them, the Five Year Plan appears to be a modest beginning. But, let us remember, that it is the first great effort of this kind, and that it is based not on our wishes, but on the realities of today. It has to be related to our present resources or else, it will be unreal. It is meant to be the foundation of bigger and better planning and progress in the future. Let us lay these foundations well, and that future will inevitably follow.

The Plan is not based on any dogmatic or doctrinaire approach to our problems, nor is it something rigid and inflexible. There is scope in it for advance and variation along any lines and at any time where such are considered necessary, and as we learn from experience, we shall improve.

It is a dynamic Plan for a dynamic nation determined to go ahead and stand on its own feet and to bring about a new social order free from exploitation and poverty, unemployment and social injustice. It is a step towards the establishment of a society, which gives security and employment to the individual, and scope and encouragement for creative activity and adventure. Properly appreciated and acted upon, it will be a great liberating force for the energies of the nation. The Plan is a big one, embracing innumerable activities all over the country, but bigger than this is the vision which draws us forward, a vision inspired by courage and hope, and a reasoned optimism. Let us have faith in our country and ourselves. The Plan is essentially a programme of work. Let us work therefore, and abandon for a while empty and destructive criticism. I invite all of you to become partners in this great enterprise of building a new India, May the New Year take us along the road to achievement. *Jai Hind.*

BUILDING THE NATION

Industrial Policy[1]

Sir, I must apologize to the House for not having been present here throughout this debate, but sometimes the claims of other works are heavy. I would have liked to have been here throughout because I am vastly interested in this subject and I should have liked to hear what members have said. I understand that many of the members have commended this resolution[2] and spoken in praise of it or in satisfaction of it at least, that some have not liked it, and that some have disliked it intensely.[3] I am glad of that difference of opinion, and I am sorry if any of the honourable members should feel that he should suppress his own opinion on such a vital matter because of some whip or some other direction of the party executive.[4]

[1] Speech in the Constituent Assembly (Legislative), 7 April 1948, on a motion regarding the industrial policy of the Government, *Constituent Assembly of India (Legislative) Debates, Official Report*, vol. V, pp. 3417–22.

[2] The resolution embodying the Government's industrial policy was placed before the Constituent Assembly on 6 April 1948. Reserving to itself full control over munitions, atomic energy and railways, the Central Government also listed six industries in which it would have exclusive rights to establish new undertakings; but the question of nationalization of existing concerns in these industries would be postponed for ten years. Eighteen industries which would be subject to central regulation were listed. The development of cottage industries and the question of industrial relations were also covered.

[3] K.T. Shah criticized the resolution as falling short of the goals of socialization. He argued that the worst enterprises had been left for the state and the best ones for the capitalists, that there was no mention of a limit on profits, and that no equality of opportunity could exist, given vast disparities in income.

[4] K.T. Shah had said that, if the terror of the whip was not applied and the House was left free to express its opinion, the resolution would stand condemned.

I have myself been concerned with the theoretical aspects of planning for a fairly considerable time. I realize that there is a great deal of difference between the theory of it and the practice of it; as in almost everything in life the theory is full of poetry as, if I may say so, was the speech of my honourable colleague, the mover of the resolution,[5] but when we come down to applying that poetry all manner of difficulties crop up. Normally, there would be those difficulties but, as we are situated today, with the peculiar situation of India after all that has happened in the course of the last seven or eight months, one has to be very careful of what step one might take which might not injure the existing structure too much. There has been destruction and injury enough, and certainly I confess to this House that I am not brave and gallant enough to go about destroying much more. I think there is room for destruction in India still of many things—they will no doubt have to be removed; nevertheless, there is a way of approach. Are we going to adopt the course of having a clean slate or sweeping away almost everything so that we might have the pleasure of writing anew, without anything else being written on that slate? That seems to be an easy way of doing things, though perhaps there never has been a clean slate even when people imagined that there was going to be clean slate.

Nevertheless, there can be more or less a clean slate; I will not say that one should never try for that clean slate. But one has to think of each country and its condition at the time and see which is the preferable course, which involves lesser dangers. It seems to me that in the state of affairs in the world today and in India, any attempt to have what might be called a clean slate, that is to say a sweeping away of all that we have got, would certainly not bring progress nearer but might delay it tremendously, which far from bringing economic progress may put us politically so far back that the economic aspect itself may be delayed tremendously. We cannot separate these two things. We have gone through big political upheavals and cataclysms and if in our attempt to get something that we liked, to go forward one step in one direction, we lose a few steps in another, then in the balance we have lost, not gained. Therefore, the alternative to the clean slate is to try to rub out here and there and to write on it, gradually to replace the writing on the whole slate—not very gradually, I hope, but nevertheless not with a great measure of destruction and strain. Maybe I have been affected by recent events, but more and more I have felt that it is wrong to destroy something that is producing or doing good. It takes a long time to build and it does not take very long to destroy, so that if this House and this country thinks that we should proceed ahead in a constructive spirit much more than in a destructive spirit, then that approach necessarily has to

[5] Syama Prasad Mookerjee, Minister for Industry and Supply.

be different. What your ideals may be is another matter, but even in the realization of those ideals do you think that the easiest way of approach will be a clean sweep and then starting anew, or to replace as rapidly as possible and as fast as you can, with your available resources and material, the existing structure with a new one? I have no doubt in my mind that we have to change this existing structure and as rapidly as possible.

I was listening to the honourable member who just spoke before me I was listening to his laments of the burdens that are put on industry, of taxation and of this and that.[6] The fact of the matter is that that lament is based on a certain view of the world which I fear cannot possibly come back. I am not thinking in idealistic terms but just in practical terms; you cannot have it back. There are going to be greater burdens of industry because the state itself is burdened so much with its social problems; it has to solve them or cease to be a social state, and if it just becomes a police state then it ceases to be and some other state takes it place. It has to face its problems, and if it is to do that it must necessarily get the wherewithal to face those problems, and the burden on industry or the like becomes greater and greater. In fact, not because you think or I think or anybody thinks, but inevitably the trend of events is to make the state more and more the organizer of constructive industry, etc. and not the private capitalist or any other person. That is just quite inevitable so far as I can see objectively. I do not rule out entirely the profit motives; I do not know how long it will last in a smaller sense, but in the larger sense of the term it will come more and more into conflict with the new sense of the social state. That conflict will go on and one must survive, and it is clear that the state will survive, not that group which represents in its pure essence the profit motive in industry. That is an inevitable development. How are you to face that development? Are you then again to try to accelerate it as many of us would like to do, because quite apart from the economic aspect, the expert aspect, we have arrived at another stage which I trust every sensitive man feels somewhat, a psychological view of looking at things. That is that sensitive people cannot put up easily today with the vast gap between human beings, the distance between them, the difference between them, the lack of opportunities on the one side and the waste on the other.

It seems so vulgar, and vulgarity is the worst thing that a country or individual should support. We are arriving at a stage which cannot tolerate it. It was not, if I may say so, vulgar 50 or 100 years ago. Although the profit motive was functioning

---

[6] J.P. Srivastava had criticized the taxation structure and said it was impossible to secure capital for any industry. Many markets had been lost to industry and neither the United States nor Britain nor any other country was anxious to provide capital goods.

very strongly and although there was probably greater suffering then, nevertheless the approach was different. Perhaps the sense of social values was different. But, in the context of the world today, it is becoming increasingly not only a wrong thing from the economic point of view, but a vulgar thing, from any sensitive point of view. So, those changes are bound to come.

How then are you going to bring about those changes? As I said, I would much rather bring them about without deliberate destruction and obstruction, because the destruction and obstruction, whatever the future may bring after them, they undoubtedly lead to a stoppage of growth at present. They stop production. They stop wealth-producing activities. One has the satisfaction of being able to do something afterwards more rapidly, no doubt, but it is not such a certain thing that afterwards you will be able to do so rapidly. One has, therefore, to compromise much. Although I hate the word compromise in this context or in any context, one has simply to do it, if one does not stick to with some kind of a notion in one's head without thinking about it.

That brings us to a transitional stage of economy. Call it what you like—'mixed economy' or anything else. It brings us to doing things in such a way as to continually add to the wealth of the country and to add not only to the wealth of the country as a whole but to the distribution of that wealth in the country and gradually arrive at a stage when the centre of gravity of the whole economy has shifted the other way. Now, I rather doubt myself whether it is possible, without a conflict or without repeated conflicts, to bring about these changes quite peacefully, because the people who are used to possessing certain vested interests or certain ideas do not easily accept new ideas and nobody likes to give up what he has got; at least no groups like it; individuals sometimes do. The conflicts are continually arising, but the point is that even those conflicts are rather foolish conflicts, if I may say so, because those conflicts cannot stop the trend of events. They may delay, and in delaying, the result is probably that those who hold on to those vested interests get even a worse deal at the end.

Now, there is another aspect which I should like the House to consider and that is this. It is an odd thing that many of our most ardent revolutionaries, who think in terms of an idealistic world, are quite extraordinarily conservative in their scientific approach to the world's problems. If I may explain myself, I have used the word 'scientific' in its narrow sense. Most of our friends—Socialists or the Communists—continually think in terms of production remaining as it is in respect of the technique of production and the methods of production. Of course, they will not admit that. They will say: 'No! It is changing.' But, nevertheless, they base their programmes more or less on a static world and not on a continually changing world with new methods of production, new techniques of production, etc. They think in terms, for instance, of changing the land system. Perfectly right, because the fundamental thing is that the feudal land system should go before you build another society. So far quite right; change the land system. They think in terms of acquiring industries, because a socialist economy means that big industries or even all of them should be owned by the state. Well, quite good. But they do not think so much in terms of the vast changes in productive methods that are coming about, which may render the present industrial apparatus or even the methods adopted in the cultivation of land completely obsolescent and obsolete. They say: Why don't you acquire this or that? They want to spend vast sums of money over acquiring things which are 90 per cent obsolete. In fact, from the point of view of technological advance, it may well be a complete waste of money to acquire obsolete machinery, factories and other things that may be there. It is true they are useful so long as new factories and new technological methods are not introduced, and if you have a vast quantity of money and resources, certainly acquire them and go ahead with other things. But if you have limited resources, then the main thing to do is not to go about thinking in terms of a static technology, but of a changing technology, thinking in terms of the state acquiring the new processes, the new changes, and not so much of the old, except when the old obstructs, when the old hampers your planning and progress.

Now, obviously, constituted as we are in India, we have not got unlimited resources. We have to think hard where to get the money; how to get the money; how to get the other resources—technical and other. If so, there has to be a certain kind of priority about what work we do. Even if you start acquiring things—suppose we decide to acquire a large number of industries—and you pass this resolution, I am quite sure when we work it out, actually in practice, it will take a good deal of time to take them one by one. However rapidly you may do it, it takes a little time, unless of course it is by the process of the 'clean slate' where you sweep an old thing away and build a new one on it. Therefore, even if you think of doing that, you have to think in terms of priorities; which industry should first be liquidated, which service, etc.; one after the other, provide the money; provide the organization; provide the technical personnel, etc. etc. So it takes time. Much more so when you have to think in terms of additional industry and new industry, new schemes plus old schemes. You have to think in terms of priorities: which must come first. I have no doubt in my mind that the priority for state enterprises must be in terms of new things as far as possible unless the old things come in the way.

I attach the greatest importance today to, let us say, the great river valley projects and schemes that have been framed, the first one of which, the Damodar Valley scheme, has passed through this legislature and others are coming up soon.[7] I think they are far more important than almost all your existing industries. Here is something new that you are building out of nothing; new land is being brought under cultivation, many new things are being created out of the enormous power produced out of the river valley projects. Now, I want that to be completely state controlled, but run, as is stated in this resolution, on the model of a public corporation.[8] I do hope that the public corporation that is going to be established is not going to be a departmentally run organization, but either wholly or more or less an independent organization. I do hope that it is not going to be run by the people who have worked in the ruts of the departments, but by persons of vision, push and drive; not the people who write on files but who do the work. Now, regarding these vast river valley schemes, of which you have got enormous ones, all the resources of India are not enough to push them through quickly. Am I going to allow those to remain undone and delay them and think in terms of acquiring a tramway system or something else here and there? Let the tramway system be acquired, if you like; but I do not want to give first priority to the tramway system of some such thing.

Now, in this resolution which has been placed before you, various lists are given—list No. 1, list No. 2, etc.—as to what Government proposes to do, and has done. There these river valley projects are mentioned rather casually. But remember what that casual mention means.[9]

It means that the state is undertaking vast enterprises all over the country which will govern the industry of this country and all your acquisition and the rest will be secondary and minor. These river valley systems are controlled by the state and they will control the economy and industry of the country completely. If you get a grip over all these things, then the process becomes swifter, but if we simply lay down rather fancy schemes then we never come to grips with any particular part of it, and really we are not advancing at all except on paper and in theory. Therefore, from the poetry of rather vague planning in air, we have to come down to the prose of the statement. Because it is a prosaic statement, therefore, there is very little poetry in it except the poetry of my honourable friend who made the speech at the

[7] The Dominion Parliament passed the Damodar Valley Corporation Bill on 12 February 1948.

[8] The resolution stated that the management of state enterprises would, as a rule, be through public corporations under the statutory control of the Central Government.

[9] The river valley projects were described as 'calculated in a short time to change the entire face of large areas of India.'

beginning. It is definitely a prosaic statement; it is meant to be a prosaic statements; the House knows it was not difficult to put in fine flourishes of language in a resolution of this kind which would have sounded so nice for the public and which would without conveying any commitment have pleased the ear and the eye and produced a general impression how fine we were. Well, we have very deliberately not done so, because we want to make it a prosaic statement of what we think we ought to do and we can do in the relatively near future and how far we can do it. How much we cannot do depends upon a multitude of factors, but, at any rate, this is a thing which is meant to be done, not a thing which is meant to be flourished about as a kind of election programme before the public.

The tempo will depend on so many factors. I mentioned these river valley schemes, because I attach the greatest importance to them. Now suppose the Damodar Valley Scheme is a thundering success, that is a bigger thing from the state's point of view, from the point of views of industrialization and from many other points of view, than the fact that this House has passed half a dozen other schemes which are not functioning. So it is the first steps that count, the first things; if we start an industry under state auspices let us make it a thorough success instead of going to acquire this and that and making a mess of many things. Of course, once you have laid a good foundation, it will be easy for you to go ahead.

Now it is obvious that this Government or this House may pass this resolution, may lay down the periods of time as to what will happen five or ten or fifteen years hence, but the fact of the matter is that we are living in an age of very swift change and transition and nobody can guarantee what will happen and when it will happen; nobody can guarantee whether there will be war or peace and nobody can guarantee what will happen even if there is peace because things change rapidly in India. We have lived during the last eight months on the verge of rapid change and very undesirable and unhealthy change in many respects. Nevertheless when we say ten years, we mean it, that is as we see things at present—and we say ten years because, so far as we can see, the state's hands will be completely full. It is not merely to give an assurance, although we wish to give an assurance to all working industries so that they may be able to function properly, but fundamentally we have got enough to do and we want to do it thoroughly; but whether I give an assurance or the House gives it ultimately events will determine the pace. Events may go faster or slower; events may break up our economy or something may happen, not only that, but a hundred and one things may happen.

When we are told—that capital is shy and it does not come in, that we cannot get capital for private industry or public loans, etc., it is a fact. Well, that too I imagine is due more to these changing conditions than to anything that we might do or anybody else might not do. For this the industrialist or capitalist himself will have to see whether he is too wary and too afraid of investing his capital if he is then well and good. It is obvious that the country cannot stand by. We should give a fair field and a fair chance to the industrialist to go ahead with certain domain and if he does not, we should go ahead as we cannot see things mismanaged or not managed because he is afraid that he won't get enough profit or something that might happen. The people cannot wait. We give a fair chance, a fair field and a fair profit and if he does not do all that, somebody else has to do it; there cannot be a vacuum. Also if any industries are mismanaged, or not managed properly, slowed down or stopped, again we have to consider what to do with that industry, because the day of an industry simply stopping, not functioning, because somebody misbehaves, either an employer or labour, and the whole community suffering is gradually passing. The community cannot afford to do that; the community must see that it gives a fair deal to labour that is a different matter. Therefore in this resolution a great deal has been said about it and that is perhaps one of the most important parts of the resolution, i.e., regarding councils and committees because unless you give a completely fair deal you cannot come down with a heavy hand in case of misbehaviour.[10] After that you may have people still misbehaving so that I would like this House to consider this resolution in this context. I have not touched on the various subjects which might be added or subtracted. I have no doubt if the House sat down it could perhaps hear and then make some changes in it but I do submit that the fundamental approach of this statement is the only right approach and the only practical approach at the present time and therefore I hope the House will adopt it.

INDUSTRIAL PEACE[11]

I appeal to capital and labour to sink their differences and work for the common good of the country.

I hope that the provincial governments, industrialists and labour will extend all their support to the Planning Commission which is to be set up shortly.

[10] The resolution stressed the importance of labour and management co-operating to increase production and proposed the establishment of a machinery to advise on fair conditions for labour and fair returns to capital. Industrial relations should also be improved.

[11] Speech at the Indian Merchants' Chamber, Bombay, 26 April 1948. From *The Times of India*, 27 April 1948.

There is now no mutual trust between capital and labour and their constant conflicts have affected the strength of the country. Many provinces have now set up industrial courts to settle disputes between them. I, however, hope that both parties will settle their differences themselves. Perhaps it is not possible to eradicate all capital-labour conflicts, but I think they can be minimized to a great extent.

In pursuing any definite industrial policy a fundamental pre-requisite is cordial relations between employers and employees. If this is not forthcoming then both are to be blamed.

It is difficult to point out which way will lead the world to permanent peace. Certainly the method followed in the last twenty five years is not the correct way as it has not established peace in the world. India wants to avoid all conflicts as far as possible.

The Government's prime objective in its plans is improvement of the lot of the common man. The future of the nation depends on how far it succeeds in that.

THE MIDDLE WAY[12]

It has been a great pleasure to me to come here. I have done so chiefly because my old friend Dr Hamied invited me and also because I consider that the chemical industry is a very important one. I have also come on a mission of curiosity and intend to find out who the chemical manufacturers of this country are and what they are doing. I have learnt something from Dr Hamied's address. Of course, I do not mean to say that I was totally unaware of their activities. Dr Hamied's address added a great deal to my knowledge of what has been done or not done and also what the Government should and should not do. He has presumably asked me and others to appreciate and admire the work of both the chemical manufacturers and the other private interests engaged in industry in India.

I have no doubt that much of their work is worthy of appreciation and occasionally some might even be worthy of admiration. Perhaps, it might be said that they have not yet attained the degree of perfection at which we aim and there might be some lapses on their part. We have, nevertheless, to look at this problem in relation to our country's economy and her needs. We have to keep before us the problem of how to build or develop our economy and, in a smaller sense, our chemical industry as well.

[12] Address at the Annual Meeting of the Indian Chemical Manufacturers' Association, New Delhi, 26 December 1950. *Jawaharlal Nehru: Selected Speeches*, vol. 2, 1949–53, pp. 44–50.

Looking at newspaper advertisements it seemed to me that one of the main industries in the country was the manufacture of some potent and powerful pills. Being unacquainted with the taste or effect of those pills and seeing the advertisements in the newspapers day after day, I began to dislike intensely the people who manufactured these things and advertised them so frequently. I may go a step further and say that I am a very bad product of the pharmaceutical age, because I have hardly ever taken any medicine, pills or drugs. However, I have no doubt that other people need these pills and I have no desire to deprive them.

Dr Hamied has referred to some large questions. He has laid down some excellent maxims and some extraordinary maxims. He has stated as an obvious fact which admits of no dispute or argument that private enterprise and nationalization can be equated with democracy and that totalitarianism and nationalization are the same. It is for the first time that I have heard such a viewpoint. I am not going to enter into any controversy about this or about what he called the dual policy of the Government. Obviously, he wants us either to plump for absolute free enterprise or for 100 per cent nationalization.

I am afraid Dr Hamied is out of touch with what is happening in the world. There is no country in the world where the free enterprise of his dream exists. It does not exist even in the United States of America which is the high-priest of free enterprise. On the contrary, it becomes less and less significant in spite of the country's policy and its aims. World conditions today create forces which compel a country to progress in a certain direction, whether it wants to or not.

There are countries like Soviet Russia and some others which have gone a long way in creating a State which is in complete control of industry. Everything else is also State-controlled. Dr Hamied wants us to choose between Soviet Russia and something which does not exist anywhere in the world. That is a very hard choice indeed and I do not see why I should be forced to make it. It is inevitable that those countries, which do not want either of the two extremes, must find a middle way. In that middle way, there is bound to be more emphasis on some factors than on others but obviously a middle way or a mixed economy, if you like to call it that, is inevitable. That is not a dogma or an axiom which can be applied to any country regardless of its conditions. It will have to be decided by each country individually with regard to its particular conditions. What may be suitable for India not be suitable, let us say, for Burma or Afghanistan or a country in Europe. We have to base our actions on objective facts and our capacities. We cannot think of this country in terms of what is happening in the United States. We must take into consideration the facts that are peculiar to and govern the situation.

The United States of America has had 150 years of consolidation and growth and its capacity for production today is colossal. All kinds of economic forces which have little relationship with the old idea of capitalism are active in that country. Of course, America is a capitalist country and she is proud of being one. But the fact is that modern capitalism in the United States of America is vastly different from what it was twenty or thirty or forty years ago. It has changed. Even economies can move in a particular direction with a momentum of their own. I was told the other day by someone who knows—I have no idea how far the figures are correct—that one person in every five in the United States of America is in some kind of State employment. That is a prodigious number and America, mind you, is a capitalist and not a socialist State. The fact that one person in five is in State employment in a capitalist country shows how the nature of the capitalist State is changing. This means that in a country where conditions are different and where the stresses of modern life are greater, the changes are also bound to be of a basic nature.

In England there has also been a considerable change. I should like to know what the response from Parliament or from the Government or from other people would be if Dr Hamied's axiom were to be stated in England. England is obviously pursuing a socialist policy and has been pursuing it with considerable courage during the last four or five years since the war ended.

So, the problem is not a simple one. There are in this world various policies, ideologies and theories. I suppose there is some truth in each of them. However, my personal feeling is that while it is very important to have a theory as the logical basis of our thought, it is not reasonable to apply it by force to all conditions. We can use a theory for the purpose of argument and for testing its validity. In practice, however, you have to take the facts of the situation and adapt either yourself or your theory accordingly. Most countries have to do it. I may say so, even Soviet Russia which seeks to base herself on a very hard and rigid theory of Marxism, interprets Marxism in a manner that suits her. The result is that her brand of Marxism has little to do with Marx. I am quite certain that Marx would be astonished if he were to see the various interpretations of his theory. Whether you approve of this or not is immaterial. The important point is that Russians, in their own way, are hard realists and continue to adapt their policy to what they consider for the moment good for their country or their party.

Coming to India, we have to consider things as they are. We cannot lay down any slogan or watchword and try to force it through to its logical conclusion. Whether it is in India or anywhere else, only those policies can succeed which promise to deliver the goods. There are no other tests. Broadly speaking, the present conflict is between the various forces represented by communism on the one side and on the other by something to which I cannot quite give a name. I cannot call it capitalism because it has all kinds of variations. What is really developing in the world is some kind of democratic socialism. It is developing gradually and in varying degrees. Whatever the two conflicting forces may be, their real test is not going to be on the battlefield. They are ultimately going to be tested by the results achieved.

We should try to understand our problems in as realistic a manner as possible, avoiding for the moment words which have long histories behind them and which confuse the mind. When we throw these 'isms' about as arguments, we get lost. Passions are aroused and the hard facts are ignored. A person who calls himself a socialist naturally has a certain general outlook and a certain set of objectives. Another person may have quite a different point of view. If you put these two persons together, they hurl harsh words at each other and nothing results. If, on the other hand, they sat down together and said, 'Well, here is a job to be done', something might result. Here in India, there is so much we want—food, clothing, housing, education, health—in fact, all the important things of life. How are we to get them? Surely, not by shouting slogans or passing resolutions about socialism or capitalism or any other 'ism'. We will have to produce the goods and distribute them properly. We must think how best to do it.

There is no doubt that American capitalism has an amazing capacity for production; in fact, it is colossal. This capacity of American capitalism was not always the same; it has changed and has been changing. Besides, the United States of America has had 150 years to achieve it in. It has a territory with huge economic resources. It had opportunity without the hampering background of conflict which other countries had to reckon with. It had neither a heavy population nor the relics of a feudal age. It was a new country with enormous space and it developed to its present level in 150 years. It is thus rather absurd to say, 'Do what has been done in America.' I would like to do it in my own way but how can I do it? I do not have the 150 years or even 100 years to settle down in and grow as America did. I have neither that enormous space not that invaluable freedom from conflict and trouble. I have neither that much time nor the same opportunity. India is a big country with a background of all kinds of conflict. Many kinds of forces are at play. I have got to solve my problems in the immediate present or in the near future, not in the next hundred years. Private enterprise in America developed gradually till it built up for itself a very strong position with enormous resources. Has private enterprise in India got the capacity or the ability or the resources to do that? It has ability and it has resources but it just has not the strength or capacity to solve the situation by itself. It is a patent fact that you just cannot do it. Is our private enterprise going to take up our river valley schemes? It cannot, because they are too big for it.

These schemes cannot pay dividends quickly. We have to wait for years and years. Therefore, the State inevitably has to take them up. In America the railways are owned by private companies. Here we own the railways. Are we not told, 'All this dislocates business. Let private enterprise have full play'? If private enterprise has full play, one of the first casualties in this country will be private enterprise itself. To be frank with you—I am talking in general terms—private enterprise in this country is not wise enough. It may be clever in making money but it just is not wise enough. It does not see what is happening all round. It does not see a changing world in turmoil but sees it in terms of an age that is dead and gone.

It so happens—and it amazes me—that here in India, in spite of enormous difficulties, we have conflicts and all kinds of unhelpful criticism and condemnation of the Government. That very fact symbolizes a certain state of affairs in India and an attitude in the minds of her people which is far from critical. There is no doubt about it. When we talk of something critical like the food situation, for instance, we use strong language without showing any awareness of the crisis. We live our lives in the same old way and though large numbers of people suffer in the country for lack of food, lack of shelter or lack of other things, most of us, especially those of us who criticize, lead our lives unaffected in any way. Asia is on the verge of a crisis. In fact, the whole world is tense with a sense of urgency but we have no such sense yet! Unfortunately, this lightheartedness in understanding what is happening all round us is not good because then realization sometimes comes as a shock. We have to take the problems of India and look at them in the context of the world. Let us deal with them as realistically as possible, having certain aims and objectives, trying to go towards them, adopting our policies with a view to realizing those objectives, without arguing so much, without having recourse to slogans or set terms.

The only objective that you can set before you in the modern world is a widespread raising of the people's standard of living. It is not the only objective but others are subject to it. No government can afford to ignore the urges of the common people. After all, democracy has its basis on those very urges and if any government flouts them, it is pushed aside and other governments take over. They may be better or worse. That is immaterial.

Dr Hamied, in his address, criticized heavy taxation on the one hand and on the other called upon the Government to provide certain urgently needed things like a synthetic petrol plant which would cost thirty or forty crores. How can we reduce the revenue by lessening the taxes and still do everything that is necessary? I don't understand. Naturally, there is a limit to our capacity to do things and there is a limit to taxation. We cannot go beyond that without disturbing the whole structure of our economy. Important things have certainly to be done and if enough money is not forthcoming, those things are not done.

I should like you, gentlemen, to look at this picture and balance things. I want you to realize that in the modern age it is not possible to go back to the old days of a dead world. No country in the wide world can go back to those days. If you think in terms of going back then you are thinking in a vacuum and that is unreal thinking. How far the State can or should come in or how far there should be co-operation are matters for consideration but the real test is results which are not the accumulation of private fortunes but the advancement of the public generally.

Community Projects

Sometimes, I begin to suspect and become a little afraid of these leads from the top that we, including myself, are always giving. We have got into the habit of doling out good advice to the country, to our people, to everybody. Nevertheless, my own experience has shown that people who give too much advice are unpopular. They are irritating. At any rate such advice does not conduce to the good of others, as it is intended to. That is to say, if we act too much from the top without adequate foundations and without that intimate relation with the lower rungs, we can hardly achieve any great results. We will achieve something, of course. So the problem becomes one of how to bring about a union of these two elements.

Obviously, it is necessary to plan, to direct, to organize and to co-ordinate; but it is even more necessary to create conditions in which a spontaneous growth from below is possible. I wonder if this Community Scheme is something which is likely to bring about a union between the top and the others. By the term top I do not mean that some people are superior; I mean those who guide, the organizers; and by others I mean the millions who will participate in the work. In fact, ultimately there should be no top and no gradations. Nevertheless, I feel that even the organizational lead should not be tossed like a ball from what is the top to what might, if you like, be called the bottom; that is to say, even the initiative for the Community Projects should come, wherever possible, from the people who are most affected by them.

Often, we like to sit in our chambers and decide everything according to what we consider to be good for the people. I think the people themselves should be given the opportunity to think about it and thus they will affect our thinking as we affect their thinking. In this way, something much more living and integrated is produced, something in which there is a sense of intimate partnership—intimate partnership not in the doing of the job but in the making of the job and the thinking of the job.

SOCIALISTIC PATTERN OF SOCIETY[13]

Comrades and Friends,

I am greatly moved at having to put this resolution before you.[14] I am moved because of a variety of reasons. I am moved, first of all, as I stand here and look at this mighty concourse of humanity and at our comrades in our struggle for freedom in this country, to see all of them here together; that is a moving sight, it is a strengthening sight. It is a sight which will increase anybody's faith in the future of the country. I am moved when I look at you and when I think of the past history of this mighty organization, which it has been our privilege and honour to serve. Here, all round us, the Reception Committee of this Congress has put up as a reminder to us some portraits of the Presidents of the Indian National Congress—those pioneers of old who started this organization, at first, in a small way. I do not say that they worked in a small way. It is easy for you and me, who reap the fruits, to imagine that they worked in a small way. They had to face all manners of difficulties and problems and it is because of the work they did that we are what we are today. So, I look back at this history of seventy years of the Congress. It is a fairly long time in a country's history, seventy years, and during this period this little seed which was sown, grew into a sapling and this sapling into a mighty tree covering the whole of India from the snows of the Himalayas to Kanyakumari in the south. All these tremendous successes in history come before me—of great men and women and great leaders of our country, each playing his or her part and taking the country one step forward.

We have met academic debaters talking loudly about big things. We have been in touch with the people of India from the fields and in the factories, in the market places, in the streets, because we represent the people, not a few high intellectuals. High intellectuals, of course, were with us but we represent ultimately the urges of the common man, the passions and the feelings of the people of India and so, as they grew, we reached out to them and reacted with each other. The Congress became the symbol of the will of the Indian people. It acted on the Indian people and the Indian people acted on the Congress, and each contributing to the strength of the other. I have no time to refer to the past history of this great movement but I want to remind you of one or two things. There were the early years of domination by Dadabhai Naoroji, the Grandsire of India, as I may call him. Then there was a

---

[13] Speech while moving the resolution on 'Socialistic Pattern of Society' at the open session of the 60th Indian National Congress, Avadi, 21 January 1995. AIR tapes, NMML.

[14] For the first draft of the resolution, see *ante*, p. 255.

great deal of struggle and chaos in the Congress, the great figure of Lokmanya Tilak arose. It is not merely that he was great; of course he was, but he represented a new thought in the Congress, a new spreading out, a new revolutionary fervour. The Congress was a different Congress after that and so it went on; and then Gandhiji, our beloved leader came into the Congress and again there was a mighty change in this organization and it spread out all over, more specially to the poor downtrodden peasantry in the country. It became fundamentally an organization representing the peasantry of India. It represented others too, but after all 80 per cent of the population of India was peasant. Now, at each stage, the Congress took a new turn reflecting the stage of development of our thoughts as a people as a whole, not as individuals, not as a number of able people laying down the law for others. We grew as a people and the people grew with us. And so, during the Gandhian era, we took step after step under Gandhiji's leadership and you will remember how each step strengthened our organization. Sometimes we stumbled and fell. The point is to know how to get up when we fall and march on and not remain there and complain. Only the weak complain, only the weak are afraid of marching on if they fall. So, though we stumbled, we got up and marched and went ahead and the nation grew in its vision and it led us to that Congress held here twenty seven years ago, when first we raised the promulgation of *Purna Swaraj*[15] and two years later, on the banks of the Ravi in Lahore, when we took that pledge.[16]

Well, we have honoured that pledge fully and completely and here we are meeting in this Congress again as proud citizens of the Republic of India, having honoured the pledge that we took twenty six years ago. But that does not mean that the journey has ended for us. There is no journey's end for a people on the march. There is going to be no journey's end for the Indian people, for we have to march on and on. There is no end to the vista opening out before us. There is no journey's end to the Congress which represents Indian people.

Having attained political freedom, obviously other things immediately came in and you will remember that at no stage in this history of our struggle for freedom did we think only of political freedom. All the time the concept of freedom moved before us. We thought of the economic aspect, we thought of the peasant, we thought of the worker and the underdog and the downtrodden and the disinherited in India. After all, what was Gandhiji but a symbol of the disinherited and the downtrodden in India, whose aim and passion in life, as he himself put it, was to wipe every tear

[15] On 27 December 1927 at the Madras session of the Congress.
[16] On 31 December 1929 at the Lahore session of the Congress.

from every eye? Well, there are very many tears and very many eyes in this country, and the world. I do not know if there is any person capable of wiping them all, but it was given to us in our generation to see a man, to serve under a man, to learn from him—a man who blessed us by coming to us and blessed this generation in India. He brought us swaraj, but that was always incidental to what he did for this country. He made us what we are; he gave us something of the spark which was in him. And, for the poor people, we became petty heroes because he showered a part of his light upon us. So this freedom struggle all the time gained in its social content, in its economic content. And now the time has come when we should march further in this direction and declare openly what we have often said that the type of society we are aiming at in India is a socialistic society. What exactly a socialistic society is, I do not propose to go into in detail. Many may argue about it and many of the pundits, *maulavies* and the academic people have argued about it and go on arguing, if you like, but I want to tell you this: Whatever it is going to be, it has to be in keeping with the Indian genius, the genius that is India. If it is something superimposed then it will not go far. I do not mean to say that we cannot learn from others. We can, we will, and we must learn from others. But whatever we learn must also be grafted on the soil of India and not be something apart from it.

We have fought for this great right of independence. Now our work is not so much to fight, although, certainly we have to fight evils within or outside us; our work is to be the builders of India. How shall we build? We have the Five Year Plan. You know that although the Five Year Plan was a cautious Plan, because we did not want to say more than we could do, yet, even now, in these three years, we have fulfilled, more than fulfilled, some of the targets of the Plan. Now that shows us our strength and shows what we can achieve. I need not go into what we have achieved, but the point is that we are now on the eve of the Second Five Year Plan and therefore, it has become necessary for us to say in what manner the Five Year Plan should be made up. Planning is essential; it is important. But what manner of planning shall we have? How shall we utilize our resources best? That is the problem. What picture should we have? We have said that we want a welfare state. Good, but remember that although a welfare state is in itself not a socialistic pattern, it is an essential part of a socialistic pattern. You may have a welfare state without a socialistic pattern but you cannot have a socialistic pattern without a welfare state. We want both for a variety of reasons. Now, do not think that we are going to achieve this quickly or rapidly. It is a very big thing. The point is that we must be set on the right path. We must look at the ideal and everything we might do should be governed by that ideal and that pattern. Therefore, it is necessary for the Congress now to state clearly that our planning in future should be in terms of a socialistic pattern of society and that we should work for that end from now on. We cannot establish it fully for many years because the problem is a big one. So, I beg to put this resolution before you.

I would like to say that when we talk of socialism and the socialistic pattern that the word 'socialism' has come to us from the West and sometimes it is a little unfortunate that it is a word with a history, and the past history of the word comes up also. Now the word 'socialism' in Europe has a past history and connotation. It is entangled with a great deal of struggle of the European proletariat and others during the last 150 years or more and it is connected together with the struggles in regard to the last War, and many other struggles. It is necessary that we should not go through the struggles of Europe to achieve our socialistic pattern. It will be foolish for us to go through those struggles and copy the mistakes of others. Apart from the fact that India is a country with a strong individuality, we have a way of doing things for ourselves in a peaceful way. I do not deny and you cannot deny that there is a class struggle in India. Where one class dominates over another there is bound to be conflict. And to deny that conflict is to shut your eyes to the facts as they are. But the point is how we meet the conflict. There was the very big conflict between British imperialism in India and Indian nationalism. We met it by peaceful methods which proved to be effective. After we attained swaraj, we had other problems; we dealt with problems of the Indian Princes and the old feudal order. We solved them by peaceful methods and negotiation. People told us we gave them too much, too big privy purses, and that we could not afford so much. I am inclined to agree that we paid large sums; but remember this, that the solution of that problem was brought about peacefully and if that had not been done, the cost of conflict would have been tremendous. Later we undertook the solution of land problem in India. I would not say that we have solved it wholly and completely, but we have very largely put an end to large landed estates, zamindaris, *jagirdaris* and *talukdaris*, again peacefully. Now, all these problems have been solved in other countries usually with bloodshed, civil wars and tremendous suffering. I think we have some reason to congratulate ourselves that we can deal in a peaceful way with these big problems that produce conflict in society.

Why, then, should we not also solve the problems of industry and the problem of bringing about a socialistic order in India through peaceful methods? Why should we think in terms of violence? Therefore, I say to you that when I use the word 'socialism', I do not use it in the historical sense in which it has evolved in Europe. Certainly, I adopt the principles, because they are common to all, but we shall have our own socialism. Our own way is to develop these things through peaceful methods and not through violence and certainly we should avoid what is much too common in people, 'adventurism'. We are not going to get socialism by revolution or by a decree or by saying suddenly that there is socialism in the country. We can only get it by hard work, by increasing our production and by distributing it equally. And so this resolution says, and I shall read it out to you now:

In order to realize the object of the Congress as laid down in Article 1 of the Congress Constitution and to further the objective stated in the Preamble and Directive Principles of State Policy of the Constitution of India that planning should take place with a view to the establishment of a socialistic pattern of society where the principal means of production are under social ownership or control, production is progressively speeded up and there is equitable distribution of the national wealth.

I put this Resolution before you because I think it represents the wish, the hope and the aspirations of the people. I put it before you not merely as an aspiration but something much more than that, as a pledge which you and I take, as a challenge of the future which we are determined to conquer.

STATES REORGANIZATION[1]

Jawaharlal Nehru: Sir, this is the seventh day, I believe, of this debate and, as you have just informed us, seventy persons have previously spoken. So, I am the seventy-first in this long succession. I have been hesitating as to whether I should take up the time of this House in this marathon race not because I am not interested in this question but I was doubtful if I could throw much light on it. I might straight off say that I am not greatly interested as to where a particular state boundary is, and I find it very difficult to get passionate or excited about it. Naturally, I have my preferences, but it does not make much difference to me whether any internal boundary of a state is drawn here or there. What is infinitely more important is what happens on either side of the boundary, what happens within the state and more especially in those great areas, which inevitably are few. Look at that from the linguistic point of view, multilingual or bilingual—as there are bound to be a large number of areas—what happens to people inside a particular state who may either linguistically or in any other sense form what might be called a minority. That seems to me a far more important proposition than where you draw the line. Because, if you once lay down those basic principles correctly, and act up to them, then the vast number of problems that arise and difficulties and legitimate grievances would inevitably disappear.

Now, for a moment, I may as well say to the House that I am not speaking particularly in my capacity as Prime Minister or on behalf of the Government and

---

[1] Speech in the Lok Sabha during a debate on the Report of the States Reorganization Commission, 21 December 1955, *Lok Sabha Debates*, 1955, vol. X. Part II, cols. 3493–514. Extracts. From *Selected Works of Jawaharlal Nehru* (Second Series), vol. 31, 2002, pp. 170–83.

I am not going to make any epoch-making pronouncement. We, in the Government, have been considering this Report and the other matters that flow from it for the last many weeks and we shall continue to consider them till we come up to this House in some form of placing the recommendations for this House to consider. And, it will not be proper for me or for any other member of the Government to express himself in any tone of finality about any matter. But, I may give expression to my own inclinations in regard to the recommendations of the Report or the other suggestions that have been made.

One thing I should like to say is that I have regretted very greatly certain criticisms that have been made in the Press, in some newspapers—I do not know how far any honourable Member indulged in such criticisms—criticisms of the Commission. One can criticize the Commission, one can criticize their recommendations, of course, that is a different matter; but criticisms of the Commission and sometimes very strong criticisms about their unfairness and all that, I think, that is a very unfair approach and it is a kind of approach which is bound to make such work now or hereafter much more difficult. We choose eminent men; they take a great deal of trouble and tell us what they think about the problem. You may or may not agree with it but to attack, in a sense, their bona fides or fairness, if I may say so, apart from its wrong approach, does indicate, to my mind, that your case is very weak. It is the old story of abusing the attorney on the other side.

May I also suggest for the consideration of this House that while Members here represent their constituencies, of course, they do something more. They are not only members of this or that particular area of India, but each Member of Parliament is a member of India and represents India, and at no time can we afford to forget this basic fact that India is more than the little corner of India that we represent. We know, all of us, that we have to face certain forces which may be called separatist, that is to say—I am not using the word in any bad sense—it nevertheless means that people's attention is being diverted more to local problems, parochial, state, provincial, and forgetting the larger problems of India. There should be really no conflict between the two but it is a question of the method in our thinking, in our minds, in considering our problems. There is the word in the English language 'parochial'. That is, a person thinks of his parish or village while he forgets the larger considerations; while he thinks too much of even of a state as big or important, he forgets these larger considerations.

Now, it has been my good fortune and privilege to travel about India a great deal and often to go abroad. Perhaps, I have had that good fortune more than most Members of this House. The result is that I am constantly compelled to think in larger terms, not only in national terms but even in international terms and see this picture of India in that context. Perhaps, that is helpful in giving a truer perspective of events. I travel about India and I see this moving drama of India and I feel excited and inspired by it. I see many things that I do not, of course like, but the major thing is this tremendous drama, that is India today moving as if by the dictates of some predestined fate and destiny towards its goal. It is a tremendous thing and we see that not only in India. I would submit to this House we see it even more if we go abroad and see this country of India in the south of Asia, from some distance, see it in proper perspective. I would beg the House to consider that there are many people in the wide world who also are beginning to feel the sense of drama and adventure about what is happening in India. Now that is the perspective. And they see also how we have got over great problems and great difficulties. It is true that we have even greater problems ahead, but in the measure in which we have succeeded in the past, that is the measure with which they judge of our strength to succeed in the future. That perspective, I submit, has some importance. We may argue as to the boundary of Bihar or Bengal or Orissa or some other state—and I have no doubt that the argument on the question is an important one and I do not say it should be brushed aside—but the word 'important' also is a relative word. There may be other things which may be more important, and one must not lose oneself in passionate excitement as to where the boundary of a state should be, provided, as I said, we have this fuller conception of India and provided we have, by Constitution, convention or otherwise, the fullest guarantees that whether a person lives on this side of the border of a state or the other, he will have the fullest rights and opportunities of progress according to his own way. In this sense I tried to approach this matter, and I felt that perhaps this larger outlook was sometimes lost sight of. We talked about linguistic provinces and some people said that this principle of linguism should be extended more and more; some people criticized my colleague, the Home Minister, because he did not quite make that the final test. May I say quite briefly and precisely that I dislike that principle absolutely 100 per cent, as it has tended to go?

Now, I want to make it perfectly clear that that does not mean that I dislike language being a very important matter in our administration or education or culture, because I do think that the language of the people is a vital matter for their development, whether it is education, administration or any other matter. But I do distinguish between the two things, this passion for putting yourself in a linguistic area and putting up a wall all round and calling it the border of your state and developing the language to the fullest extent, because I do not think that the people can really grow except through the language. I accept that completely, but it does not follow in my mind that in order to make them grow and their language, you

must put a barrier between them and others, that you must put a wall around and
call that this is this language area or that. For a state, broadly speaking, there are
language areas in India; of course, you cannot ignore them and there is no need to;
they are welcome as they are; they represent the development of history through
the ages. But considering them as something opposed to the others and putting a
hard and fast line between the two areas is, I think, carrying it too far. As a matter
of fact, it just does not matter where you draw your line. If you judge it from the
purely linguistic point of view, you go against the wishes of some—may be many.
There are invariably bilingual areas, and if they are not today bilingual areas, are
you going to prevent people from going from one state to another? Are you going
to stop, contrary to the dictates of our Constitutions, the movement of population,
the movement of workers or of other people from one state to another? You cannot.
Therefore, whatever fixed line you may even draw, if that movement is free, people
will go, will be attracted by one side or other, and again change the linguistic
composition of that state or the border area. Are we going to sit down every few
years or ten years and say, 'Now the ratio of this particular *tehsil* or *taluk* has changed
and, therefore, it should be taken out of this state and put into another'? It is quite
impossible if you think in that way.

Therefore, you must realize that while there are clearly marked linguistic areas
of great languages, there are also almost always between two areas bilingual areas,
from the language point of view, and sometimes even trilingual areas. And wherever
you may draw your line, you do justice to one group and injustice to another. What
is our difficulty in these problems is raised in this Report and there are many
difficulties. By looking at it purely from the language point of view, the difficulty
is that there is good reason, good logic and good argument for every case, on both
sides of the case. That is the difficulty. If there is logic only on one side, we decide
it easily; but there is logic on both sides and the two logics conflict. there is argument
on both sides. You may balance the two and say that this argument is stronger than
that; by and large, the case of one side is somewhat better, but the fact is that the
case of the other side is pretty good too. Are you to measure merely in a balance—
maps and census figures have become the fashion now—how many individuals
are supposed to speak in this or that language? Because there is a slight majority in
this case, this kind of a thing may be all right. It might be done sometimes, but it
leads us ultimately to all kinds of fantastic conclusions.

Therefore, I submit that we must consider this matter separating the question
of language in the sense that we must be clear that the language has to be developed,
more especially all the great languages of India which are mentioned in the
Constitution—but I would go a step further—and even those that are not

mentioned in the Constitution like those in the North East Frontier Areas and elsewhere ought to be developed; secondly, that the development of one language should not be and cannot be at the expense of the other. It is a strange notion that the development of one language comes in the way of another language in India. I am absolutely convinced that the development of any one of the great languages of India helps the development of the other languages of India. It is my privilege, however, unworthy I might be, of being the President of the Sahitya Akademi, started a year or two ago where we deal with all the languages of India and try to encourage them. The more we discuss these matters, the more we see that every encouragement, development and growth of the language results in the other Indian languages also getting some advantage of growing. And we, of course, are trying to have translations of one from the other and so on. I would go a step further and say that the knowledge of a foreign language helps the growth of an Indian language. If we are cut off from foreign languages, we are cut off from the ideas that come in those foreign languages—with not only the ideas but the technology which is part of modern life. Therefore, let us not think of excluding a language. I do not for instance understand—I may be quite frank—the way some people are afraid of the Urdu language. I am proud to speak Urdu and I hope to continue to speak Urdu. I just do not understand why in any state in India people should consider Urdu as a foreign or something which invades into their own domain. I just do not understand it. Urdu is a language mentioned in our Constitution. Is it intended to live in the upper atmosphere or stratosphere without coming down to earth? I just do not understand it. It is this narrow-mindedness that I object to....

People go into arguments in regard to philology, in regard to other things. Take the Punjabi language. We heard learned arguments about the origin of Punjabi and Gurmukhi script and how far it is connected with Hindi and how far it is independent of Hindi; whether it has descended from Sanskrit, etc., as if it was of the slightest significance, to what source it belongs. What matters is what people do today. Let scholars go into the past of Gurmukhi, Hindi or anything. What is done today? If people in Punjab or elsewhere are accustomed, or if they wish to have, to use or to speak a certain language and to use a certain script, I want to give them every freedom, every opportunity and every encouragement to do that. Because, as a matter of fact, speaking from the strictly narrow, practical and opportunist point of view, the more you try to suppress it the more opposition there is, and the more, if I may say so, it survives the suppression. Everybody knows that in regard to language there are intimate rather passionate ideas connected with it in people's minds—something very intimate. I can understand the passion with regard to any language—Hindi or any other. But the person who feels passionately about a language must also remember that the other fellow also feels passionately about it. That is the difficulty. Therefore, the safest and the only course is to give every freedom and opportunity to all of them. Let them develop in the natural course of events. They will adapt themselves; they will affect each other and influence each other and grow more and more important, if they have the capacity or remain less developed. It is not for any person or for me to go about and say that any language—let us say, the Punjabi language—is an undeveloped language. It may be. It does not matter. We should try to develop it then and allow the natural forces to increase the importance and the use of this language. Any attempt to decry or deny a language is bad not only from that language's point of view but from the point of view of other languages and those who use the other languages. It is the only correct policy both from the point of view of good policy and even if you look from the narrower points of view.

I am dealing with this question of language because it has somehow come to be associated with this question of states reorganization. I repeat, if I may, that I attach the greatest importance to the language but I refuse to associate it necessarily with a state. Inevitably, of course, in India as it is, there are bound to be states where one language is predominant. If that is so, let it be so; we encourage that. But there are also bound to be areas where there are two languages; as I have said, we should encourage both of them. We should make it perfectly clear that the dominant language of that state should not try to push out or suppress or ignore in any way the other language of the state. If we are clear about that, then the language issue does not arise.

Other issues may arise—economic and others. With language of course other aspects, cultural aspects which are connected with them may arise. Then the two should be treated on the same basis. That is to say, every culture, every manifestation of culture should be encouraged. Culture is not an exclusive thing. The more inclusive you are, the more cultured you are. The more barriers you put up, the more uncultured you are. That is the definition of culture. Therefore, culturally too, we should encourage every aspect of culture. If, as the world develops and changes, something falls out, let it fall out. But if you try to push it down or push it back, then you are probably not likely to succeed and in fact it brings in conflict which injures your own culture possibly.

Thinking as I do in this matter, I personally welcome the idea of bilingual or multilingual areas. For my part, I would infinitely prefer living, and my children being brought up, in bilingual and trilingual areas than in a unilingual area. Because of that, I think, I would gain wider understanding of India and of the world and a wider culture—not a narrow culture, however big that narrow culture may be.

The House will forgive me, if I mention a rather personal thing. This is in relation to my daughter. When I has to face the problem of her education—unfortunately, I was a bad father and I was not with her for years and years—my attempt was this; when she was a little girl I sent her to a school—not in UP as I wanted her, as a child, to pick up some of India's languages—in Poona; I sent her to a Gujarati school in Poona because I wanted her to know the Marathi language and the Gujarati language and their influence. I sent her subsequently to Shantiniketan because I wanted her to understand the Bengali background—not only the language but the cultural background. Whether I succeeded or she succeeded or not—that is another matter. My point is that my outlook was such. I should like her to go down south and learn Tamil or Telugu or Malayalam. But of course, life is not long enough to allow one to go to every state.

MEGHNAD SAHA: May I interrupt? What is the percentage of people who have the capacity to learn more than one language? Ninety per cent of the people have no capacity for learning a second language and you must legislate for those ninety per cent of people....

JN: The honourable Member has put a question: What is the percentage of people who can learn another language? Well, if I may say so, I imagine that the percentage is very very large. I will tell you what I mean by it. You and I may have some difficulty in picking up another language because we proceed by grammar and all that. But you take persons—pick them out from the Delhi bazaar and put them in an environment of another language. You will find in three months they will talk that language which you will not know. I know and I can tell you another instance. In our foreign missions, our secretaries and others are supposed to learn the language of that country. They do try to learn in a scientific way. Before they know anything of that language, some of the lower staff who have to work there pick up the language and talk in it. So, it is not merely a question of learning a language correctly but being in a position to understand it and thereby entering into the life of other people; that is important. There is nothing so difficult as trying to understand another people unless you can speak to them directly without an interpreter. An interpreter is a great nuisance.

Therefore, I would say that the first question for us and the most important question in this entire Report is the last portion—the last chapters in which they mention certain safeguards. Whether they are enough or not is another matter. Add to them if you want. But the point is that there should be clear safeguards laid down, possibly in the Constitution, otherwise, by some other way, so that a fair deal could be given to every language everywhere in this country. There should be no argument about that. We should not say: we are in a majority and therefore our language should prevail. Every language has equal right to prevail even if it is a minority language in the country, of course there have to be some good numbers. You cannot have it for every small group. I understand that the Bombay Corporation has schools in fourteen languages, because Bombay is a great city with all kinds of language groups there.

Secondly, if I may venture to lay down a rule, in every matter it is the primary responsibility of the majority to satisfy the minority. The majority by virtue of its being a majority naturally has strength to have its way, it requires no protection. It is a bad custom, a most undesirable custom, to give statutory protection to minorities, it is not good. Sometimes it is right that you should do that to give an encouragement, let us say to backward classes, but it is not a good thing. Therefore, by its being in the stronger position it is the duty and responsibility of the majority community, whether it is linguistic, whether it is religious, whether it is caste— whatever it may be—to pay particular attention to what the minority there wants, to win it over. It is strong enough to crush it if other forces do not protect it. Therefore, I am always personally in favour, wherever such a question arises, of the minority there, whether it is a linguistic minority or a religious minority.

Talking about religion in the broad sense of the word. Obviously in India the votaries of the Hindu religion outnumber others tremendously. Nobody is going to push them from their position; they are strong enough. Therefore, it is their responsibility, and special responsibility that people following other religions in India, which may be called minority religions, have the fullest liberty and a feeling of satisfaction that they have their full play. If that particular principle is applied then I think most of these troubles and grievances would disappear.

About a month ago I think, or less, at that tremendous meeting in Calcutta which was a kind of public reception to the Soviet leaders who were here—much has been said about *Panch Shila*; as the House knows everybody talks about *Panch Shila*—I ventured to say that this *Panch Shila* was no new idea to the Indian mind— maybe, to other minds also it is not new—and that, in fact, it was inherent in Indian thinking, in Indian culture, because *Panch Shila* ultimately is the message of tolerance. And I quoted at that mighty meeting—I do not know whether is was very proper on that occasion or not—Asoka's edicts and said: 'This is the basis of Indian culture and *Panch Shila* flows from it.'[2] Naturally it is not an imposed thing on us. We may misbehave as we sometimes do—that is a different matter—but the basic Indian thought is that, and it has continued for these long ages.

---

[2] For Nehru's speech on the occasion, see *post*, pp. 312–17.

Now, we thought of this *Panch Shila* and peaceful co-existence in the wide world, warring world, and we have gained a measure, a considerable measure of respect and attention because of that. Why have we done so? Well, partly, I would submit, because our thinking has been correct and based on some principles which are not so opportunist, and partly also because our thinking has been correctly laid down, has not been very divergent from the action we have taken; that is, there has been an approximation in the ideals we have laid in regard to foreign policy and the action we have taken. I do not say they absolutely coincide, but there has been an approximation, and whenever thought and action fit in strength follows. It is the conflict between one's so-called ideals and one's action that leads to bad results and to frustration in the individual, or the group, or the nation. Where a nation is fortunate, or a group, or an individual, to be able to act according to his own ideals, well, then it achieves results. It is in our struggle for Independence and freedom that we were fortunate in being able, largely, to combine our ideals with our day to day activities as well as given strength to us as individuals and as a nation.

Therefore, we have succeeded in this measure in our foreign policy, and may I, as an interlude, just mention two matters not only because they are relevant, but because we have been criticized with regard to them in foreign countries? The two questions are Goa and Kashmir. We are criticized by some people that we, who talk loudly about peace and loudly about anti-colonialism and all that—well, it is said by our critics—follow a different policy in Kashmir and Goa. Now, I think that possibly when history comes to be written Kashmir and Goa will be the brightest examples of our tolerance, of our patience and the way we have suppressed our anger and resentment at many things in order to follow that broad idealistic policy that we have laid down.

Now, I was saying that what I am concerned with is not so much the boundaries here and there. I am concerned with two things: first the principles, that is, the principle of life wherever you may live, on whichever side, and; secondly, the manner of approach to this problem, that is to say: how do we discuss these matters, how do we decide them, how do we accept the decisions made. That is vital. That is more important than what you decide. A person is judged more by that. Anybody can decide things according to his own wishes, but when a group meets, of varying opinions, how do they decide? There is the method of democracy, of discussion, of argument, of persuasion and ultimate decision and acceptance of that decision even though it goes against our grain and our opinion. That is the democratic method; or else, simply the bigger lathi or the bigger bomb prevails and that is not the democratic method. Whether you consider this matter in problems of atomic bombs or street demonstrations the question is the same. That is to say, I am not objecting to demonstrations, but I am objecting to the violent part of it, the violence of it. There are democratic ways of demonstration too. I am objecting to the violence coming in these matters and that violence is, in quality the same perhaps, the there is the violence of atomic bombs. At any rate the violence of the atomic bomb has a tremendous course, tremendous destruction, but it does not poison your personal thinking so much, which smaller violences do. When you begin to hate your neighbour you cannot pull on with your neighbour. That is a more dangerous thing from the point of view of degradation of the individual. That hatred seeps in, the hatred of your neighbour and it is bad enough. Or course, to hate a country or a whole nation is bad but somehow that spreads out. That hatred is not good, but the hatred of an individual, group or a community, the hatred of a Hindu for a Muslim or the hatred of a Muslim for a Hindu or a Sikh, that type of thing is much worse. It poisons your daily life.

· So, I submit what is more important is the method of decision. Do we believe in peaceful democratic methods or means or not? That is the test question in this matter, because we feel passionately. Let us admit that many of us feel very strongly about our point of view on this matter and no doubt they have reasons for feeling strongly. I do not object to that but we must be strong enough, in spite of our feeling strongly, to realize that it is far more important that this question should be discussed calmly, deliberately and peacefully, and whatever decisions are arrived at by the final authority—and the final authority of course is this Parliament—must be accepted, because there is no absolute finality about any decision. But also, at the same time, nobody wants the whole question to be brought up and discussed again and again frequently. If one can do it calmly or objectively, one can do it, so we need not think that we are tied down to a particular decision forever. At the same time, we should accept it and work it with all goodwill. Therefore, the basic question is one of approach, of goodwill. It really does not matter what the decision is.

Now, the two or three most important questions appear to be, let us say, the questions in regard to the State of Bombay or Punjab or any other. Now, what do we aim at? What can we aim at? Obviously to me, speaking for myself, I do not care two pins as to what happens to them provided that the people of Punjab or the people of Bombay have goodwill for each other. That is the basic thing. It does not matter how you divide or sub-divide one state or two states or three or four states. That is a matter which we could consider on administrative, economic, and linguistic and other grounds. But the basic thing is that, after having done that, do you create goodwill and co-operation amongst the people who live there; because, if you do not, it does not matter how much you justify the decisions made by census figures and arguments and maps. If you do not create that goodwill, you fail completely, because we have to live and work together.

We have in India, as I ventured to say a little earlier, a moving sight. What is happening in India? We—this Parliament and the people of India—are working hard to weave this pattern of India's destiny, with its variegated, many-coloured facets and many languages and yet, it is under one Government that we are weaving gradually at present. Now, if, instead of weaving it, we take the scissors and the knife and start tearing it and making holes in it, that is bad. What is the pattern you give? Therefore, the basic thing is the goodwill that accompanies a decision and we should remember it.

Some honourable Members here may well remember that I delivered quite a number of speeches in Hyderabad opposing tooth and nail, if I may use the word, the disintegration of the State of Hyderabad. That was my view. I would still like the State of Hyderabad not to be disintegrated, but circumstances have been too strong for me. I accept them. I cannot force the people of Hyderabad or the other people to come in a particular line because I think they should do so. I accept the decision and I adjust myself to the change that Hyderabad be disintegrated. If it is going to be disintegrated, the Commission has suggested that the Telengana area, the remaining part of Hyderabad State, should remain for five years and then it may be decided. We have no particular objection, but logically speaking, considering everything, it seems to me unwise to allow this matter to be left to argument. Let it be taken up now and let us be done with it.

When I read this Report first rather hurriedly, I may assure this House—because some people seem to doubt it—that I had seen not a single line of the Report before it was officially handed to me, and I knew very, very little about what it contained before I got it. So I read it as something almost new. Because of that, many parts of it and many proposals that it contained were new to me. I had absolutely no notion what they are going to suggest about Bombay, Punjab, Madhya Pradesh and about any other place. I had no notion at all. The thing which for the moment rather surprised me somewhat was the proposal about Madhya Pradesh for the simple reason that it was quite novel to me. I have not thought of it in those terms at all. I said so in the broadcast[3]—not criticized—but I said that some parts of the Report came as a surprise to me. They did; but I thought about it, we discussed it amongst ourselves. The more we discussed, the more we talked, I became more and more convinced that it was the right proposal. I had no preconceptions and prejudices

---

[3] On 9 October 1955. See *Selected Works* (Second Series), vol. 30, pp. 525–6.

about this or that. So, the House will notice how my mental approach to all these problems was—to keep an open mind and try to understand the various aspects of it and in particular to arrive at a decision which is an agreeable one and which creates goodwill as far as possible. Because of this, apart from official approaches to this problem, we have met literally hundreds and hundreds of persons in groups of five, ten or twenty, who were coming from almost every state of India and putting forward there viewpoints. We have listened to them and we have discussed it with them, because we want the greatest measure of agreement and cordiality about this and because we attach more importance to a decision having that goodwill, even though it might be logically not a good decision: for, logic is a very feeble and unworthy substitute of goodwill. I would rather have goodwill than logic, and co-operation. We have proceeded that way. How far it will succeed wholly in creating that goodwill I do not know. But I am quite positive that, however much the Government may or may not succeed, this House can succeed if it wants to create that and give that lead to the country in deciding these things rightly or wrongly but with goodwill, and accepting the decisions made. Then, if something is wrong about the decisions, we can consider them quietly later on.

Now, take two of the major problems—the questions of Bombay and Punjab.[4]

An Honourable Member: Bihar also.

JN: With the greatest respect for our friends in Bihar and Bengal and Orissa,[5] I would say that nothing is more unimportant than their problem. I am really astonished at the amount of heat, about these three or four states, which has been imported.[6] We can consider it and decide it. But what does it matter if a patch of Bihar goes this way and a patch of Bengal or Orissa goes the other way? I cannot get excited about it provided always that they get fair treatment. That is the vital and important point.

---

[4] See *Selected Works* (Second Series), vol. 31.

[5] The SRC had suggested minor boundary adjustments between West Bengal and Bihar—a portion of the Purnea district east of the river Mahananda and the Purulia sub-district of the Manbhum district minus the Chas thana should be transferred from Bihar to West Bengal. No changes were suggested for Orissa.

[6] The SRC Report aroused discontent both in Bihar because of the transfer of certain areas to West Bengal, and in West Bengal because it fell short of their expectations. Strong feelings were evoked in Orissa because of the rejection of their claims to certain areas of Bihar and Madhya Pradesh. Subsequently twenty leading Congressmen including Ministers, MPs and MLAs, resigned from the Party on 17 January and demonstrators disrupted train and air traffic and attacked Government buildings in Cuttack and Puri.

About Bombay, which undoubtedly is one of our major difficulties, I think there are arguments advanced on the part of Maharashtrians, on the part of others in Bombay, and I have no doubt at all that the arguments advanced about the Maharashtrians have great force. But, unfortunately, I see the force in the other arguments too. Obviously, nobody can say that it is a one-sided affair. Then, how does one deal with it? Honourable Members know that the Congress Working Committee, after considerable discussion, suggested three states, but speaking for myself, I hate them and believe that the recommendation made by the States Reorganization Commission was the best in the circumstances. But, I do not wish to compel others to accept it, because the Maharashtrians, Gujaratis and others are the people who have to reside there. Who am I to push my opinion down their throats, more especially the Maharashtrians who played such a vital part in India's history and who have to play such a vital part in the future of India? But I do think that was a fair and equitable decision which would have promoted co-operative working and which could, if necessary later, have been added to or amended. There is nothing to prevent it, I still think that it will be the best thing. I do not know if the time is past for considering that matter afresh by the people most affected by it.

Take Punjab. People talk about unilingual and bilingual states. I have already laid stress on the importance I attach to language; and, in relation to Punjab, I would lay stress on the importance I attach to the Punjabi language, because, apart from the very important fact of a large number of the Sikhs or all the Sikhs wanting it—that is the major factor good enough for me; it does not come against me—I do not know why the Hindi-knowing people should object. I say that a language should not be considered something exclusive or excluding others; we must be inclusive in our thinking. But, apart from that, the minor modulations of a language represent the growth of a particular specific culture in a group. The folk songs of Punjab are an immensely important part of the Punjabi culture. It does not matter to me for the moment how many books on technology exist in the Punjabi language in the Gurmukhi script. If they do not exist, it is a great drawback from the national point of view. Either that drawback will be made good, or it will suffer and it will not advance with us in the future. But I do wish to give every encouragement to the Punjabi language, not at the expense of Hindi. There is no question of expense of Hindi, Hindi is strong enough, wide enough and powerful enough in every way to go ahead. They should co-operate with each other. This whole outlook of one language trying to push out the other is a wrong outlook. So, I have laid stress on this linguistic point. If you look at the Punjab from the linguistic point of view, from the point of view of numerous proposals made, you will find that there is no proposal conceivable which makes the Punjab completed unilingual, that is to say, unilingual in the sense the entire thing being based on Punjabi in Gurmukhi script. So far as the speaking part is concerned, it might well be said that nearly all Punjabis speak Punjabi, whatever they may say. In fact, even Hindi or Urdu is half Punjabi, so that, if you look at it from the communal point of view, it is a bad attempt. It does not matter how much you may divide Punjab, but the Hindus and Sikhs are intermixed completely. You may, by adjustments, make one 45 per cent and the other 55 per cent, the one 30 per cent and the other 70 per cent and so on. But, you do not change the basic fact that both are completely mixed up in each village. And, therefore, the only way for Punjab to exist and prosper, rather, even to exist, is for both to pull together. There is no other way. Of course, the Punjabis are people with very great virtues, but among their great virtues, the virtue of pulling together has not been known. Perhaps it may be due to their greater vitality. They are very vital people. Even today Punjab is probably the most prosperous of our states, from the common people's point of view. Nowhere in India do people drink more milk and lassi than in the Punjab. They have a future before them of great advance, with Bhakra Nangal and other schemes; that is a tremendous future and it surprises me that they should waste their great energies when they have all this work before them. Again I would say, if, as they are, the Hindus in the Punjab are in a majority—I am not for a moment talking about the shape of things to come regarding boundaries, I am not going into it—it is their duty to win over the Sikhs, and, it is the duty of the Sikhs to win over the Hindus. This business of going against each other, trying to trip each other and weaken each other is not, if I may say so, mature politics. It is immaturity and we have grown out of it in India.

There are one or two things I should like to say before I finish. We have to examine all these matters, all these changes, from the point of view of our economic development, the Second Five Year Plan, etc. It is highly important. It is true that in drawing up the Second Five Year Plan, there has been an attempt made to draw it up for almost each individual district so that if the district changes over to another area, it does not affect it so much. But, if you support the whole state, practically all your energy and resources will be spent in the next two or three years in settling down and not in the Five Year Plan. One should like to avoid it.

Finally, the more I have thought about it, the more I have been attracted to something which I used to reject seriously and which I suppose is not at all practicable now. That is the division of India into four, five or six major groups regardless of language, but always, I will repeat, giving the greatest importance to the language in those areas. I do not want this to be a thing to suppress language, but rather to give it an encouragement. That, I fear, is a bit difficult. We have gone too far in the contrary direction. But, I would suggest for this House's consideration a rather feeble imitation of that. That is whatever final decisions Parliament arrives at in regard to these states, we may still have what I would call zonal councils, i.e., a group of three, four or five states, as the case may be, having a common council. To begin with, I would say that it should be an advisory council. Let us see how it develops. Let it be advisory, let the Centre also be associated with it for dealing with economic problems as well as the multitude of border problems and other problems that arise. There can be, let us say, five such zonal areas.[7]

H.V. KAMATH: A common High Court.

JN: There may be, as the honourable Member suggests, in some places a common High Court, a common Governor, etc., but, a common economy is more important. We are having these big schemes, river valleys and others. It will be very helpful. In the main, I want them to develop the habit of co-operative working to break down the wall. It may be that, later, the advisory zonal councils may develop into something more important. I think, we should proceed slowly and cautiously so that people may not suspect an undermining of their state's structure. So, we could have, let us say, five: one for the north, one for the south, one for the east, one for the west and one for the Centre.

H.V. KAMATH: *Dakshin, Purva,* etc.

JN: Something like that. I would submit that for the consideration of this House.

---

[7] It was suggested to group the states into five zonal councils to 'deal with matters of common concern, promote inter-state concord and arrest the growth of acute consciousness'. Common Public Service Commissions, High Courts and Governors in certain regions were also contemplated.

LANGUAGE ISSUE[1]

Mr Speaker, Sir, a week ago today[2], I returned to Delhi after visiting many countries and great cities in the West, and meeting many leading personalities there. I tried to understand the great movements that were taking place there, the thoughts in the minds of people there and the changes that had taken place. Even more so, I tried to understand what reflection there was of India in the minds of the people that I met in Europe.

I was interested in that naturally, because even as I watched something of the stuff of history being made in Europe, I wanted to know how far the history we might be making here was reflected in the minds of people in Europe. I found they were greatly interested, indeed sometimes more than interested, in what was happening in India, because they felt that something very significant was happening here, something that would not only change India, but would affect other countries and other continents. And I thought then of the work that we do here in India, the great problems that face us, and the tremendous responsibility of this Parliament of India. This Parliament of India indeed has this responsibility of making the history of India.

That was one thought that struck me. Another thought that struck me as I travelled from country to country was of how the old frontiers had gradually meant less and less. Within an hour or two, I travelled from the capital of a great country to the capital of another great country. There were problems, certainly many

[1] *Selected Works of Jawaharlal Nehru* (Second Series), vol. 34, 2005, pp. 114–24.
[2] Statement in the Lok Sabha, 30 July 1956, *Lok Sabha Debates*, vol. VI, Part II, 16 July–3 August 1956, cols 1504–22. Extracts.

problems and many conflicts, but this idea of national frontiers became less and less important somehow in the modern scheme of things.

I mention this because here we are considering with considerable heat and passion not the frontiers of nations but the borders inside the nation between two States or provinces. If the frontiers of a nation become relatively less important than they were, and if in the course of a few years, they may almost be ignored for many matters, how much less important are these problems of State boundaries which we are considering? I do not wish to minimize their importance, but I do wish this House to consider this question in proper perspective. We are apt to lose that perspective in the heat of debate or otherwise. I know that this question which we are considering, and this Bill and its provisions, have moved people strongly, deeply and that even now there is a great deal of feeling about them. I do not suppose that the most ideal solutions, whatever they might have been, could possibly have been pleasing to everybody.

So far as I am concerned—indeed, I might say, so far as Government here is concerned—it is of no great significance to us what part of India goes into this State boundary or that. Yes, certainly we must consider what is more desirable from various points of view. But in the ultimate analysis, it does not make much difference where one little part is from the Government point of view. From the individual's point of view or the State's point of view, it has certain importance; I do not deny that.

Therefore, the Government of India approached this question, if I may use the word, more or less objectively and without any particular desire to impose this decision or that. We have been told that we did not go through the proper procedure of consultation and decision, etc. But I think any person who knows what has happened in the last six, seven or eight months in this country, will also know that the amount of consultation and discussion about this matter that we have had is without parallel. In fact, many people say—and perhaps rightly—that we overdid this: it would have been much simpler if we had not tried to consult hundreds of thousands of persons in this process and thereby perhaps added to the confusion. However, it is a fact that this question has roused people. But I wish this House to realize this, and first of all look at this picture in proper perspective, lest we forget that perspective and get lost in the passions of the moment. Secondly, to realize that however important these questions of borders might be, they are, after all, administrative divisions inside the country. Thirdly, whatever we may decide today, surely nobody prevents us afterwards, subsequently, from making any variation.

I realize that nobody wants to decide things and change them everyday. That is a different matter. But nothing is final in the sense that it cannot be changed in the future.

Now, our difficulty has been that we have tried too much perhaps to balance respective viewpoints, to try to find a common way, to find as large a measure of agreement as possible. And naturally, in doing so, we have often succeeded in displeasing many people. Yet I would beg of you to remember that in this very very complicated business which affected the whole of India, by far the greater part of India has accepted, broadly speaking, the proposals that are made. True, very important questions remain; among them perhaps the one that has been talked about most is the question of Bombay and Maharashtra.

Now, I have felt—I say so with respect—that perhaps the approach to these questions has been too much marred by strong language and by direct or indirect reproaches, and, if I may use the word, by running down this group or that group, this community or that, not only in regard to Bombay, but in regard to other places too—whether it is Bengal, Bihar or other places. I would beg this House to consider whether it helps in the slightest the consideration of these problems by running down any province, any community, in any part of the country, by considering one part more capable, more courageous, more independent or more nationalistic— whatever it may be. We are all here as Members chosen by some constituency or other in India. Naturally, we are interested in that constituency. But I submit that we are here as something else also. I am not here merely as Member for the eastern part of Allahabad district. I consider myself the Member for India here, and I do submit that every Member of Parliament is a Member for India. We are not members of some local municipality or district to consider the particular interests of that area only and forget the rest of India. We have to consider every question, I hope to the best of our ability, in relation to the whole country. I am not Prime Minister of Allahabad district. I am Prime Minister of India by the grace of this House, and I have to think or try to think in terms of India. I may make a mistake. Of course, I make mistakes; all of us make mistakes. But I do submit that when we begin to challenge each other's bona fides, then any discussion and any consideration of any problem on merits becomes a little difficult.

Let us consider these problems from this larger point of view, realizing that even if some decision which we dislike is made it does not make a terrible lot of difference, realizing that if the mistake is made, it is a mistake in a narrow sphere and it can be corrected later—because the greatest possible mistakes and the greatest possible error in this is having a wrong mind and a wrong approach to this problem and creating an atmosphere of conflict—which is so vital to the development of any big thing in India. That is the basic approach.

Some honourable Members may well say, 'It is all very well; your intentions may be very good, but where have you landed us with your good intentions?' It is perfectly true that we have landed ourselves in a bit of mess. I admit it and I admit my responsibility for it because, naturally, as Prime Minister and otherwise also, I am at least partly responsible for it. I do not wish to run away from it. It sometimes happens that in trying to avoid one difficulty one lands in another. But there it is.

I do not wish to go into the past history of all these eight months' debate and consideration; but we have arrived at a certain stage now and we have to look at the picture as it is. Many things could have been done, large bilingual States and many other things might have been done; they might be done later too. I do not rule that out. But, what exactly can we do at the present moment so as to promote and help to bring about this larger atmosphere of co-operative endeavour. In a decision which we take—the decision may please somebody or displease somebody; it may be a right or wrong decision—the main thing to consider is what is the final result of it in terms of goodwill or ill will. That is the main thing.

On several occasions, in regard to this very matter of Bombay and Maharashtra, we varied previous decisions. Each time we varied it—I am talking about the earlier stages—we landed in a fresh difficulty. We did it at the suggestion of somebody, some respected colleague of ours, and then, they themselves wanted something else. Ultimately we landed ourselves in this difficulty that any attempt to change it probably resulted in a worse situation than the first one.

Honourable Member, Shri Deshmukh said, he preferred a City State formula to the present state of affairs.[3] So did we and that was our first decision and, the honourable Member will remember that on one occasion, he told us not only on his behalf but responsibly and authoritatively on behalf of others too that we should adopt the City State formula.[4] We adopted it although we had come to some other conclusion because we were anxious and eager to please. But not 48 hours had passed when we were told: 'No; go back upon that; we won't approve that.' We

---

[3] Deshmukh stated that the government's decision to have central administration for Bombay city 'places Maharashtra in a worse position than even if Bombay had been made into a city state.' He added that with the status of a city state, Bombay would not have to wait for five years for deciding whether it should join Maharashtra or not.

[4] On 23 August, G.B. Pant, Home Minister, told the Rajya Sabha that Deshmukh had informed the Cabinet on 8 January 1956 that Maharashtra leaders had authorized him to say that they would prefer a city state for Bombay.

went back upon it and so we shifted about in our anxiety to arrive at some decision which carried the largest measure of agreement and consent.

The honourable Member referred to what he called two crucial decisions which were taken without consultation. I am in a difficulty about this matter because I am really, totally and absolutely unable to follow him. I do not know where he gets his facts from. I consulted my papers, my Cabinet records and everything. There are two decisions—I leave out for the moment the statement that I made in Bombay. The first decision was taken, I say, absolutely and repeatedly with the consultation of everybody and my colleagues in the whole Cabinet. I have no doubt about it. Finally, I say—leave out the intermediate stages—this Bill itself was placed before the Cabinet. The Bill, after all, contains it and it was the Cabinet that adopted it before it came to this House. That is the usual procedure. I do not understand how anyone can say without forgetting all these that this decision was adopted without consultation. There was more consultation than on any other subject that I have had since I have been Prime Minister.

The other matter is a small matter: what mistakes I might have made or anything said about me. Shri Deshmukh was kind enough and good enough to say that he did not refer to me when he said that there was a certain animus.[5] I thank him for that statement, but it is a small matter after all as to what I am and what I may be. But, it is a much bigger matter as to what our method of Government is, what the procedure we follow in our Cabinet and the Government of India and in this Parliament and elsewhere. It is no small thing. Are we following wrong procedures; are we overriding everybody and just imposing some individual will, mine or a small committee's will over this Parliament, over the country? That is a vital matter. It is more vital than, I say, this whole States Reorganization Bill. If we go wrong, how are we to function? It is a charge the honourable Member has made; it is a very serious charge.[6] It is not easy to reply to it and to justify my own conduct. But I do submit that he has done little justice to his colleagues in the Cabinet and even less justice to himself when he made that charge. He has functioned in this Cabinet for

---

[5] Speaking in the Lok Sabha on 30 July, Deshmukh said: 'I believe there is some evidence of animus against Maharashtra among important personages of the Congress Party....' Refuting the contention that he was 'interested in making such a charge' against Nehru, Deshmukh said, 'I am well aware that he (Nehru) is constitutionally incapable of animus against anybody.'

[6] This refers to the charge made by Deshmukh in the Lok Sabha on 25 July and 30 July that the decision regarding Bombay city was taken without consulting the Cabinet.

[7] See *Selected Works* (Second Series), vol. 32, pp. 227–32.

six years or more and he has been a valued and respected member and colleague of ours. Now, he makes this charge against his colleagues after six years of functioning together, a charge however much I may be guilty of or deserve, I do submit it is a very very unfair charge on all my responsible colleagues in the Cabinet.

However, there was this question of the statement that I made at Bombay. Now, what is the crucial decision and the statement that I made in Bombay? Repeatedly I had said at Amritsar Congress[7]—and at various other places that statement had been made repeatedly—that Bombay will be given an opportunity to decide by some democratic process what it should do and where it should go to. For my part, I would be exceedingly happy if Bombay went to Maharashtra. I have absolutely no reason against it and I shall be completely and absolutely frank in this House that I think there are many valid arguments, good arguments for Bombay going to Maharashtra. But I also say that other valid arguments are also to be considered on the other side. In this difficulty we thought, many of us thought, that the best way was to allow Bombay to decide. It may have been done even now. But, as I pointed out, the conditions have been such that so much passion has been aroused that it was not yet the right time to decide that. Let things cool down. I have repeatedly said, 'Let normality prevail and then let it be decided by them'. I do not naturally mean that you will have a plebiscite or referendum and all that; but, if there is a good atmosphere, I have no doubt that it would be far simpler to settle this matter without any such cumbrous procedure. I was hoping for that and I still hope for that. In Bombay at the meeting of the All India Congress Committee,[8] I was not to my thinking making any great decision or announcement on a very big thing. I was merely stating what I had stated repeatedly—my view—and I am something; after all, I am the Prime Minister of India. And a Prime Minister is a Minister and he can lay down the policy of the Government—it may be repealed or it may be anything. I know something about democratic procedure; I know something about party procedure; I know something as to what the Prime Minister's duties are, and in the Constitution we have and in the Constitution that Britain has, the Prime Minister is a linchpin of Government. To say that the Prime Minister cannot make a statement is a monstrous statement itself. I entirely fail to understand where the honourable Member has got his acquaintance of democracy and what under the present Constitution of India and England the Prime Minister is and what he can do and what he cannot do. I am something more than the Prime Minister: we are something more; we are the children of the Indian Revolution.

[8] The meeting was held at Mumbai on 2–3 June 1956.

And although we may be toned down here and although we may forget much that we did before, we still have something of the revolutionary fire in us.

I venture to say that many of us know a little more about the Indian people, about those poor people, about those peasants than some other who talk about peasants. We have spent a good deal of our lives with those peasants and poor people, and it does not behave any person to talk of moneybags, in the sense of referring to our Party or to our Government.

I made that statement in Bombay, a simple statement, if I may say so, to give an assurance that this was not a final thing; a statement which said, 'Let peace be restored first and then this matter may be decided calmly'. I do not mind which way it is decided. I am perfectly prepared to plead the cause of Maharashtra with others. 'Animus' is a big word. I have no disinclination to Maharashtra, but 'animus' is a big word. I do attach much importance to this question being solved in a calm manner so as not to leave any headache behind.

I do not entirely agree with all that Shri Patil[9] said; I agree with much but I do not agree with something that he said. But I say that the main thing is that if you do something with Bombay this way or that way and as a result give headache to that party, the Maharashtra, it will do little good to Maharashtra to get that headache. By all means, let it get it in a friendly way, in a co-operative way, and it will be good for Maharashtra, it will be good for Bombay, and good for the country. That was the trouble I had in the way to do these things.

I do venture to submit not in this matter only but in almost every matter in an individual's life or in a national life, that the older I grow, the more I feel that what is more important is the manner in which things are done than the things themselves. Means are more important than ends. More and more I feel that. All our trouble in this business has been not that the ends were not good but the means employed somehow tarnished the ends, made difficulties and actually came in the way of achievement of those ends. That has been the difficulty. I am not blaming anybody. If I am to blame, I am quite prepared to blame myself. It is not a question of blaming anybody, but I believe it is a fact that if you employ the wrong methods and gain something, that end is prevented. Other considerations come in, passions come into play. Because of this difficulty I wanted this question to be considered in a calmer atmosphere. The more I thought, the more I felt it was good to postpone this particular decision for some time. I say five years, but I am not making any rigid limit. That, oddly enough—what is called the crucial decision—was, apart

[9] S.K. Patil, President, Bombay Pradesh Congress Committee.

from being a repetition of what I said, an indication that our minds are not closed on this, an indication that this is not a finality that is coming in, but that the matter is left open for the future and wherever opportunity arises, it can be done. It was, to my humble thinking, a hand spread out to Maharashtra instead of against them, and, if I may say so—I do not know if it is quite proper for me to say so—the day before I made that statement in the All India Congress Committee, I had the privilege of meeting quite a number of leading gentlemen from Maharashtra—I do not say they all represented Maharashtra, but some did—and we talked about these matters. I told them my difficulties and said, 'This Bill is there, what can we do about it?'. I said that we can see that this matter is not closed, but is opened after a period. Then they said, 'Can you not make your statement in the All India Congress Committee?' I Said, 'Certainly', and I made that statement.

It is not conveying any firm decision of Government as such or that the Cabinet and the Government have decided it. I made a statement. I know that when a Prime Minister makes a statement, it is an important thing, it is not a casual thing. That statement itself, if you examine it, was 'the door being left open' and that there is no finality about it, it can be varied, it could have been varied slightly here or there, if you accept what the Bill contains, because it refers to my talk in Bombay about the Bill, which was, of course, Government's decision, etc. In order to lessen the shock of the Bill to those who do not like it, I found a way by which this can be varied or changed a little. It is really to lessen the shock of the Bill that I did so rather than to come in the way of Maharashtra.

Some people talked about a big bilingual State, and for my part, obviously I welcome it. I do not mind if Bombay is a City State. I do not mind if any chunk of territory were to go from one side or the other. Maybe I do not have a sense of provincialism in me. I can consider economic reasons, geographical reasons. Geography is important, of course. Of course, geography of little patches becomes less important in this age of fast travel, etc. But the one thing that is really important, I feel, is this. Stress has been laid on this in the Report of the Commission—how linguistic minorities are to be treated—because it just does not matter where you put your boundaries, between this and that, they are bound to be overlapping. You can put people speaking in one language in a closed house, in a closed province. But there are bilingual areas, maybe trilingual areas, whatever the percentage may be. How are you to treat them?

The House will remember that in the Commission's Report, there is a special reference in the concluding chapter to certain measures, certain protections, certain precautions, certain assurances, certain statutory provisions so as to give them protection—protection to the linguistic minorities. Now I am anxious that this should be done, and done in the form of words. At any rate this charge has some truth and I do believe that a language is not given protection or a group representing a certain language is not given protection when it happens to be in a minority or almost equal, whatever it is. That difficulty and that complaint must be removed altogether from India and removed in a way not merely by some pious protestations but by some active and precise instructions to that effect. One cannot get rid of all the evils of this world, but anyhow one should go as far as possible to prevent this happening. If this can be done, then the linguistic complaint goes or ought to go from every part of India. If I may say so, this fact, I am told, is in the Constitution, but nonetheless I do not think everybody realizes it.

I do think that all the fourteen languages mentioned in our Constitution are our national languages—not Hindi only, but all the fourteen languages. Hindi, not because of any linguistic superiority, but because it is spread over a larger area and for various reasons and facility and the rest, we have said, should be an all-India language; it should become an all-India language gradually and, after a certain period, for official purposes. But, all are national languages. We want to encourage them. And I am convinced that the encouragement of one language in India leads to the encouragement of others. The outlook that we can encourage one language by crushing others is completely wrong from any point of view—literary, or linguistic point of view. In this matter, for instance, I feel that any kind of application, letter or petition of any kind can be presented to courts: it can be done in any of the fourteen languages of India and no court will reject it. It may be, of course, that the court may be unable to deal with it if it is totally unaware of it because no court can keep fourteen translators. That does not matter. It is a matter of convenience. But, a court in Delhi has to accept an application put in Malayalam or Tamil or Telugu or Kannada. Let them get it translated. Maybe, it will delay matters. But it is none of your business to say that you cannot get it. It is one of our national languages.

If that is so about every language in India, it may be so especially in regard to the actual languages represented in a certain area. There should be no difficulty. Certainly those languages should be given that official position in that area, in applications and others. After all Government issues notices and others so that they may be understood. That notices is (sic) not merely to encourage or discourage a language. It should be issued in the language of that area, regardless, I say, of whether it is sixty or forty per cent—whatever the percentage—provided of course there are sufficient number of people to be approached in that way.

I just mentioned about the frontier. We are, as the House knows, facing tremendous technological changes. We have got this marriage of science and technology and industry and that is producing enormous changes in the world. If you think of those changes, the problem that we face—such problems as in this particular Bill—becomes quite extraordinarily insignificant. Of course they have importance. I do not mean to deny it. I would beg of you to consider it in this particular context and consider the way the country is changing, we are changing, what our future is going to be. I am intensely interested in the future of India; so are the Members of this House. We work for it. We may pause but India will continue. We have laid the foundation of that future today. About our future, one thing is quite certain. It is not going to be a repetition of the past. The world is changing too rapidly and it is of the utmost importance that, in building that future, we should develop this all-India outlook. The provincial outlook is not going to pay either the province much less India. We cannot have it. I may come from UP, my ancestors might have come from Kashmir, but I consider myself an Indian. I feel that I have inherited every great deed and great tradition of India from cape Comorin to the Himalayas. Sometimes, there are comparisons in this House that the people of this province are brave, that the others are not so brave and that the others are businessmen and these people are *saudagars* and so on. All this thinking which we find is unfortunately the reflex of the caste system—a bane and curse to this country which should be dealt with as such. We are too much immersed in these things. Which province is there in India, which State is there in India, which has not got a proud tradition of its own? Go to the south—the Tamils; there is a great language and there are great traditions—military and the rest. Go to Andhra— famous Andhra empires. Go to the Malayalees, go to the Kannadigas—the Vijayanagar empire. Whether you go north or south or east or west, each area, each part of India has got great traditions, great stories of the past, best culture— even military glory they have in store.

I inherit all that legacy. Do you think that I can confine myself to the story of Allahabad, although it is an ancient city, because I was born at Allahabad! I claim to have a right to the glory of Andhra, or Tamil Nad or Maharashtra or Gujarat or any part.

Maharashtra—everybody knows the vital part it has played in India's history, military way, scholarly way, literary way, in learning and in so many ways and lastly in the struggle for freedom. The Maharashtrians or Gujaratis or the Tamilians do not require protection. They are big enough. But the people who do require protection are our border people....

We talk of geography. Geography is important and will remain important though it fades away in this air age. But geography has made India of the past, with Himalayas and the two seas surrounding. Whatever internal divisions and dissensions and conflicts we had in India in the past few thousands of years, the concept of India has remained. The concept of India, Bharat or Hindustan—call it what you like—has remained and has kept us mentally together. It mattered not so much in the old days and that is why politically we were apart. But is does matter today, in the age we live, when we must not only be integrated in that manner—that is not good enough—but we must emotionally and intellectually be integrated. The painful thing that has happened in the last few months is to display, not to ourselves but to the world, how we are not so integrated in our minds and hearts. We have to get over that.

Even accepting the mistakes, even accepting or realizing that somebody else has committed the mistake, even accepting that the Government of India has committed the mistake, it will take time. It may be true. You can of course change the Government of India. You can change the decision—whatever it is—but keep, above all, the major thing in mind, that is, we have to face the situation as it is today and how we can preserve this big thing, that is, India, uninjured in any manner. If we are making any mistake today let us calmly and quietly deal with it sometime later.

As for Bombay, I understand, I concede, the logic, the fairly strong logic. The logical aspect on behalf of Maharashtra, I do not deny. There are logical arguments on the other side too. Maybe, one is more powerful than the other. But, I look at it in the context of the present moment, after we have arrived through a devious and tortuous way, at a certain position. How are we to deal with it? Are we to go on quarrelling and quarrelling about that or allow matters to settle down and deal with it in a proper way? According to our Constitution, it is always open to this House to deal with a matter whenever it chooses and, apart from that, we purposely say that we are not limiting this, we are not making it absolutely final; the thing will be open and in the meanwhile let us keep as many bonds as possible to prevent this kind of thing happening....

LETTER TO K.M. MUNSHI[1]

New Delhi
4 August 1956

My dear Munshi,[2]

Thank you for your letter of 4 August.[3]

A curious situation has arisen here in regard to Bombay, Maharashtra and Gujarat. Till three days ago, there was no talk of a bilingual State and we were proceeding with the Bill as it is. It is true that Pantji and I and others had said that we would have liked a bilingual State if that had been feasible.

Suddenly the back-benchers in Parliament began to move and to our surprise a great majority of the Members of Parliament signed a representation to me asking for a bilingual State.[4] This majority included not only a large number of Congressmen but a number of members of the Opposition. This put me in an odd position. As Leader of my Party or of the House, I could not very well order them to vote against the very thing which I had approved of. If I left it to a free vote of the House, there was no doubt that the bilingual State would win. Thus we were

---

[1] JN Collection.

[2] Governor of Uttar Pradesh.

[3] Munshi suggested that there should be a bigger bilingual state in western India, with Bombay city as its capital. Such a state should have regional councils on the lines of the regional formula for Punjab, Munshi added.

[4] One hundred and eighty members of Parliament submitted a memorandum to Nehru on 3 August endorsing the idea of a bilingual Bombay state. An amendment seeking to establish a composite state of Bombay was moved in the Lok Sabha by Frank Anthony, Tulsidas Kilachand, Jaipal Singh and eight others.

really cornered. For my part, I was not at all unhappy about it. But quite apart from my wishes in the matter, we were driven by circumstances into a certain direction.

SCIENCE AND ETHICS[1]

SCIENTISTS AND AN INTEGRATED VIEW OF LIFE[2]

Mr Governor,[3] Mr President,[4] Friends and Comrades,

You have been welcomed on behalf of the Agra University and on behalf of the Uttar Pradesh Government.[5] I should like to add to that welcome, not only on my own behalf but on behalf of the Government of India. More particularly, I should like to extend a warm and cordial welcome to the distinguished scientists who have come from other countries to participate in the labours of your Congress.[6] It has become a very agreeable and helpful feature of this annual session of the Indian Science Congress to have these distinguished visitors from abroad, to give us the benefit of their learning and experience and to build up the bonds of scientific co-operation between India and the other countries, many of whom are more advanced than India in scientific work.[7] We welcome that not only because, in a

---

[1] *Selected Works of Jawaharlal Nehru* (Second Series), vol. 31, 2002, pp. 126–33.

[2] Speech at the inauguration of the forty-third session of the Indian Science Congress, Agra, 2 January 1956. AIR tapes, NMMI.

[3] K.M. Munshi, Governor of Uttar Pradesh.

[4] M.S. Krishnan.

[5] Over 1,200 scientists and technologists from India and abroad attended the seven-day session.

[6] Fifty delegates from other countries including B.A. Houssay of Argentina, Liu Chung-lo of China and D.M. Fedotov and A.V. Topchiev of the Soviet Union, attended the session, the largest number being from the Soviet Union.

[7] The Polish, Chinese and Soviet delegations presented their latest scientific papers, medical journals, scientific books and periodicals at the Indian Science Congress.

selfish way, it is helpful to us to have them here and have the benefit of their experience, but also because it is fundamentally a good thing to develop this scientific co-operation between different countries, as all kinds of co-operation between different countries is to be welcomed.

You meet here at the beginning of the year, and in the course of the last ten years or so, almost every year I have had the privilege of being present at your session. It is a good thing to meet early in the year and give, perhaps, some new direction, or some additional direction to people's thinking in this country. As we are at the beginning of the year, I wish all of you a good year. I did not say 'Happy New Year', though I hope you will have your due measure of happiness. But, somehow, to talk about happiness seems rather inane. We all want happiness, and I hope we shall deserve and get it. But what is more necessary is a year of certain achievements, of taking some steps forward towards the great causes that we serve and, I hope, science serves.

One small matter, if I may mention, that this Science Congress almost always meets on the 2nd of January, thereby making most of the delegates travel on New Year's Day and spend the New Year's Day in railway trains or aeroplanes or wherever they may be. Perhaps, it might be better to allow the delegates to rest in peace on New Year's Day wherever they might be and come a day or two later. Let them think on New Year's Day, think of what they have done and what they propose to do, and have a quiet time. Well, that is for you to decide. This is a very minor matter.

In the old days, long long ago, I suppose that learned men and high priests used to gather, from time to time, to share experiences and to try to probe into the mysteries of nature. It may be that modern scientists, or some of them, may rather look down upon those ancient efforts, though I hope very few do so, because after all even those, what you might consider from your modern standpoint as unscientific efforts, were the basis for further advance, even though they might have dealt with alchemy of metaphysical research of something with a much broader basis, that is philosophy. Anyhow, the high priests of those days, presumably, dominated the scene, and they may sometimes have exploited their position and misled the multitude; they may have tried to instil the fear of certain mysteries in the multitude, so as to keep up their vested interests as high priests. Nevertheless, basically, that was a search for truth, to understand the nature of things, the nature of the practical world, as well as to explore the nature of some other worlds, if there are such, or wherever they may be. Now, gradually those times, led, through many steps, to the beginnings of science as we see it today and science developed, and now it overshadows the world, not only in its external achievements but in men's thinking, and the scientists of today now occupy the position of the high priests of the mysteries. It is true that the true scientist does not function, and does not want to function, in a mysterious way and science and knowledge is largely an open secret to those who care to see and understand it, as it should be. Nevertheless, it becomes so complicated that few people, perhaps, have the capacity to understand it, or have the will to take the trouble to understand it, and for most it becomes some kind of a mystery which is beyond their reach. Nevertheless they profit by it, of course, or suffer from it, or both, and the world as we see it becomes, essentially something that has grown out of science or its application, and science is likely to dominate us more and more in the future. Therefore, it is a thing of the highest importance, what scientists do, in what atmosphere and temper they work, how far scientists help a certain direction in the world's development, in the world's thinking, and how far they give it a wrong direction.

Scientists, presumably, are searchers after truth and truth is a difficult thing to aim at. And if you search after truth you must not be afraid of the consequences of that search, even though it may sometimes force you to look down into the pit of hell. If you are afraid of the consequences of your search then you cannot go too far. That is so. You search for it, whether it is good or bad. Nevertheless, I take it that such a thing as pure objectivity in any individual, even in a scientist, is not quite possible or, if I may say so, desirable. You cannot isolate yourself from the life of the world, from the joys and sorrows, from the possible dangers to the world or the possible benefits that might come to the world from your activity. You must have some function in life, to aim somewhere, not merely to look with wide open eyes at what is happening, in fact, to give some turn to events where you can. The moment you become functionless, any of us, we become rather passive spectators of events, than have any hand in directing them. I do not suppose, that scientists would like to be called merely passive spectators, or anyone for that matter. Therefore, some kind of broad ideal has to be before us, apart from, of course, the search for truth. What is that broad ideal?

Well, there may be many ideals, but obviously that ideal must have some relation to the problems of today—let us put it in the narrowest way: a problem that Indian scientists have to deal with is, the development of the Indian people, the betterment of the Indian people, raising their standards, increasing their wealth, removing inequality, and so on and so forth; planning, if you like, in its widest sense to help in that process, to direct it properly, that is a big problem which takes all our time and energy, or ought to take. Or let us go a step further and think of certain world problems. Now, I am not going to discuss these great world problems, and I think all of us are too apt to express our opinions in regard to them with a measure of arrogance, as if we could solve the problems of the world, if only our views were accepted by the world. That is not a becoming attitude for anyone however wise he might consider himself. Nevertheless, to surrender to the problems of the world and feel helpless is also not becoming. But without considering any particular problem, big as they are, we can, all of us and more especially men and women of science, perhaps consider the basic approach to those problems. What do I mean by the basic approach? Shall I say, the basic temper in which those problems should be approached; the temper of science, the temper of reasonableness, the temper of finding out the truth or—whether that is a temper of science or not I do not know—the temper of peace. I think that really is more important, the more I think of it, than any positive step that might be taken towards the solution of a problem. That is, the methods employed to consider or to solve a problem. You may put that in a phrase, which has been often used, that means are more important or at least as important as ends; means govern ends. Means are apt to divert you from the ends you have in view, if they are not the right means. That is a basic proposition in which, for my part. I believe. But apart from that, means count. If you and I meet together to settle a problem it makes all the difference in the world if we are aggressively hostile to each other or if we try to understand each other. Nothing will come if the approach of two individuals or two groups or two nations is that of aggressive hostility, and anger and hatred. Only evil can flow out of that meeting—out of an approach of hatred; while it is possible that if the approach is different, something else, that is good might come out of it. I suppose this principle was good at any time. But when we arrive at a stage that a false step may lead to tremendous consequences, far reaching disaster, then of course, it becomes much more important for us not to take that false step, not to approach each other with that frame of mind, which is likely to lead to a false step.

We talk about atomic power, atomic bomb, hydrogen bomb, and there is general realization of the tremendous danger to the world in case these are used, or even, many people think, in case that this experimentation of them in the shape of explosions goes on. You know better what that dangers might be. I suppose no one knows exactly. Even the best scientist can largely guess. But everyone recognizes those infinite dangers. Do we recognize, quite as much, that the other source of great danger is the kind of atomic bombs that we nurse in our minds and bosoms; as individuals and, much more so, nations? It is out of that, that the other bomb comes and is used. That is the source, the origin, and perhaps, that is a more dangerous thing in the final analysis than the other bomb you talk about. In fact, that leads to the other. How then do we deal with this matter? We have seen even in recent political history that wherever the great leaders of the world meet together in a friendly atmosphere and talk in friendly terms to each other, even without doing much else, it changes the whole atmosphere of the world. Tensions are relaxed. People feel better. A burden is off the back of the world, because something intangible—which you cannot measure or weigh—but something that is enormously important took place. That is, the hostility inside our minds, for the moment, if not faded away, seemed to be much less and the world was happier for it. How important it is, therefore, for us to deal with this atomic bomb in our minds and heats? I remember my leader, Mahatma Gandhi, saying more than once, that if you have a sword in your heart, have it out and use it rather than nurse it in your bosom all the time, for if that is allowed, if you go on nursing the swords and atomic bombs in your minds and hearts all the time it will corrupt you, it will spoil you and it will spoil others. The Governor, who was just speaking, talked about moral values, spiritual values and the like. Call them what you like, the point is that it becomes increasingly important, it is important what you do as scientists or as people of lesser clay, but is it at least as important, if not more important, as to what you nurse in your mind and bosom, as to what you are ultimately. Maybe the scientist might say that, that is somewhat outside his scope, outside his beat. Obviously, it is not, and if it ever was, it can no longer be so in the future; and no scientist is worth his salt if he is just a narrow scientist and has no larger view of things. Every scientist, to some extent every human being, has to be a bit of a philosopher, has to think of the consequences of his action. He is not an automaton just working in a particular direction and not caring what happens to his work, or to the consequences of his work. He is dealing with far too serious matters.

Therefore, the present conflict has arisen in the minds of many great scientists, some of the greatest, as to how far they are justified in using their ability towards an end which might perhaps be evil, which might perhaps bring large-scale destruction to the world. It is a legitimate conflict in the mind, and the scientist who does not feel that at all, may perhaps be a good scientist, I do not know, but he is a bad human being, a bad and insensitive human being. We cannot, in life today, isolate life in various compartments. You cannot, even in the purely scientific sphere, isolate the study of one science and remain ignorant of the others. They overlap as life, as every part of life, overlaps. You have to see the whole picture and you have to see life as a whole, as something integrated, whichever way you look. I referred to our Five Year Plan. Whether that Five Year Plan is good or bad, it does not go far enough or goes too far, you may consider that, but if it is any good as a plan it must look at India's life as a whole.

And so, in this larger sphere of the world, scientists have to look at life as a whole and the consequences of what they are doing and direct people's thinking in the right direction. It is important. It is difficult for any one of us as individuals, whatever positions we may occupy, however high or important that position may be, it is difficult for us to live in an ivory tower or to isolate ourselves from our surroundings. We can only influence events in a certain individual, however important he might be. He is conditioned, each one of us is conditioned, by a thousand and a million factors within him and outside him. He has to work subject to that conditioning. Yet he has the ability to change that conditioning also and to get out of that shell to some extent. But even if he had that ability to do so, how is he to affect the others' conditioning, the thousands and millions of others? Not the biggest autocrat or dictator can go beyond certain limits. But he can go, but each individual can, to a small extent or to a slightly more extent, help in that process. Of course the amount of effect that his action might have, will largely depend upon the receptiveness of people's minds. A right thing said, when people are not receptive, will fall flat. The biggest truth may not be listened to because people's minds are not attuned to it, are not receptive to it, just as even some discovery, some invention may have no great future till the time is ripe for it. All this industrial revolution which began in the western world, with the fly shuttle, or this or that or steam, it succeeded because the time was ripening for it. Similar things had been done 50 years or 100 years before in parts of Europe and they had fallen flat. Time was not ready for them. So a certain receptiveness was required. Of course one may try to produce that receptiveness. But, anyhow, in order for a truth to be appreciated the time must be ripe. The time must be ripe in your external circumstances and even more so in people's minds. Now, I think that the tremendous developments in science, which might for the moment be considered as symbolized by the hydrogen bomb or atomic energy, of course there are many developments in many directions, but anyhow atomic energy and the bomb have struck popular imagination powerfully. Indeed they had to. Nobody can help being struck. If you are hit on the head by a hammer, you are struck, you think of the hammer, you cannot avoid the hammer. So, people's minds have been struck powerfully by these manifestations of science. On the one hand, there is the reaction of fear at this tremendous destructive power. On the other hand, a hope that this might be used, if properly handled, for the benefit of humanity. So I believe that people's minds are receptive, and therefore it becomes all the more important for scientists, on the one hand, and people like politicians and others engaged in public affairs, on the other, to take advantage of the receptiveness of the public mind all over the world.

It is not only receptive but, if I may use the word, it almost waits for the direction to be given. You may call that the people's, well, active or negative desire for peace. By negative desire I mean, the fear of war has become so great that one negatively tries to shelter oneself and go away from it and wants peace; not the other, it is perhaps something slightly different from the active desire for peace. Anyhow, the desire for peace, the desire rather for the avoidance of war, which might be so terrible. That itself, the shock of these recent events has made people all over the world think a great deal about the ways of how one can avoid these disasters. It is for this reason that I say that there is a certain receptivity in the public mind all over the world.

Now, politicians of course talk a lot, sometimes very good sense, sometimes rather nonsense. They talk so much that it is difficult to find so much good sense. Inevitably, they have to talk about other matters too. Also, they are conditioned by their circumstances a good deal. Nevertheless, I think there is a happy trend even in the utterances of politicians the world over to realize the basic nature of this problem, which in a sense essentially becomes a moral problem, and to direct people's attention. Unfortunately, while they talk, they themselves are too conditioned to act firmly in that direction, because they have to bring up the level of their people's thinking also. But, anyhow, so far as scientists are concerned, they are, I imagine, somewhat freer and not so limited and conditioned in their actions or thinking as politicians are. And, after all, it is the scientists who have given this terrific power, which can be used for good or ill. Therefore, it seems to be important that they take a lead in this matter and help the people to think aright and not say that their duty is to keep outside these arguments and these basic issues and principles, they only objectively go on making experiments and finding bigger and bigger, let us say, bombs. It is not quite good enough. We have to take a much more integrated view of life, whether it is in the individual or the group or the nation or the world. Manifestly, all these developments in science, not only the atomic bomb, but in communications and so many other things, have made this world a very narrow place to live in and we stumble against each other all the time, and if we do not develop the capacity, not only for co-operation outwardly, but that mental approach to co-operation, inevitably we come into conflict with each other; we are too near each other, we just cannot avoid each other. And therefore, this crisis in the world today, where you have to choose between active cooperation or active hostility, warfare and conflict. The middle stages have somehow gone. You cannot live your lives in this country or that outside the sphere of these big influences and controversies and conflicts. We all realize that.

Now, I have to deal from day to day with the world where politicians function, being myself of that tribe, and naturally I find myself, on the one hand, pushed by my own urges, on the other hand, conditioned and limited by many other factors. The only way, in a sense, for a person, the only place where he can be completely free from the conditioning factors of this human being is if he isolated himself, I suppose, took *sanyas* and went on a mountain top. There, of course, he will be conditioned much more by nature. He won't be conditioned by human beings but he will be a complete slave of nature. One cannot isolate oneself. So one is conditioned by these factors. A person who deals with large numbers of human beings is conditioned; while he may condition them, he is conditioned by those large numbers of human beings. The larger your sphere of action, the larger your sphere of influence, the larger the number of factors that condition your action. That is so. Nevertheless, one can function in a particular direction to the best of one's ability and strength. But what I am trying to point out is, that the scientist ought to have, and I believe, has a somewhat greater freedom of functioning and of directing people's thoughts, because the politician is suspect. He is believed, maybe even as he says or does the right thing to have some ulterior motive behind him. If a country's government even says or does the right thing, another country, which is suspicious of this, will believe some trickery about that. Well, we cannot help that and can only get over that by gradually knowing each other better and laying stress on the better aspects of human beings and not on the evil aspects. After all, we are all a mixture of good and evil and this business of any country or any individual thinking that he, or his action, is all good and the outer is all evil, shows a certain immaturity of judgment and outlook, because we are all mixtures of good and evil, and it would be a good thing if we approached all these problems with a measure of humility. The great men always have a measure of humility about them. Perhaps the greatest scientist of this century, Einstein, was a man full of humility, and that, I should hope, is a true sign of a great scientist, the humility he has, or of any other person.

So the thing to aim at, how to counter this hostile approach to each other and, I believe, how to deal with this intangible atmosphere—which comes in the way of people finding out the good in the other—and which only spots the evil in them, which there is, as there is the good. Science today, after its tremendous victories in the domain of the physical world, physics and chemistry and all that, is dabbling more and more in the inner urges and nature of man. Perhaps that may help, I do not know. Anyhow, it has become very important to know what man is. We have seen what man can do, and no doubt we will see more. But what man is, and how he can, how the good elements in the man can be encouraged and the wrong elements discouraged, becomes one of the important problems of our times. I believe quite firmly, as a matter of scientific truth, though I cannot justify it of course, that every action has a certain consequence; every good action has necessarily a good consequence, regardless of anything else; every evil action has necessarily an evil consequence. Of course that good action may be smothered, the consequences of the good action may be smothered by other things. It is a different matter. Or, the consequences of the evil action may be somewhat improved by other factors in science. If that is so, then evil means utilized must have, as true as the law of cause and effect, evil results, regardless of your motive, regardless of your aim; they must have that result. If that is so, then if you nurse hatred and violence in your hearts, well, you not only spread the area of hatred and violence but you draw out the hatred and violence in the other party and it becomes a conflict of the greater hatred, of greater violence. And there is no end to that conflict. On the other hand, if you give out goodwill and friendship, there is not a shadow of a doubt that you draw out the goodwill and friendship of the opposite party and thereby increase the fund of goodwill and friendship all over the world. In other words, evil can never put an end to evil, or violence put an end to violence. Other methods have to be adopted.

You will forgive me for this dissertation on subjects somewhat outside the problems before you. But I do believe that these are basic and, situated as I am in responsible position, I have to think about these matters. They impinge themselves upon my mind, and other matters, however important, really take a second place. And therefore I have ventured to place these thoughts of mine before you.

I thank you.

SCIENCE AND TECHNOLOGY[8]

It has almost become a custom for the Science Congress to do me the honour of inviting me year after year to inaugurate its sessions[9]. I believe, I have been doing this for ten years or so. I consider this a great privilege and honour for a variety of reasons, although I sometimes fear that repetition of a practice makes it rather stale.

I come here every year in a dual capacity. As the head of the Government, I come to convey the greetings of the Government to the delegates, both those who come from abroad, and those from our own country, to tell them of the Government's keen desire the help and encourage the pursuit of science and the applications of science. I come also in my personal capacity because I am deeply interested in the work that has been done in India and abroad in the various fields of scientific activity. Those fields become ever wider and wider, and are impinging today on realms which might almost be considered to be unknown and which

[8] *Selected Works* (Second Series), vol. 36, pp. 20–5.

[9] Inaugural address at the forty-fourth session of the Indian Science Congress, Kolkata, 14 January 1957. AIR tapes, NMML.

threaten the future of the human race. Every sensitive person, therefore, must necessarily be interested in what science and scientists do.

I am coming here today from Hirakud where yesterday I performed or helped in the opening ceremony[10] of a very magnificent piece of work of Indian engineers, the great Hirakud Dam which, I am told, is the longest in the world. A day before, that is, day before yesterday, I participated in a completely different function at Nalanda, a great university centre 1,500 years ago in Magadha, which is now Bihar.[11] At this great university centre, where the ruins of this University of Nalanda still exist, my mind went back to the old days, when the Buddha flourished and went to Nalanda or Rajbir and when his message had powerfully affected the Indian people. And so, I wondered at the close association of this ceremony at Nalanda and the memories of the Buddha coming to me and of subsequent events of that University, and the next day at a product of modern science—this Hirakud Dam— and today, I am here before you at this Science Congress. And the centuries seem to come together before me, and again I thought, how India is a bundle of centuries, where you can find almost every century represented here from the remote past to the modern age. Somehow we jog along with the past and the present, and even work for the future together, and the cow and the tractor march together in this country. I do not know what the future will hold. It does not seem terribly incongruous that the cow and the tractor are side by side.

So, my mind wandered, again going back to Nalanda. I thought of the message of the Buddha which was, apart from its religious significance, a message of tolerance, a message against superstition and ritual and against dogma. It was a message essentially in the scientific spirit. He asked no man to believe anything except what he could prove by experiment and trial. All he asked was the people to experiment and trial and thus to seek the truth and not to accept anything by the word of another even though he might be the Buddha. That seems to me the essence of the Buddha's message and it struck me that the message, far from being out of date had a peculiar significance even today.

Then I found greater rigidity coming into people's thinking, in whatever plane they may function. The spirit of dogma which had badly affected the religious quest and made minds rigid and their practices conform to ritual which have no significance. I found that the rigidity of this dogma which had applied itself chiefly to religion was apparently projecting itself in the realm of politics and economy. The idea that you are in possession of the truth, the whole truth, and every bit of

---

[10] See the preceding item.
[11] See *Selected Works* (Second Series), vol. 36, pp. 185–8.

the truth—that kind of rigidity, with certain forms of religious approach—had narrowed men's minds, perhaps to some extent even in the scientific region. The tolerant and objective approach not only looked into the heavens without fear, but also looked down into the pit of hell without fear. All this becomes narrower because of this dogmatic and rigid approach to life's problems, the feeling that you have got the key to them and, the other person who does not accept your thesis, is your enemy and has to be combated. And so apparently the key to life's problem is combat, violence and destruction of the person who does not hold your own opinion.

It seems to me that somehow people in the Buddha period were more advanced in tolerance, not in technology, not in the development of science, but in some other phases, not only in compassion but in the tolerant approach. It struck me that quite apart from the religious issue, there might be something worthwhile in the pagan view of life; not from the religious point of view, because the pagan view of life is a tolerant view of life. While it may hold to one opinion, it respects the opinion of others, and thinks, there may be truth in the other opinion too. It takes the universe and the mysteries of the universe, tries to fathom them no doubt, in a spirit of humility and it thinks that truth is too big to be grasped suddenly, and whatever one may know, there is much else to be known, and others may possess a part of that truth. So, while it worshipped its gods, it also honoured the unknown gods whom it did not know.

I venture to say all this because during the last two days, physically and mentally, I have wandered between various centuries; 2,500 years ago when the Buddha was here, 1,500 years ago when that great University of Nalanda was flourishing and attracting students from distant countries. I was there this time to celebrate that occasion when a great traveller from China became a student of the Nalanda University and spent seven years there and has written about his experience during that period.[12] And then the next day this great engineering feat, the Hirakud Dam, and the other advances in engineering or other departments of science and technology that are taking place in India. And then my mind travelled to the problems we have to face in India and the world. The overwhelming problem of course is this: whether we or any other country or people will continue to function in peace, serving at the altar of science and using them for the good of humanity, or whether we shall distort the power that science gives us and use it for evil purposes.

The scientist is supposed to be an objective seeker after truth, and science has grown because, in a large measure, the great scientists have sought truth in that

[12] Huen Tsang was at Nalanda from AD 637–42.

way. But no man, I suppose today, not even a scientist, can live in a world of his own, in some kind of an ivory tower, cut off from what is happening, cut off from the effects of his own work, which are so powerfully affecting the destiny of humanity. And therefore science today has perhaps begun to overlap the borders of morals and ethics. If it divorces itself completely from the realm of morality and ethics, then the power it possesses may be used for evil purposes. But above all, if it ties itself up to the gospel of hatred and violence, then undoubtedly I feel it has taken the wrong direction and that will bring much peril to the world. I plead with scientists here and elsewhere to adhere to the temper of science, to remember that this temper is essentially one of tolerance, one of humility, to the great truths which they are seeking to discover and which they are unveiling from day to day, realizing that much remains still for them to discover in future, but always remembering that somebody else also may have a bit of the truth. They do not have the monopoly; nobody has a monopoly, no country, no people, no book. Truth is too vast to be contained in the minds of human beings, or in books, however sacred they might be.

I remember that once a deputation went to Cromwell, the English dictator, some hundreds of years ago, and insisted on his following a certain line—rather hard line. Cromwell's reply became rather well known; he said, 'I beseech you gentleman in the bowels of Christ, to consider whether it is possible that you may be in the wrong.'[13] But we all think ourselves in the right. That would not matter so much if we did not want to impose our right on the other persons, forcibly if necessary, and that creates conflict; and when you have a great power, the conflict is all the greater, and the consequence and the disaster are all the greater.

Let us be a little humble; and let us think that the truth may not perhaps be entirely with us; others may possess it too. Let us cooperate with the others; let us, even when we do not understand what the others say, respect their views and their ways of life, etc. Emperor Asoka has left memorials to himself and his thinking all over this great land—memorials which you can see today, great pillars of stone carved with his message, or on the rock or elsewhere. Among the many messages that he gave, the one which I think we should all remember not only in this country, but elsewhere is this one. Remember the period when he spoke; 2,300 years ago. People in those days spoke more in terms of religion than other matters. But what he said had a wider application. Addressing his own people, he told them, 'If you reverence your faith, while you reverence your faith, you should reverence the faith of the other who differs from you. In reverencing the faith of others, you will exalt

---

[13] Oliver Cromwell, English soldier, politician and General. He made these remarks in a letter to the General Assembly of the Kirk of Scotland on 3 August 1650.

your own faith and will get your own faith honoured by the others.' I do not quote the exact words but this is the sense of it. Now apply that message of toleration not only to the field of religion but to the other activities of human life today, politics, economics and science, and you will find that it puts things in a different context. It is a context which is not very much in evidence today in the world, where opinions that differ are not liked, where ways of life that differ are not liked, where the tendency is to suppress the view, or the opinion or way of life that one does not approve of, where ultimately science itself becomes vitiated by this narrow outlook. That would have been bad enough at any time but when we have these new weapons forged by the work of scientists hovering above us and the possibility of their being used, then it becomes far more important and vital as to how people think today, how people react to other people's thinking, whether their minds are full of hatred and violence and intolerance, or whether they grow more in tolerance and in appreciation of others. Then it becomes much more important today than in Buddha's time or any other time, because a mistake today carries you very far, may carry you very far.

And so the burden falls a great deal on scientists, men and women of science, who have given to humanity many good things, and will no doubt give more of the good things of life, but who have also given great power, which may be used for good or evil. It is not good enough for the scientist to say that I have done my job by unveiling truth of releasing sources of power, let others use them. He may not control it of course but he has to go on with his quest for truth whether it leads the world to destruction or not, because it is absurd for our scientists to stop research for truth, simply because humanity may use his discoveries for evil. That cannot be done. The world marches on, and so we have got caught in these inner conflicts today, at the national and individual level. Many countries cannot keep pace, or many individuals cannot keep pace with the changes that are taking place. We adapt ourselves outwardly to the changes, but mentally we do not keep pace with them.

The rhythm of history goes on developing and each individual country sometimes does not fall in line with that rhythm. Or it lives in some old rhythm of its own, and thus conflicts arise; while chiefly because of the work of the scientists, development in communications and all that, there has to be fundamentally one basic rhythm for the world today, or else there is conflict.

I have ventured to place before you some thoughts that have been coursing through my mind and more specially during the last two to three days, as I have wandered from 500 BC to today, and seen these various centuries at work in India, and to some extent in the distant world. But here we are in the middle of the twentieth century. After all, the past is there only for us to learn from, both from its successes and failures. We have to live in the present and we have to build the future; and here in India as, no doubt, elsewhere people are engaged in building this future, and we seek your sympathy, your cooperation, your earnest and passionate attention to this great work of building up not only our country, but building up a world of peace and tolerance and compassion.

it is possible, to those wider vistas of mind and thought in history, because without that it narrows its scope and it cannot evoke very much response from the average mind. All of us in a greater or lesser measure make history. History ultimately is some kind of a resultant of millions and millions of human lives, but it is true that some individuals perhaps play a greater part in the making of history. It has been given to us in the present age to play some part in the making of history, and for a person who does that it becomes an even more important thing to understand the processes of history so that he might not lose himself in trivial details and forget the main sweep. Because fate and circumstances placed me in a position to be an actor in the saga, or the drama of India, if you like, in the last twenty or thirty years in common with many others, my interest in history became not an academic interest in things of the past and of long ago, but an intense personal interest. I wanted to understand those events in relation to today and to understand today in relation to what had been, and try to peep into the future, however dimly, with the help of that understanding. I do not know if that quest helped me very much or not in any real understanding, because events have happened in the last few years which I can only say are past all understanding—great wars and the like—and all one's conceptions of an ordered progress of humanity have been shaken. Well, whether these studies have helped to understand or not, they have been a very fascinating pursuit and I sometimes feel how delightful it must be to carry on that pursuit in the calmer atmosphere of a university or some institute, cut away from the provocations and disturbances of the type of life that I lead. But that is merely a kind of nostalgia from which I suppose many of us suffer who do not like the particular job they are placed in.

I welcome you all here, and I hope your labours will not only bear fruit in building up true history which is something much more than dates and events, but will also I hope help, shall I say, in binding together people. History shows us both the binding process and the disrupting process and today in the world as always I suppose—today a little more obviously—the binding or the constructive forces are at work, as also the disruptive or the fissiparous forces, and in any activity that we are indulging in, we have the choice of laying emphasis on the binding and constructive aspect or the other. We must not, of course, give way to wishful thinking and emphasize something which we want to emphasize and which has no relation to fact. Nevertheless, I think it is possible within the terms of scholarship and precision and truth to emphasize the binding and constructive aspect rather than the other, and I hope the activities of historians and of this Commission will be directed to that end. I welcome you again.

A New Perspective of History[2]

I never studied history in the formal way but informally I have been greatly interested in history, chiefly because of my seeking to understand the past rather in terms of the present and even of the future to come. I have approached it as an exciting story. I have approached it as a developing drama, leading up to the present and making me wonder where it will lead to in the future. I never got into the habit of trying to learn the names of kings, dates, etc. And I confess I am singularly ignorant of names and dates except those I could not help picking up.

The whole course of history has fascinated me. Being an Indian, facts relating to the past of India interested me more. Being an Asian, facts relating to Asia also interested me more. But on the whole what has interested me really is the story of man developing himself wherever he might be. It is from that point of view I have tried to co-ordinate such little knowledge of history as I possess.

I remember about 40 years or more ago one of the earliest books dealing with world history came out, namely H.G. Wells' *Outline of History*. It is very easy to criticize Wells, but his was a new approach. and it was a great success. He did try to bring in one compass the tremendous story of man. He did also something which was new for most European leaders, that is, he paid some attention to what was happening in Asia; his world was not merely the Mediterranean world in ancient times, as had been imagined in Europe. China came in, and India, the Middle East and the other countries. Since then this type of history has become more common. Other forms of history, social histories and the like, have been written and they attract much more attention than the political histories of the past.

So far as Asia is concerned, we have been grossly maltreated by most historians from other countries. And as a reaction to that, sometimes our own historians have perhaps gone too far. I suppose it is difficult for any person with strongly held ideas to write what might be called an impartial history. Sometimes I have wondered if impartiality was not the quality of a weak mind. There must be a positive quality in a human being. If there is this positive quality, that aspect of the mind impresses itself on the subject which it deals with and perhaps slightly distorts it. I do not know how we can get over this difficulty. On the one side, there is the nationalist history which, starting from a strong nationalist bias, praises everything that is national at the expense of other things and, on the other side, there is the reverse of this. In the case of India, a Western scholar, especially from the United Kingdom, inevitably tended to look at the history of India as if the past few thousand years

---

[2] From inaugural address to the Asian History Congress, New Delhi, 9 December 1961.

were a kind of a preparation for the coming British dominion in India. And there was the nationalist reaction to it. It seems to me that our historians burrow too much into details and thereby lose sight of the main theme. Both these approaches were limited and both failed to look at the picture in a broad way. In the main, the nationalist approach and imperialist approach distort history. They sometimes suppress history.

We have had examples of some kind of an organized approach or a philosophy of history, and this has led to curious results. One of the books which I had occasion to read in the leisure moments of my prison life was Spengler's *Decline of the West*. I was rather fascinated by it, as one is fascinated by some evil thing. I dislike intensely its sweeping approach. It seems to me that as soon as we start looking at history with any preconceived approach, it turns us away from some patent facts which do not fit in with our theory. And we select things which agree with our own thinking. It does not do harm provided we can get the main currents of history right and if stress is placed on one aspect in order to draw attention to it. The stress on the social aspect has certainly been very helpful in balancing one's approach to history.

The old idea of writing a history of any one country has become progressively out of date. It is impossible today to think of the history of a country isolated from the rest of the world. The world is getting integrated. We have really to consider history today in a world perspective.

What is the basic philosophy of history? I try to think of history as a process that leads man to higher and better stages of progress. Then I find to my surprise that those higher stages have been represented by great men in the long past. Having been fascinated by the scientific and technological civilization which has been built up in Europe and in America, I gradually come to a stage when it seems to me to have stopped. I begin seeking for something deeper than merely the physical aspect of civilization. I find that my mind is more interested in what Plato or the Buddha said, which has a timelessness about it. So I wonder if our present-day history, having fulfilled its destiny in so far as science and technology are concerned, is at all moving on to a higher plane of human existence. I do not presume that the average historian will be able to answer such a question unless he himself becomes a great seer who can pierce the veil of the future. But he can help in putting things in proper perspective.

The immediate object of the History Congress should of course be to straighten out all the twists which Asian history has received at the hands of Europeans. While some of them are very fine historians, their approach has nevertheless been based on Europe being the centre of the world, and naturally that affects their appreciation of the histories of Asian countries.

WHAT IS CULTURE?[3]

I have come here with pleasure, because I have always looked forward to furthering
the cause of India's cultural association, not only with the neighbouring countries
to the East and West but with the wider world outside. It is not a question of merely
wanting such cultural association or considering it good; it is rather a question
of the necessity of the situation which is bound to worsen if nothing is done to
prevent it. I earnestly hope that the formation of the Indian Council for Cultural
Relations will lead to a better understanding between our people and the peoples
of other countries.

There is a great deal of confusion in my mind and I shall state quite frankly
what it is. All kinds of basic questions crop up from what is going on in the world
around us. Nations, individuals and groups talk of understanding one another and
it seems an obvious thing that people should try to understand one another and to
learn from one another. Yet, when I look through the pages of history or study
current events, I sometimes find that people who know one another most, quarrel
most. Countries, which are next door to one another in Europe or in Asia, somehow
seem to rub one another up the wrong way, though they know one another very
thoroughly. Thus knowledge, by itself, does not lead to greater co-operation or
friendship. This is not a new thing. Even the long pages of history show that. Has
there been something wrong in individual nations or in the approach to this
question? Or is it something else that has not worked as it should have done? When
we talk of cultural relations, the question that immediately arises in my mind is—
what exactly is the 'culture' that people talk so much about? When I was younger
in years, I remember reading about German 'kultur' and of the attempts of the
German people to spread it by conquest and other means. There was a big war to
spread this 'kultur' and to resist it. Every country and every individual seems to
have its peculiar idea of culture. When there is talk about cultural relations—
although it is very good in theory—what actually happens is that those peculiar
ideas come into conflict and instead of leading to friendship they lead to more
estrangement. It is a basic question—what is culture? And I am certainly not
competent to give you a definition of it because I have not found one.

One can see each nation and each separate civilization developing its own
culture that had its roots in generations hundreds and thousands of years ago. One
sees these nations being intimately moulded by the impulse that initially starts a

[3] Speech at the inauguration of the Indian Council for Cultural Relations, New Delhi,
9 April 1950. *Jawaharlal Nehru: Selected Speeches*, vol. 2, 1949–53, pp. 356–62.

civilization going on its long path. That conception is affected by other conceptions and one sees action and interaction between these varying conceptions. There is, I suppose, no culture in the world which is absolutely pristine, pure and unaffected by any other culture. It simply cannot be, just as nobody can say that he belongs one hundred per cent to a particular racial type, because in the course of hundreds and thousands of years unmistakable changes and mixtures have occurred.

So, culture is bound to get a little mixed up, even though the basic element of a particular national culture remains dominant. If that kind of thing goes on peacefully, there is no harm in it. But it often leads to conflicts. It sometimes leads a group to fear that their culture is being overwhelmed by what they consider to be an outside or alien influence. Then they draw themselves into a shell which isolates them and prevents their thoughts and ideas going out. That is an unhealthy situation, because in any matter and much more so in what might be called a cultural matter, stagnation is the worst possible thing. Culture, if it has any value, must have a certain depth. It must also have a certain dynamic character. After all, culture depends on a vast number of factors. If we leave out what might be called the basic mould that was given to it in the early stages of a nation's or a people's growth, it is affected by geography, by climate and by all kinds of other factors. The culture of Arabia is intimately governed by the geography and the deserts of Arabia because it grew up there. Obviously, the culture of India in the old days was affected greatly, as we see in our own literature, by the Himalayas, the forests and the great rivers of India among other things. It was a natural growth from the soil. Of the various domains of culture, like architecture, music and literature, any two may mix together, as they often did, and produce a happy combination. But where there is an attempt to improve something or the other which does not naturally grow and mould itself without uprooting itself, conflict inevitably arises. Then also comes something which to my mind is basically opposed to all ideas of culture. And that is the isolation of the mind and the deliberate shutting up of the mind to other influences. My own view of India's history is that we can almost measure the growth and the advance of India and the decline of India by relating them to periods when India had her mind open to the outside world and when she wanted to close it up. The more she closed it up, the more static she became. Life, whether of the individual, group, nation or society, is essentially a dynamic, changing, growing thing. Whatever stops that dynamic growth also injures it and undermines it.

We have had great religions and they have had an enormous effect on humanity. Yet, if I may say so with all respect and without meaning any ill to any person, those very religions, in the measure that they made the mind of man static, dogmatic and bigoted, have had, to my mind, an evil effect. The things they said may be good but when it is claimed that the last word has been said, society becomes static.

The individual human being or race or nation must necessarily have a certain depth and certain roots somewhere. They do not count for much unless they have roots in the past, which past is after all the accumulation of generations of experience and some type of wisdom. It is essential that you have that. Otherwise you become just pale copies of something which has no real meaning to you as an individual or as a group. On the other hand, one cannot live in roots alone. Even roots wither unless they come out in the sun and the free air. Only then can the roots give you sustenance. Only then can there be a branching out and a flowering. How, then, are you to balance these two essential factors? It is very difficult, because some people think a great deal about the flowers and the leaves on the branches, forgetting that they only flourish because there is a stout root to sustain them. Others think so much of the roots that no flowers or leaves or branches are left; there is only a thick stem somewhere. So, the question is how one is to achieve a balance.

Docs culture mean some inner growth in the man? Of course, it must. Does it mean the way he behaves to others? Certainly it must. Does it mean the capacity to understand the other person? I suppose so. Does it mean the capacity to make yourself understood by the other person? I suppose so. It means all that. A person who cannot understand another's viewpoint is to that extent limited in mind and culture, because nobody, perhaps, barring some very extraordinary human beings, can presume to have the fullest knowledge and wisdom. The other party or the other group may also have some inkling of knowledge or wisdom or truth and if we shut our minds to that then we not only deprive ourselves of it but we cultivate an attitude of mind which, I would say, is opposed to that of a cultured man. The cultured mind, rooted in itself, should have its doors and windows open. It should have the capacity to understand the other's viewpoint fully even though it cannot always agree with it. The question of agreement or disagreement only arises when you understand a thing. Otherwise, it is blind negation which is not a cultured approach to any question.

I should like to use another word—science. What is a scientific approach to life's problems? I suppose it is one of examining everything, of seeking truth by trial and error and by experiment, of never saying that this must be so but trying to understand why it is so and, if one is convinced of it, of accepting it, of having the capacity to change one's notions the moment some other proof is forthcoming, of having an open mind, which tries to imbibe the truth wherever it is found. If that is culture, how far is it represented in the modern world and in the nations of today? Obviously, if it was represented more than it is, many of our problems, national and international, would be far easier to solve.

Almost every country in the world believes that it has some special dispensation from Providence, that it is of the chosen people or race and that others, whether they are good or bad, are somewhat inferior creatures. It is extraordinary how this kind of feeling persists in all nations of the East as well as of the West without exception. The nations of the East are strongly entrenched in their own ideas and convictions and sometimes in their own sense of superiority about certain matters. Anyhow, in the course of the last two or three hundred years, they have received many knocks on the head and they have been humiliated, they have been debased and they have been exploited. And so, in spite of their feeling that they were superior in many ways, they were forced to admit that they could be knocked about and exploited. To some extent, this brought a sense of realism to them. There was also an attempt to escape from reality by saying that it was sad that we were not so advanced in material and technical things but that these were after all superficial things; nevertheless, we were superior in essential things, in spiritual things, in moral values. I have no doubt that spiritual things and moral values are ultimately more important than other things but the way one finds escape in the thought that one is spiritually superior, simply because one is inferior in a material and physical sense, is surprising. It does not follow by any means. It is an escape from facing up to the causes of one's degradation.

Nationalism, of course, is a curious phenomenon which at a certain stage in a country's history gives life, growth, strength and unity but, at the same time, it has a tendency to limit one, because one thinks of one's country as something different from the rest of the world. The perspective changes and one is continuously thinking of one's own struggles and virtues and failings to the exclusion of other thoughts. The result is that the same nationalism, which is the symbol of growth for a people, becomes a symbol of the cessation of that growth in the mind. Nationalism, when it becomes successful, sometimes goes on spreading in an aggressive way and becomes a danger internationally. Whatever line of thought you follow, you arrive at the conclusion that some kind of balance must be found. Otherwise something that was good can turn into evil. Culture, which is essentially good, becomes not only static but aggressive and something that breeds conflict and hatred when looked at from a wrong point of view. How you are to find a balance, I do not know. Apart from the political and economic problems of the age, perhaps, that is the greatest problem today, because behind it there is a tremendous conflict in the spirit of man and a tremendous search for something which it cannot find. We turn to economic theories because they have an undoubted importance. It is folly to talk of culture or even of God when human beings starve and die. Before one can talk about anything else one must provide the normal essentials of life to human beings. That is where economics comes in. Human beings today are not in the mood to tolerate this suffering and starvation and inequality when they see that the burden is not equally shared. Others profit while they only bear the burden.

We have inevitably to deal with these problems in economic and other ways but I do think that behind it all there is a tremendous psychological problem in the minds of the people. It may be that some people think about it consciously and deliberately and others rather unconsciously and dimly but that this conflict exists in the spirit of man today is certain. How it will be resolved, I do not know. One thing that troubles me is this: people who understand one another more and more begin often enough to quarrel more and more. Nevertheless, it does not follow from this that we should not try to understand one another. That would amount to limiting oneself completely and that is something which really cannot be done in the context of the modern world. Therefore, it becomes essential that we try to understand one another in the right way. The right way is important. The right approach, the friendly approach, is important, because a friendly approach brings a friendly response. I have not the shadow of a doubt that it is a fundamental rule of human life that, if the approach is good, the response is good. If the approach is bad, the response is likely to be bad, too. So, if we approach our fellow human beings or countries in a friendly way, with our minds and hearts open and prepared to accept whatever good comes to them—and that does not mean surrendering something that we consider of essential value to truth or to our own genius—then we shall be led not only towards understanding but the right type of understanding.

So, I shall leave you to determine what culture and wisdom really are. We grow in learning, in knowledge and in experience, till we have such an enormous accumulation of them that it becomes impossible to know exactly where we stand. We are overwhelmed by all this and, at the same time, somehow or other we have a feeling that all these put together do not necessarily represent a growth in the wisdom of the human race. I have a feeling that perhaps some people who did not have all the advantages of modern life and modern science were essentially wiser than most of us are. Whether or not we shall be able in later times to combine all this knowledge, scientific growth and betterment of the human species with true wisdom, I do not know. It is a race between various forces. I am reminded of the saying of a very wise man who was a famous Greek poet:

What else is Wisdom? What of man's endeavour or
God's high grace, so lovely and so great?
To stand from fear set free, to breathe and wait,

To hold a hand uplifted over Hate,
And shall not Loveliness be loved for ever?

Synthesis is Our Tradition[4]

To endeavour to understand and describe the India of today would be the task of a brave man. To describe tomorrow's India would verge on rashness.

What is India? That is a question which has come back again and again to my mind. The early beginnings of our history filled me with wonder. It was the past of a virile and vigorous race with a questing spirit and an urge for free inquiry and, even in its earliest known period, giving evidence of a mature and tolerant civilization. Accepting life and its joys and burdens, it was ever searching for the ultimate and the universal. It built up a magnificent language, Sanskrit, and through this language, its arts and architecture, it sent its vibrant message to far countries. It produced the Upanishads, the Gita and the Buddha.

Hardly any language in the world has probably played that vital part in the history of a race which Sanskrit has. It was not only the vehicle of the highest thought and some of the finest literature, but it became the uniting bond for India, in spite of its political divisions. The Ramayana and the Mahabharata were woven into the texture of millions of lives in every generation for thousands of years. I have often wondered, if our race forgot the Buddha, the Upanishads and the great epics, what then will it be like! It would be uprooted and would lose the basic characteristics which have clung to it and given it distinction throughout these long ages. India would cease to be India.

Gradually deterioration set in. Thought lost its freshness and became stale, and the vitality and exuberance of youth gave place to crabbed age. Instead of the spirit of adventure there came lifeless routine, and the broad and exciting vision of the world was cabined and confined and lost in caste divisions, narrow social customs and ceremonials. Even so, India was vital enough to absorb the streams of people that flowed into her mighty ocean of humanity and she never quite forgot the thoughts that had stirred her in the days of her youthful vigour.

Subsequently, India was powerfully influenced by the coming of Islam and Muslim invasions. Western colonial powers followed, bringing a new type of domination and a new colonialism and, at the same time, the impact of fresh ideas and of the industrial civilization that was growing up in Europe. This period

[4] Extracts from 'India Today and Tomorrow', Azad Memorial Lectures, New Delhi, 22 and 23 February 1959, published by Indian Council for Cultural Relations.

culminated, after a long struggle, in independence and now we face the future with all this burden of the past upon us and the confused dreams and stirrings of the future that we seek to build.

We have all these ages represented in us and in our country today. We have the growth of nuclear science and atomic energy in India, and we also have the cow-dung age.

In the tumult and confusion of our time, we stand facing both ways, forward to the future and backwards to the past, being pulled in both directions. How can we resolve this conflict and evolve a structure for living which fulfils our material needs and, at the same time, sustains our mind and spirit? What new ideals or old ideals varied and adapted to the new world can we place before our people, and how can we galvanize the people into wakefulness and action?

For the present, in India we are rightly absorbed in the Five Year Plans and in a tremendous effort to raise our people's living standards. Economic progress is essential and a pre-requisite for any other type of advance. But a doubt creeps into our minds. Is this by itself enough or is something else to be added on to it? The Welfare State is a worthwhile ideal, but it may well be rather drab. The examples of States which have achieved that objective bring out new problems and difficulties, which are not solved by material advance alone or by a mechanical civilization. Whether religion is necessary or not, a certain faith in a worthwhile ideal is essential to give substance to our lives and to hold us together.

Change is essential but continuity is also necessary. The future has to be built on the foundations laid in the past and in the present. To deny the past and break with it completely is to uproot ourselves and, sapless, dry up. It was the virtue of Gandhiji to keep his feet firmly planted in the rich traditions of our race and our soil and, at the same time, to function on the revolutionary plane. Above all, he laid stress on truth and peaceful means. Thus he built on old foundations, and at the same time, oriented the structure towards the future.

When Islam came to India in the form of political conquest it brought conflict. It had a twofold effect. On the one hand, it encouraged the tendency of Hindu society to shrink still further within its shell; on the other, it brought a breath of fresh air and fresh ideals, and thus had a certain rejuvenating influence. Hindu society had become a closed system. The Muslims who came from outside brought their own closed system with them. Hence the great problem that faced India during the medieval period was how these two closed systems, each with its strong roots, could develop a healthy relationship. Wise rulers like Akbar and others realized that the only hope for the future lay in some kind of harmony being established.

The philosophy and the world outlook of the old Hindus was amazingly tolerant; and yet they had divided themselves up into numerous separate caste groups and hierarchies. The Muslims had to face a new problem, namely how to live with others as equals. In other countries where they had gone, their success was so great that this problem did not really arise. They came into conflict with Christendom and through hundreds of years the problem was never solved. In India, slowly a synthesis was developed. But before this could be completed, other influences came into play.

The new liberal thought of the West and industrial processes began to affect the mind and life of India. A new nationalism developed, which was inevitably against colonialism and sought independence, and yet which was being progressively affected by the new industrial civilization as well as the language, literature and ways of the West.

Ram Mohan Roy came, seeking some kind of a synthesis between old India and modern trends. Vivekananda brought back something of the vigour of old Indian thought and dressed it in a modern garb. Political and cultural movements grew up and culminated in Gandhiji and Rabindranath Tagore.

In Europe there had been a fierce conflict between science and traditional religion, and the cosmology of Christianity did not fit in at all with scientific theories. Science did not produce that sense of conflict in India and Indian philosophy could easily accept it without doing any vital injury to its basic conceptions.

In India, as elsewhere, two forces developed—the growth of nationalism and the urge for social justice. Socialism and Marxism became the symbols of this urge for social justice and, apart from their scientific content, had a tremendous emotional appeal for the masses.

Living is a continual adjustment to changing conditions. The rapidity of technological change in the last half century has made the necessity of social change greater than ever, and there is a continual maladjustment. The advance of science and technology makes it definitely possible to solve most of the economic problems of the world and, in particular, to provide the primary necessities of life to everyone all over the world. The methods adopted will have to depend upon the background and cultural development of a country or a community.

Internationally, the major question today is that of world peace. The only course open is for us to accept the world as it is and develop toleration for each other. It should be open to each country to develop in its own way, learning from others, and not being imposed on by them. Essentially, this calls for a new mental approach. The Panchsheel, or the Five Principles, offer that approach.

There are conflicts within a nation. In a democratic apparatus with adult suffrage, those conflicts can be solved by normal constitutional methods.

In India we have had most distressing spectacles of conflicts based on provincialism or linguism. In the main, it is conflict of class interests that poses problems today, and in such cases vested interests are not easy to displace. Yet we have seen in India powerful vested interests like those of the old princes and of the big *jagirdars*, *talukdars* and *zamindars* being removed by peaceful methods, even though that meant a break-up of a well-established system which favoured a privileged few. While, therefore, we must recognize that there is class conflict, there is no reason why we should not deal with it through these peaceful methods. They will only succeed, however, if we have a proper objective in view clearly understood by the people.

We have deliberately laid down as our objective a socialist pattern of society. Personally I think that the acquisitive society, which is the base of capitalism, is no longer suited to the present age. We have to evolve a higher order more in keeping with modern trends and conditions and involving not so much competition but much greater co-operation. We have accepted socialism as our goal not only because it seems to us right and beneficial but because there is no other way for the solution of our economic problems. It is sometimes said that rapid progress cannot take place by peaceful and democratic methods. I do not accept this proposition. Indeed, in India today any attempt to discard democratic methods would lead to disruption and would thus put an end to any immediate prospect of progress.

The mighty task that we have undertaken demands the fullest co-operation from the masses of our people. The change we seek necessitates burdens on our people, even on those who can least bear them; unless they realize that they are partners in the building of a society which will bring them benefits, they will not accept these burdens or give their full co-operation.

Whether in land or industry, or in the governmental apparatus, institutional changes become necessary from time to time as functions change. A new set of values will replace those that have governed the old acquisitive society based on the profit motive. The problem before us is ultimately to change the thinking and activities of hundreds of millions of people, and to do this democratically by their consent.

India today presents a very mixed picture of hope and anguish, of remarkable advances and at the same time of inertia, of a new spirit and also the dead hand of the past and of privilege, of an overall and growing unity and many disruptive tendencies. Withal there is a great vitality and a ferment in people's minds and activities.

It is a remarkable thing that a country and a people rooted in the remote past, who have shown so much resistance to change in the past, should now be marching forward rapidly and with resolute steps.

What will emerge from the labour and the tumults of the present generation? I cannot say what will tomorrow's India be like. I can only express my hopes and wishes. I want India to advance on the material plane—to fulfil her Five Year Plans to raise the standards of living of her vast population; I want the narrow conflicts of today in the name of religion or caste, language or province, to cease, and a classless and casteless society to be built up where every individual has full opportunity to grow according to his worth and ability. In particular, I hope that the curse of caste will be ended, for there cannot be either democracy or socialism on the basis of caste.

Four great religions have influenced India—two emerging from her own thought, Hinduism and Buddhism, and two coming from abroad but establishing themselves firmly in India, Christianity and Islam. Science today challenges the old concept of religion. But if religion deals not with dogmas and ceremonials, but rather with the higher things of life, there should be no conflict with science or *inter se* between religions. It might be the high privilege of India to help in bringing about this synthesis. That would be in India's ancient tradition inscribed on Ashoka's Edicts.

Tomorrow's India will be what we make it by today's labours. We have started on this pilgrimage with strong purpose and good heart, and we shall reach the end of the journey, however long that might be.

What I am concerned with is not merely our material progress, bur the quality and depth of our people. Gaining power through industrial processes, will they lose themselves in the quest of individual wealth and soft living? That would be a tragedy, for that would be a negation of what India has stood for in the past and, I hope, in the present time also as exemplified by Gandhiji.

Can we combine the progress of science and technology with this progress of the mind and spirit also? We cannot be untrue to science, because that represents the basic fact of life today. Still less can we be untrue to those essential principles for which India has stood in the past throughout the ages.

How Deep is Our Nationalism?[5]

What we are discussing here, whatever we may say about Assam or Bengal, is really ourselves: how we behave, how we feel, how we are excited against each other, how superficial is the covering of what we like to call 'nationalism' which bursts open at

---

[5] From speech in Lok Sabha on Assam disturbances, 3 September 1960.

the slightest irritation. It is amazing how all higher considerations are swept away when communal passions are roused. It is not only the Assamese or the Bengalis who are guilty in this regard; each one of us is a guilty party.

When we talk loudly of our nationalism, each person's idea of nationalism is his own brand of nationalism. It may be Assamese nationalism, it may be Bengali, it may be Gujarati, UP, Punjabi or Madrasi. Each one has his particular brand in his mind. He may use the words 'nationalism of all India', but in his mind he is thinking of that nationalism in terms of his own brand of it. When two brands of nationalism come into conflict, there is trouble.

We live in a closed society—not one closed society, but numerous closed societies. There is a Bengali closed society, a Marathi closed society, a Malayali closed society, and so on. This is not all. For, when you go abroad you will find that, wherever Indians are living in large numbers, they have a separate Gujarati club, a separate Malayali club, a separate Bengali club, and so on.

A Voyage of Discovery[6]

I have come to this country to learn something of your great achievements. I have come also to convey the greetings of my people and in the hope that my visit may help to create a greater understanding between our respective peoples and those strong and sometimes invisible links, stronger even than physical links, that bind countries together. The President referred the day before yesterday, in language of significance, to my visit as a voyage of discovery of America. The United States of America is not an unknown country even in far-off India and many of us have grown up in admiration of the ideals and objectives which have made this country great. Yet, though we may know the history and something of the culture of our respective countries, what is required is a true understanding and appreciation of each other even where we differ. Out of that understanding grows fruitful co-operation in the pursuit of common ideals. What the world today lacks most is, perhaps, understanding and appreciation of one another among nations and people. I have come here, therefore, on a voyage of discovery of the mind and heart of America and to place before you our own mind and heart. Thus, we may promote that understanding and co-operation which, I feel sure, both our countries earnestly desire. Already I have received a welcome here, the generous warmth of which has created a deep impression on my mind and, indeed, somewhat overwhelmed me.

---

[6] Speech in the House of Representatives and the Senate, Washington DC, 13 October 1949.

During the last two days that I have been in Washington I have paid visits to the memorials of the great builders of this nation. I have done so not for the sake of mere formality but because they have long been enshrined in my heart and their example has inspired me as it has inspired innumerable countrymen of mine. These memorials are the real temples to which each generation must pay tribute and, in doing so, must catch something of the fire that burned in the hearts of those who were the torchbearers of freedom, not only for this country but for the world; for those who are truly great have a message that cannot be confined within a particular country but is for all the world.

In India, there came a man in our own generation who inspired us to great endeavour, ever reminding us that thought and action should never be divorced from moral principle, that the true path of man is the path of truth and peace. Under his guidance, we laboured for the freedom of our country, with ill will to none and achieved that freedom. We called him reverently and affectionately the Father of our Nation. Yet he was too great for the circumscribed borders of any one country and the message he gave may well help us in considering the wider problems of the world.

The United States of America has struggled to freedom and unparalleled prosperity during the past century and a half and today it is a great and powerful nation. It has an amazing record of growth in material well-being and scientific and technological advance. It could not have accomplished this unless America had been anchored in the great principles laid down in the early days of her history, for material progress cannot go far or last long unless it has its foundations in moral principles and high ideals.

Those principles and ideals are enshrined in your Declaration of Independence, which lays down as a self-evident truth that all men are created equal, that they are endowed by their Creator with certain inalienable rights, that among these are life, liberty and the pursuit of happiness. It may interest you to know that, in drafting the Constitution of the Republic of India, we have been greatly influenced by your own Constitution. The preamble of our Constitution states:

We, the people of India, having solemnly resolved to constitute India into a Sovereign Democratic Republic and to secure to all its citizens:

Justice, social, economic and political;
Liberty of thought, expression, belief, faith and worship;
Equality of status and of opportunity; and to promote among them all Fraternity assuring the dignity of the individual and the unity of the Nation;

In our Constituent Assembly do hereby adopt, enact and give to ourselves this Constitution.

You will recognize in these words that I have quoted an echo of the great voices of the founders of your Republic. You will see that though India may speak to you in a voice that you may not immediately recognize or that may perhaps appear somewhat alien to you, yet that voice somewhat strongly resembles what you have often heard before.

Yet, it is true that India's voice is somewhat different; it is not the voice of the old world of Europe but of the older world of Asia. It is the voice of an ancient civilization, distinctive, vital, which, at the same time, has renewed itself and learned much from you and the other countries of the West. It is, therefore, both old and new. It has its roots deep in the past but it also has the dynamic urge of today.

But however the voices of India and the United States may appear to differ, there is much in common between them. Like you, we have achieved our freedom through a revolution, though our methods were different from yours. Like you we shall be a republic based on the federal principle, which is an outstanding contribution of the founders of this great Republic. In a vast country like India, as in this great Republic of the United States, it becomes necessary to have a delicate balance between central control and State autonomy. We have placed in the forefront of our Constitution those fundamental human rights to which all men who love liberty, equality and progress aspire—the freedom of the individual, the equality of men and the rule of law. We enter, therefore, the community of free nations with the roots of democracy deeply embedded in our institutions as well as in the thoughts of our people.

We have achieved political freedom but our revolution is not yet complete and is still in progress, for political freedom without the assurance of the right to live and to pursue happiness, which economic progress alone can bring, can never satisfy a people. Therefore, our immediate task is to raise the living standards of our people, to remove all that comes in the way of the economic growth of the nation. We have tackled the major problem of India, as it is today the major problem of Asia, the agrarian problem. Much that was feudal in our system of land tenure is being changed so that the fruits of cultivation should go to the tiller of the soil and that he may be secure in the possession of the land he cultivates. In a country of which agriculture is still the principal industry, this reform is essential not only for the well-being and contentment of the individual but also for the stability of society. One of the main causes of social instability in many parts of the world, more especially in Asia, is agrarian discontent due to the continuance of systems of land tenure which are completely out of place in the modern world. Another— and one which is also true of the greater part of Asia and Africa—is the low standard of living of the masses.

India is industrially more developed than many less fortunate countries and is reckoned as the seventh or eighth among the world's industrial nations. But this arithmetical distinction cannot conceal the poverty of the great majority of our people. To remove this proverty by greater production, more equitable distribution, better education and better health, is the paramount need and the most pressing task before us and we are determined to accomplish this task. We realize that self-help is the first condition of success for a nation, no less than for an individual. We are conscious that ours must be the primary effort and we shall seek succour from none to escape from any part of our own responsibility. But though our economic potential is great, its conversion into finished wealth will need much mechanical and technological aid. We shall, therefore, gladly welcome such aid and co-operation on terms that are of mutual benefit. We believe that this may well help in the solution of the larger problems that confront the world. But we do not seek any material advantage in exchange for any part of our hard-won freedom.

The objectives of our foreign policy are the preservation of world peace and enlargement of human freedom. Two tragic wars have demonstrated the futility of warfare. Victory without the will to peace achieves no lasting result and victor and vanquished alike suffer from deep and grievous wounds and a common fear of the future. May I venture to say that this is not an incorrect description of the world of today? It is not flattering either to man's reason or to our common humanity. Must this unhappy state persist and the power of science and wealth continue to be harnessed to the service of destruction? Every nation, great or small, has to answer this question and the greater a nation, the greater is its responsibility to find and to work for the right answer.

India may be new to world politics and her military strength insignificant in comparison with that of the giants of our epoch. But India is old in thought and experience and has travelled through trackless centuries in the adventure of life. Throughout her long history she has stood for peace and every prayer that an Indian raises, ends with an invocation to peace. It was out of this ancient and yet young India that Mahatma Gandhi arose and he taught us a technique of action that was peaceful; yet it was effective and yielded results that led us not only to freedom but to friendship with those with whom we were, till yesterday, in conflict. How far can that principle be applied to wider spheres of action? I do not know, for circumstances differ and the means to prevent evil have to be shaped and set to the nature of the evil. Yet I have no doubt that the basic approach which lay behind that technique of action was the right approach in human affairs and the only approach that ultimately solves a problem satisfactorily. We have to achieve freedom and to defend it. We have to meet aggression and to resist it and the force employed must be adequate to the purpose. But even when preparing to resist aggression, the ultimate objective, the objective of peace and reconciliation, must never be lost sight of and heart and mind must be attuned to this supreme aim and not swayed or clouded by hatred or fear.

This is the basis and the goal of our foreign policy. We are neither blind to reality nor do we propose to acquiesce in any challenge to man's freedom from whatever quarter it may come. Where freedom is menaced or justice threatened or where aggression takes place, we cannot be and shall not be neutral. What we plead for and endeavour to practise in our own imperfect way is a binding faith in peace and an unfailing endeavour of thought and action to ensure it. The great democracy of the United States of America will, I feel sure, understand and appreciate our approach to life's problems because it could not have any other aim or a different ideal. Friendship and co-operation between our two countries are, therefore, natural. I stand here to offer both in the pursuit of justice, liberty and peace.

THE CONCEPT OF MAN[7]

I am grateful to you for this opportunity of attending the last session of this Symposium. I must apologize for not having attended the opening session to welcome you all here. I looked forward to it greatly, not merely to perform the formal function of opening but rather, as the President suggested, to participate in some way in your discussions and talks and to try and gather some light from those discussions. I was greatly disappointed that I could not do so. It is good of you to ask me to speak but I feel somewhat hesitant because of the presence of very eminent friends who have come from distant countries. There are specialists and men and women of great experience; and for me to say something about the great subject of your debate appears rather presumptuous to me. If I had the chance and the occasion to attend some of your sessions, I would have listened to what was said, perhaps, sometimes participated or put a question but mostly listened. I would have listened, because I have been anxious to find out what you had in your mind and to find out how that would help me to understand for myself some of the problems that confront us. Most of us, I suppose, are burdened with the complexity of our present-day problems. We live our day to day lives and face our day to day difficulties but somehow that is not enough. One seeks something behind that daily round and tries to find out how one can solve the problems that affect the world. For one whom circumstances have placed in a position of great responsibility, it is particularly

[7] Address at the UNESCO symposium in New Delhi, 20 December, 1951.

difficult to avoid thinking about these problems. During the last few weeks I have been going about this great country and seeing multitudes of human beings, surging masses of my countrymen and countrywomen. I have thus invariably thought of what was going to happen to these people, what they were thinking and in which direction they were going. These questions apply to us also because we are in the same boat. And then I think of the multitudes in other countries. What about those vast masses of human beings? Some of us here are functioning on the political plane and presuming to decide the fate of nations. How far do our decisions affect these multitudes? Do we think of them or do we live in some upper stratosphere of diplomats and politicians and the like, exchanging notes and sometimes using harsh words against one another? In the context of this mighty world, its vast masses of human beings and the tremendous phase of transition through which we are passing, politics becomes rather trivial. I have no particular light to throw on the problems that you have been discussing; rather I would like to put some of the difficulties that I have in my mind before you and I hope that when I have occasion to read some of the reports of what you have been saying to each other, perhaps, those addresses might help me to understand the methods of solving some of these problems.

Now, one of my chief difficulties is this: somehow it seems to me that the modern world is getting completely out of tune with what I might call the life of the mind—I am leaving out the life of the spirit at the moment. Yet, the modern world is entirely the outcome of the life of the mind. After all, it is the human mind that has produced everything that we see around us and feel around us. Civilization is the product of the human mind and yet, strangely enough, one begins to feel that the function of the mind becomes less and less important in the modern world or, at any rate, is no longer so important as it used to be. The mind may count for a great deal in specialized domains; it does and so we make great progress in those specialized domains of life but, generally speaking, the mind as a whole counts for less and less. That is my impression. If it is a correct impression, then there is something radically wrong with the civilization that we are building or have built. The changes that are so rapidly taking place emphasize other aspects of life and somehow prevent the mind from functioning as it should and as perhaps it used to do in the earlier periods of the world's history. If that is true, then surely it is not a good outlook for the world, because the very basis on which our civilization has grown, on which man has risen step by step to the great heights on which he stands today, the very foundation of that edifice, is shaken.

In India we are more particularly concerned about the primary necessities of life for our people. We are concerned with food for our people, with clothing, shelter and housing for our people, with education, health and so on. Unless you have these primary necessities, it seems futile to me to talk about the life of the mind or the life of the spirit. You cannot talk of God to a starving person; you must give him food. One must deal with these primary necessities, it is true. Nevertheless, even in dealing with them one has to have some kind of ideal or objective in view. If that ideal or objective somehow becomes less and less connected with the growth of the human mind, then there must be something wrong. I do not know if what I say is true or whether you agree with it and I do not know, even if it is true, what can be done to improve it.

I am, if I may say so, a great admirer of the achievements of modern civilization, of the growth of and applications of science and of technological growth. Humanity has every reason to be proud of them and yet if these achievements lessen the capacity for future growth—and that will happen if the mind deteriorates—then surely there is something wrong about this process. It is obvious that ultimately the mind should dominate. I am not mentioning the spirit again but that comes into the picture, too. If the world suffers from mental deterioration or from moral degradation, then something goes wrong at the very root of civilization or culture. Even though that civilization may drag out for a considerable period, it grows less and less vital and ultimately tumbles down. When I look back on the periods of past history, I find certain periods very outstanding. They show great achievements of the human mind, while some others do not. One finds races achieving a high level and then apparently fading away—at least fading away from the point of view of their achievements. And so I wonder whether something that led to the fading away of relatively high cultures is not happening today and producing an inner weakness in the structure of our modern civilization.

Then the question arises in my mind as to which environment is likely to produce the best type of human being. You talk about education and that obviously is very important. But apart from school or college education, the entire environment that surrounds us naturally affects the development of the human being. What kind of environment has produced these great ages of history? Are we going towards that environment or going away from it, in spite of the great progress that we have made in many departments of human life? The Industrial Revolution that started about 200 years ago brought about enormous changes, largely for the good. That process, I take it, is continuing and the tempo of change becomes faster and faster. Where is it leading us to? It has led us in one direction towards great conflicts and possibly greater conflicts are in store for us which threaten to engulf a large part of humanity in a common cataclysm.

There is an essential contradiction in this race between progress and building up on the one hand and this element on the other, which is likely to destroy all that we have built up. Most of us seem to live as if both are inevitable and have to be put up with. It is very odd that we wish to build and build and build and at the same time look forward to the possible destruction of all that we build. The destruction may externally be through war but what is perhaps more dangerous is the inner destruction of the mind and spirit, after which the destruction of the outer emblems of the mind and spirit may follow. Is it, I wonder, some resultant of the growth of the Industrial Revolution that is over-reaching itself? Have we lost touch with the roots that give strength to a race, humanity or the individual just as a city-dweller, perhaps, loses touch with the soil and sometimes even with the sun, living an artificial life in comfort and even in luxury? He lacks something that is vital to the human being. So whole races begin more and more to live an artificial life, cut off, if I may say so, from the soil and the sun. Is that not so? These ideas trouble me. This growth of a mechanical civilization, which has obviously brought great triumphs and helped the world so much, gradually affects the man and the mind. The mind which produced the machine to help itself gradually becomes a slave of that machine and we progressively become a mechanically minded race.

I suppose the vitality of a group, an individual or a society is measured by the extent to which it possesses courage and, above all, creative imagination. If that creative imagination is lacking, our growth becomes more and more stunted, which is a sign of decay. What then is happening today? Are we trying to improve in this respect or are we merely functioning somewhere on the surface without touching the reality which is afflicting the world and which may result in political conflict, in economic warfare or in world war?

So, when there are discussions on the concept of man as visualized in the Eastern ideal or the Western ideal, they interest me greatly from a historical point of view and from a cultural point of view, although I have always resisted this idea of dividing the world into the Orient and the Occident. I do not believe in such divisions. There have, of course, been differences in racial and national outlook and in ideals but to talk of the East and the West as such has little meaning. The modern West, meaning thereby a great part of Europe and the Americas, has, more especially during the last 200 years or so, developed a particular type of civilization which is based on certain traditions derived from Greece and Rome. It is, however, the tremendous industrial growth that has made the West what it is. I can see the difference between an industrialized and a non-industrialized country. I think the difference, say between India and Europe in the Middle Ages, would not have been very great and would have been comparable to the difference between any of the great countries of Asia today.

I feel that we think wrongly because we are misled in our approach. Differences have crept in and been intensified by this process of industrialization and mechanization, which has promoted material well-being tremendously and which has been a blessing to humanity. At the same time, it is corroding the life of the mind and thereby encouraging a process of self-destruction. I am not, for the moment, talking or thinking about wars and the like. We have seen in history races come up and gradually fade away, in Asia, in Europe and other places. Are we witnessing the same thing today?

It may be that this will not take effect in our life-time. In the past anyway, one great consolation was that things happened only in one particular quarter of the world. If there was a collapse in one part of the world, the other part carried on. Now, the whole world hangs together in life and death so that if this civilization fades away or collapses it will take practically the whole world down with it. No part of it will be left to survive as it could in olden times. During the so-called Dark Ages of Europe, there were bright periods in Asia, in China, in India, in the Middle East and elsewhere. In the old days, if progress was limited, disaster was also limited in extent and intensity. Today, when we have arrived at a period of great progress, we have also arrived at a period of great disaster and it is a little difficult for us to choose a middle way which would enable us to achieve a little progress and, at the same time, to limit the scope of disaster. That is the major question. A person who has to carry a burden of responsibility is greatly troubled by the practical aspects of this question. I should have liked your conference to throw light on this question. Am I right in saying that the mental life of the world is in a process of deterioration, chiefly because the environment that has been created by the industrial revolution does not give time or opportunity to individuals to think? I do not deny that today there are many great thinkers but it is quite likely that they might be submerged in the mass of unthinking humanity.

We are dealing with and talking a great deal about democracy and I have little doubt that democracy is the best of all the various methods available to us for the governance of human beings. At the same time, we are seeing today—by today I mean the last two decades or so—the emergence of democracy in a somewhat uncontrolled form. When we think of democracy, we normally think of it in the rather limited sense of the 19th century or the early 20th century use of the term. Owing to the remarkable technological growth, something has happened since then and meanwhile democracy has also spread. The result is that we have vast masses of human beings brought up by the industrial revolution, who are not encouraged or given an opportunity to think much. They live a life which, from the point of view of physical comfort, is incomparably better than it has been in any previous generation but they seldom have a chance to think. And yet in a democratic system, it is this vast mass of human beings that will ultimately govern or elect those who govern.

Are they likely to elect more or less the sort of persons they need? That becomes a little doubtful. And I think it may be said without offence—and I certainly can say without offence, for I belong to that tribe of politicians—that the quality of men who are selected by this modern democratic method of adult suffrage gradually deteriorates. There are outstanding individuals chosen, no doubt, but their quality does deteriorate because of this lack of thinking and because of the application of modern methods of propaganda. All the noise and din and the machinery of advertisement prevent men from thinking. They react to this din and noise by producing a dictator or a dumb politician, who is insensitive, who can stand all the din and noise in the world and yet remain standing on his two feet. He gets elected while his rival collapses because he cannot stand all this din. It is an extraordinary state of affairs. It is all very well for us to praise the growth of democracy and I am all for it. The point that I wish to make is not in regard to democracy but rather in regard to the fact that modern life does not encourage the life of the mind. If the life of the mind is not encouraged, then inevitably civilization deteriorates, the race deteriorates and ultimately both collapse in some big cataclysm or just fade away and become as other races and civilizations have become.

ON MUSEUMS[8]

I am grateful to you for inviting me to inaugurate this Centenary Celebration because I am deeply interested in museums in my own layman's way. I am not an expert in anything but I have dabbled in a large number of activities. I am interested in many things and am even interested in experts, though from a distance. It is obvious that experts have their use but they often think that they function only in a world of experts, with the result that they somehow lose touch with the common man or the layman who is not an expert. I merely mention this, because I feel that experts exist in some upper sphere unconnected with humanity at large and very few persons even find their way there except, as I said, experts.

Now, museums I think are very necessary from a variety of points of view and some of the most exhilarating times that I have spent have been in museums—not in this country but chiefly in Europe—and I have always been sorry that I could

---

[8] Speech at the Centenary celebration of the Madras Government Museum and the opening of the National Art Gallery, Madras, 27 November 1951.

not spend more time there. What exactly a museum is and what purpose it serves are questions which can be answered in many ways. I suppose it is some kind of congealed history or a bit of the past locked up in your cabinets and placed so that you may have a glimpse of it. It is a place where you collect beautiful objects and it is good to have beautiful objects for people to look at. More and more people seem to lose all idea of what beauty is and to surround themselves with articles which certainly are not beautiful, whatever else they may be. It is quite extraordinary how people are losing any real appreciation of beauty. What is the reason? I am not talking of India only but of many other countries, too; whether it is symptomatic of the modern age or not, I do not know; but the fact remains that we are becoming more and more shoddy. What is worse, however, is that we sometimes seem to take pride in this fact. Therefore, it is desirable to collect articles of beauty. Even in a matter like children's toys, may I ask why they should be given horrible golliwogs as presents? I do not know. No doubt, children are interested in animals and they should have them. Why not have beautiful things and why not train them in the appreciation of beauty from their childhood instead of giving them toys which are caricatures of what they see? Such toys no doubt excite their curiosity but, at the same time, make them insensitive to beauty. Because of this tendency, which appears to me to be growing throughout the world, because of this lack of appreciation of any kind of beauty, it is desirable to collect articles of beauty from the past and the present so that we may at least have some standard to judge by and so that the people who come to the museums may see for a while articles of beauty, even though they may not generally see them in their daily lives.

There is another aspect of the museum which I called congealed history. Do people go there just to see odd things oddly displayed, just to see, as an oddity, something that existed five hundred or a thousand years ago or do they go to see something that might have significance for them even today? I do not know how history is taught because, at college, I hardly learnt history in the normal way. I read it myself and, therefore, my reading was not guided by experts at all. It was casual, though widespread, reading and I was fascinated by it. My fascination for history was not in reading about odd events that happened in the past but rather in its relation to the things that led up to the present. Only then did it become alive to me. Otherwise it would have been an odd thing unconnected with my life or the world. It must somehow be connected in a series—something of the past leading to something else and that something else leading to the present. Then alone can history live for us.

Let us apply that to the museum. A museum which is really meant to interest and educate must be something which connects its objects with the things the visitors are used to seeing in their lives and in their environments. It should not be just a symbol of the distant, unconnected past. I do not know how far our experts think on these lines and prepare their museums on these lines. It is not the normal antiquarian's view of things. An antiquarian is necessary, of course, to collect these antiquities but an antiquarian who himself becomes an antique piece is not much good. He must have some relation to the modern world. Then only can we make antiquity a living reality in terms of the modern world. Forgive me for these personal reflections. It seems to me incorrect for us to treat any period of the past as something cut off from subsequent periods or from the present and if I look at it that way it does not interest me much. If there is the slightest connection between that and my present-day thoughts and activities it is a blessing and a matter of interest to me. I am giving these rather personal reactions, because I think it might interest some of you, gentlemen, especially those connected with museums. If I may say so with all humility, the greatest danger in the world is that people, in their zeal to specialize, lose all perspective. They become specialists at a particular job and very fine specialists at that but they lose the larger view of things and, therefore, perhaps they may be said to be only specialists and nothing more. Some of you may know these lines from Wordsworth:

> A primrose by a river's brim,
> A yellow primrose was to him
> And it was, nothing more.

They bring to mind the botanist who studies the Latin names of flowers but loses all sense of the beauty of flowers. In other words, we become experts in something but lack wisdom in everything else. In our world, which is so learned in so many subjects, there is very little wisdom. Perhaps, that is because we all know something about a very little part of life and very little about the larger scheme of things.

Now, coming back to the museum, it is a collection of all kinds of things of beauty or things of utility from the past and present and should convey to us some idea of the larger scheme of life. It should ultimately lead to or at least help in an understanding of the present scheme of things. I like the museums of antiquity but there is another type of museum which perhaps the antiquarians consider to be of a lower species. That is the type which may be represented by, let us say, Deutsches Museum of Munich and some other museums in Paris and London, where one can see modern life, modern activity, the growth of science from the pre-scientific period. Such museums are fascinating and contain more education than years of courses in college or university. They also represent something I should like to see grow as part of general education and school or college education.

Lastly, the whole point of museums, whether they be museums of antiquity or museums of modern life, is that larger and larger numbers of people should visit them and learn from them. They should not be confined to the visiting Directors of Museums from other countries. More and more people should come and learn and, in fact, facilities for learning should be provided. That is to say, some arrangement should be made for lectures to be given to ordinary folk who come there and for guides to explain to them what these things are and arouse their interest in them, especially school children and college boys and girls. That is the main purpose of museums. I would not very much mind if no adult came to the museums, because his mind is made up and is not always capable of learning much; but in the formative period of childhood and youth, it is essential that people should come to museums and learn. Their minds will be affected by the objects which they see there. I should like this aspect of education through the museums to be developed, not by appeals to the public but by encouraging and inviting people to come, inviting not only the people who would normally come but also those who would not otherwise come, persuading them to bring their children and explaining things to them so that they may widen their vision and feel that the world is a bigger thing than they normally believed it to be. As I grow old, I tend to philosophize and dole out advice to others. But I am happy to be here to participate in the Centenary Celebration of the oldest of India's museums. I hope it will flourish and expand and, if I may say so, expand in the direction that I have indicated.

The Sixteenth Year[9]

We are again assembled here today on this auspicious occasion of the sixteenth anniversary of free India. Sixteen years ago today, we met here, below the Red Fort, and our National Flag fluttered here for the first time. We shall never forget that day when India attained freedom after a long and hard struggle and great suffering. We were kind of intoxicated with happiness and celebrated the day with fervour. We thought our days of toil were over and we would be able to build our country. But, very soon, the country was overtaken by a terrible calamity. In the wake of the partition of the country, there were riots in Pakistan and on this side of the border. These were ghastly events which shocked us and pained us. But we faced the situation and gradually brought it under control. Then came the assassination of Mahatmaji

---

[9] English rendering of the Independence Day address, delivered in Hindi, Delhi, 15 August 1963.

at the hands of an Indian. We could not have suffered a more rigorous sentence. Nevertheless, we asked ourselves what Gandhiji would have wanted us to do— would he want us to mourn and bewail or fight those evil forces and ideologies which could destroy the country. We faced them and triumphed over those forces.

A fresh wind began to blow again across the country and we decided to devote all our energies to build a new and prosperous India so that the people could move forward and strengthen the nation. Big plans were prepared which we have been implementing for the last 10 or 12 years. I believe, and I think you will agree with me, that the face of India has changed in these 10 or 12 years and is still changing. New cities have been built, thousands of new factories have been set up. Projects have been implemented and everywhere a measure of prosperity is discernible. No doubt, we are still very far from our goal. But these achievements cannot be denied. In recent years, our attention has, however, strayed from the fundamentals. We became complacent and felt that our freedom was secure and there was none who could threaten it. We had not yet grasped that freedom is not secure by itself. We did not realize that freedom calls for eternal vigilance, year in and year out, day in and day out. In the absence of vigilance, dangers arise. We had become standard-bearers of peace in the world and India was rightly regarded as a country which stood for peace. We still stand for peace. But weakness goes ill together with peace. Peace can be secured by strength and endeavour, not by complacency. That way alone can peace be secure in the world and our voice can be heard with respect.

All of a sudden, aggression was committed on our borders last year by a country which we had looked upon as a friend. This naturally shocked us and we had to pass through hardships and difficulties. This also had its good consequences, because we were shaken out of our complacency and once again a climate of preparedness and sacrifice was generated. I still remember how our people, the ordinary people, offered to the nation all their possessions, cash, gold and silver. Those who had the least gave the most. People forgot their mutual conflicts, put them aside and realized that their first duty was to face the danger to the freedom of the country. The spirit of unity manifested itself in the country, which proved that notwithstanding the apparent differences, there is an underlying unity which comes to surface at the right time.

Our morale was high. We strove to prepare for defence and to raise our strength, and the country did become strong. But popular enthusiasm is not enough in national preparedness. Preparing for the defence of the country means a thousand different activities to make the equipment and material which the defence forces need. Backing this all, are the countless farms of India which produce foodgrains and other foodstuff. Preparedness therefore means all-round effort, everyone in this place striving hard to produce to the limit of his capacity so that our economy is strengthened. We have attended to these matters and some progress has been made and is still continuing.

But again the state of complacency is returning because the hostilities have ended. In place of the unity and harmony that were witnessed, the old controversies and conflicts which weaken the country have reappeared. Unfortunately, this is our old failing, reasserting itself when we are not face to face with danger. But we are facing continuous danger on our borders and it becomes our first task to defend the country against it. Other things can wait. Who will respect that country which cannot defend its independence and its territorial integrity? Such a nation is even powerless to make any progress. No doubt, at this moment the biggest task facing us is to raise the strength of the country, increase production and banish poverty so that everyone has an equal opportunity for progress, and the millions of our people and our children have a chance to lead a better life and to get the good things of life. But all this presupposes that we uphold our honour and make our freedom secure. Any slackening in this respect will leave the country disheartened, weak, powerless. A free country which wants to maintain its freedom gives top priority to its defences. Everything else comes afterwards. On this question there can be no argument, although there is scope for discussion. We have to speak with one voice. The unity of India, which is most vital to us, comes first—the unity which manifested itself last year and early this year but which we have been neglecting after the fighting stopped. It is unfortunate that again conflicting and dissenting voices have begun to be heard and small and big controversies have erupted.

Ours is a free country and everyone has a right to free discussion and criticism which one can freely exercise. But with rights go duties and obligations. Anyone who neglects his duties cannot protect his rights. The national duty today is to defend the country, to maintain unity and increase the nation's strength, irrespective of religion or State. Everybody has his rights but if we neglect this duty we weaken our claim to those rights. There are several rights which cannot be fully operated today. All our citizens are entitled to a happy life, to be freed of the burden of poverty and to expect opportunities of progress for their children. We are marching towards that goal and we hope that the day will come when it will be achieved. The fact, however, remains that we are far from that goal and we can reach it only when we fulfil our duties.

When I say that the country is facing dangers on the borders, I am not suggesting that something is about to happen. Rather that this new situation that has arisen has created new dangers on our borders, which we appear to have forgotten. Of course, we have to station our troops and our Air Force to guard against this menace, but the Army or the Air Force alone cannot protect the country. Nowadays, the defence of the country requires all the people, men and women, to do something or the other in that cause. The defences have to be strengthened by the endeavour of the entire nation, by its unity and ability to work together, in farms and factories or wherever we happen to be. We should all prepare ourselves to meet the danger so that we could strengthen our country and thus strengthen the Army.

It is a strange world in which we live, a world which is changing. On the one hand, there is a danger of a world war in which nuclear weapons may be used. On the other hand, there are also some favourable trends. Recently a treaty was concluded in Moscow on nuclear tests by the United States, the Soviet Union and Britain. We and other countries acceded to the treaty later. The agreement does not eliminate the danger of war but it shows a way to bring war and warlike tendencies under control and to ensure peace in the world. Seven or eight years ago, we had made this proposal in the United Nations, which it has now given the shape of a treaty in Moscow. We were the first to raise our voice for this kind of arrangement. We are, therefore, particularly happy that our proposal has been acted upon and hope that a move having been initiated, further progress will continue to be made and the world would be rid of the nuclear danger. Young men and women today face a life full of dangers as well as hopes. It is a good thing that we live in such times because in a situation like this a nation can become strong and courageous. Soft living is not good for any nation because it weakens the people. I wish to congratulate the people, particularly the young men and women and the children, that they live in an age full of tests and trials more difficult than the examinations they have to take in schools and colleges. The tests in life are harder and bigger and no book can help us in facing them. To face these tests and trials and to emerge victorious, we need character, a stout heart and mind. As the years roll by and free India grows up, we have to grow in strength along with it and never permit ourselves to become complacent. We may have two, three or even a thousand different views, but so far as the unity of India and its security and prosperity are concerned, we have to speak with one voice. There is no scope for difference of opinion in this matter. We can argue about the approaches and methods, but whenever we take any action we should ask ourselves whether by that step we are serving India, strengthening its unity, helping in the defence of the country or weakening it. This should be our yardstick in whatever we do because often we are carried away in the heat of factional controversies and weaken the country. We should remember all this because the days to come will not be easy ones. However we look at the situation, we are going to face a difficult time.

After the attack on our borders, we were compelled to take certain measures which we did not like. The military expenditure had to be increased, more than double, and for that taxes had to be levied and increased. Nobody likes taxes, neither the taxpayer nor the government. But when the country is in danger, those who are talking about their profits and not about the danger hardly serve the country. Money we can earn and spend, but the country has to go on for ever. Recently, when aggression was committed, everywhere, whether in our Parliament or in the country at large, we rose to the occasion and despite the hardships, we faced it with firmness and dignity. No matter how much we have to suffer, even at the cost of our lives, we have to face the danger of aggression so that India may live.

Now, we have to face all kinds of dangers, internal and external, and in so doing if we have to carry heavier burdens, we should be prepared to do so. When nations go to war, the people have to carry tremendous burdens and sometimes a country is laid waste. We are not facing such a war at the moment. Nobody knows what the future holds for us. But to avert such a war we have to be ever vigilant and we have to undergo hardships.

We have a reputation for being a peace-loving people. The fact that we are expanding our defence capacity and giving military training to our young men does not mean that we have given up our principles and policy of peace. We shall follow that policy in any situation and try to resolve disputes with other countries by peaceful means, if it is possible to do so. We do not like war which can bring ruin to the country and cause hardships to the people. But there could be no peace without honour, certainly not by submission to evil, out of fear. If the people are seized by fear, they weaken the country and tarnish its fair name. Thus, while we prepare with all our strength for the defence of the country, we shall tread the path of peace. Whenever we can solve any problem in the world, any issue concerning us, we shall always resort to a peaceful course, but not to the detriment of India's honour. To uphold that honour we shall prepare in full measure. This preparedness does not merely mean arms and armaments. It means that every man, woman and child in the country has to offer something, has to be ready to work with determination and in co-operation with others. Very few people in our country know how to march in step. Marching in step is not in itself a virtue but it stands for working together. An army is strong because the soldiers work together, march in step. They are disciplined and follow rules. We have to teach to our countrymen discipline, the outlook of a soldier.

It would be a good thing for our future if we prepare ourselves in this manner and when we are out of the present danger, we would be a strong country with courage and confidence in ourselves. Then we would be able to march on the road to prosperity with ease. Nations become great by self-confidence, not by relying on others. You can be friends with others, but you have to rely on yourselves. There can be co-operation with others, but you have to do your own thinking and work with your own hands. Any country which forgets this and is frightened and loses self-confidence begins to decline, faces ruin and lowers itself. What greater indignity can there be for India than that fear should grip us and we lose confidence in ourselves? Whatever work is there, it is we who have to do it, although we have friends in the world and we have to maintain that friendship and take their help. The big countries in the world have helped us and we are grateful for that, not only for the help but for their sympathy. We have to march ahead towards our goal on the path we have chosen for ourselves, and we shall attain that goal. We have to remember this principle and ensure the progress of the country. Relying on ourselves and with the help of friends, we have to solve our economic problems, and so change our country that it would be able to stand on its legs.

I particularly want that the millions of our children have an opportunity for growth, for education and to serve the country and to serve themselves. Let us build an India in which these opportunities are available and there are no differences of high and low. This is our vision of India. Of course, the Planning Commission and other offices of Government are working for this purpose, but as you know the Government and the Planning Commission can only show the way. The work has to be done by millions of our people. If they cannot do it, neither the Planning Commission nor the Government can achieve anything. Whether it is defence or development, it is the people who have to carry out the work, not those sitting in offices. Our task is to awaken the 450 million people of India and to show the path. It is for them to march along that road and reap the benefit. Whatever happened on our border this year was, I think, all to the good because it will strengthen and fortify us. It would prepare the country for progress, provided we do not lose heart. Our people have never trodden the path of cowardice.

I again congratulate you on the 16th anniversary of our freedom and hope that you will remember the day. Free India is still a child, for what are sixteen years in the life of a country? Of course, ours is an ancient country. I hope it makes progress, becomes strong and holds its head high in the world. Let us remember these things, particularly the fact that we are all brethren in this country; wherever we live, and whatever our religion, we have to work together. Whoever forgets this fact does not serve the country well.

Study of the Past[10]

Mr President and Distinguished Delegates, I am somewhat embarrassed at this moment, specially after hearing what Professor Kabir, the President, has said about me. I must confess to you that I do not claim to be a scholar or historian. What I am, it is difficult for me to say—a dabbler in many things—but I certainly feel a certain feeling of embarrassment standing before this distinguished audience of Orientalists because, apart from dabbling in many things, I have not studied carefully the work of Orientalists. I have always thought their work important and occasionally I see what they have done to understand what the past has to show to us and to relate it, so far as that was possible, to the present. That does not entitle me to speak with authority before this audience about subjects that interest you.

Why is a person an Orientalist? I suppose the very idea involves people from outside the 'oriental' sphere, as it may be called, looking into the ancient lives and thoughts of those who lived in this part of the world. I have been a resident, born and bred here, and I can't look at these things as an outsider can do. Of course, even looking at it from inside, the mind can be adapted to look at it from the point of view of an outsider also.

I suppose that the original study by western scholars of oriental lore was conditioned chiefly by intellectual curiosity. And I feel grateful to the many eminent scholars in Europe who have studied these subjects and shed a great deal of light on them, studied them from the point of view of modern scholarship and criticism and not merely as an Indian is likely to do in regard to India, being over-burdened by, shall I say, the very thoughts and feelings of our forebears. Many of our people also are now adapting the modern scientific methods to study them.

But what is the object of the study apart from curiosity? It is, I suppose, to learn how people thought and acted in the old world. It is extraordinary how in some countries, and one of them is India, these old ideas and thoughts have clung to the people through the ups and downs of history and still continue to affect their lives.

I would say that there is something important, something lasting in those thoughts, which have lasted in spite of all manner of events that have happened not only in India but in other countries, too. At the same time, those thoughts have got tied up with many others that certainly are not of permanent value, such as the various customs and attitudes which we find a little difficult to discard, although they have no particular virtue and may have many disadvantages attached

---

[10] Speech at the International Congress of Orientalists, New Delhi, 4 January 1964.

to them. But it is for scholars to distinguish between the real thing and the dross attached to it, which has grown round it through the ages.

India is one of the few countries which have had a more or less continuous tradition over a long time. That tradition is based on the thinking which was current in India a long time ago. It is also based on all manner of customs that have gradually grown and covered our lives, and which we now find difficult to get rid of.

Among the other ancient countries, whose ancient history you study, there has been a definite break with that ancient period. That break, I think, has not yet fully come about in India. India is different from what it was, of course, but there has been no serious break, as in many other countries, and so India offers a peculiar ground for study. How these old ideas and thoughts have continued and influenced our people and what among them may have some application today deserves study. We have to find some way of evolving a certain synthesis between the old and the new.

We cannot entirely discard the old and uproot ourselves from it. I do not think it will be desirable to do so. Undoubtedly, if we want to give it up, or circumstances force us to give it up, we become rootless. We have to live in the modern age, adapting the past to our ways.

Many of you, ladies and gentlemen, are interested in finding out facts about the old and the very old from various points of view. The chief concern that fills my mind is how to find a synthesis between the old and the new, because I do not find it good enough entirely to discard the old and, obviously, I cannot discard the new. The two have to be brought together. Maybe that the new as we know it, important as it is, lacks somewhat of the depth of the old. I am not talking of India only, but of other countries, too, with ancient civilizations.

There was a certain depth in the traditional way of living, a certain something that even now has a meaning. With life today, with its rush and hurry and technical developments which are, of course, very important in their own way, we are apt to lose something of the depth that the old civilizations gave us. And that is why I have tried to think of how the two can be harmonized. Possibly, when I talk of the old world, I talk about some writers and thinkers only, and not of the mass of people in the old world. But I suppose even the masses were to some extent governed by the thinking of the age.

I suppose we live now, as we always live, to some extent, in a transitional age. Only, today the transition is much more rapid due to the enormous advance that science and technology have made and are making. That makes it still more difficult for us to adapt ourselves continuously to the changes that are going on all the time. Perhaps I am thinking of this problem, living in this new world, and also in a little of the old world. This sort of thing helps us to keep our balance and not become something without roots.

Well, you, ladies and gentlemen, are interested in discovering the ancient past of various countries and finding out what they stood for. That is interesting, of course. Why is it interesting? What was there in the thinking of the old which has still some meaning for us? Whether it was Plato, let us say, or somebody else, or some of our ancient sages or old people of China, Confucius and others, what is it which they said and is of value to us today? That I suppose is one of the chief aims of these studies.

Sometimes, I find that the specialists in these studies look upon them as museum pieces unconnected with life's everyday happenings, or they lose themselves in them.

How can you bring about this connection between the two? It is a strange world we live in, ever changing, and opening out new avenues. But all the progress which we make is essentially in our knowledge of the external world and the forces that control it, in technology and science, and not very much, I suppose, in the knowledge of ourselves. We go back to our ancient saying, whether Greek or Indian or of any other country, which always laid stress on a person knowing himself before he seeks to learn about the world. Well, the ancient way of thinking really concentrated on knowing oneself, but neglected to learn about the external world in which one lived. Today, we concentrate the external world, which is very necessary and very good, but we perhaps ignore the individual, and do not know enough about him.

These two approaches, the external approach and the internal approach, have to be, I suppose, combined in order to make us realize what we are and how we are to face our problems. This is what I am suggesting to you, though I am not sure if it is outside the scope of the Orientalists who are here; but I do suggest that it is desirable for us to learn something of ourselves, apart from learning something of the outside world about us. Perhaps in this era of tremendous changes and of confusion, it would be helpful if we thought quietly about ourselves and of the world at large, and not merely in terms of the atom bomb and how to escape from it. Of course, we all want to escape from the atom or hydrogen bomb. We all want to have peace without which there can be no progress. But, in addition to that, it may be necessary to think a little more deeply—what we are, what the world is and where our life is leading us to.

I am a politician tied up with day-to-day occurrences and have little time to think of the deeper things of life. Nevertheless, sometimes I am forced to think of them and to wonder what all this is about that we indulge in and whether it is worthwhile our doing the many things that we do. Yet, I do believe that there is some force which fashions our destiny, which in spite of all these dangers leads us forward. Perhaps the human race is as a whole going forward, not in the merely material sense, but also in other ways, and out of this tremendous confusion of today something better will arise. It is in the fashioning of that better world that, perhaps, the old thoughts of our forebears could help us. And, therefore, a study of them in an understanding way ought to prove very useful to us.

In India, there is a wealth of ancient material to be studied. I do not know how many, but I was told there are still in Sanskrit alone about 50,000 or more books listed in catalogues—many of them not seen, nor read or considered carefully. This is apart from the other visible evidence of the ancient thinking in the form of temples and other structures. I suppose it is the same case in other countries also. And so a study of these must throw some light not only on past thinking, apart from the past way of life, but also help us in the present, because after all our history is a very short one, going back a few thousand years and in these few thousand years all these changes have taken place. If we could discover the essence of things from a study of the past and the present, we might be able to serve the cause of the future a little better, and not leave it to take whatever shape it chooses.

You will realize, distinguished delegates, that I have nothing specific to say to you. Therefore, I am rambling on various odd things that strike me. I think the subjects in whose study you are engaged are highly fascinating. There is still, I believe, the question of the script of the Mohenjodaro period which has not been solved and the solution of which may throw further light on that period and subsequent periods. Those are interesting pursuits, no doubt, but, for me their interest lies chiefly in the light they throw on our knowledge of the development of the human being.

The work of Orientalists, which, perhaps, some consider as not very useful from the point of view of the modern world, seems to me of extreme importance because it throws light on our past thinking and past action. So, I hope that your labours at this conference and elsewhere will lead to more and more knowledge of our past, which will help us to see the present in a proper perspective and not as something cut off from the past.

Profiles

NEHRU ON HIS CONTEMPORARIES

Sarojini Naidu[1]

It has been my painful duty, Sir, as Leader of this House, to refer from time to time
to the passing away of the illustrious sons and daughters of India. Recently I referred
to the passing away of a very eminent son of India, Sir Tej Bahadur Sapru. Then
the Governor of a province suddenly died. He was a very distinguished servant of
the State. When we refer to these distinguished sons or daughters of the country,
we say often enough that it will be difficult to replace them, that they are
irreplaceable, which may be true enough in a partial manner. But, today, I, with
your leave, would like to refer to the passing away early yesterday morning of one
about whom it can be said with absolute truth that it is impossible to replace her
or to find her like.

She was for the last year and a half or a little more the Governor of a great
province with many problems and she acted as Governor with exceeding ability
and exceeding success as can be judged from the fact that everyone in that province,
from the Premier and his Ministers and Government to the various groups and
classes and religious communities down to the worker and the peasant in the field,
had been drawn to her and had found a welcome in her heart. She had succeeded
very greatly as a Governor and as a great servant of the State in an exalted position.
But it is not as a Governor that I should speak much of her, for she was much
greater a person than Governors are normally supposed to be. What she was exactly
it is a little difficult for me to say, because she had become almost a part of us, a part

[1] A commemorative speech on Shrimati Sarojini Naidu, in the Constituent Assembly
(Legislative), New Delhi, 3 March 1949.

of our national heritage of today and a part of us individuals who had the great privilege of being associated with her for a multitude of years in our struggle for freedom and in our work.

Sir, it is a little difficult to see persons with whom you have been so closely associated in proper perspective, and yet one can do that to some extent. And thinking of her one sees a person to whom any number of epithets and adjectives might be applied. Here was a person of great brilliance. Here was a person vital and vivid. Here was a person with so many gifts, but above all with some gifts which made her unique. She began life as a poetess. In later years, when the compulsion of events drew her into the national struggle and she threw herself into it with all the zest and fire that she possessed, she did not write much poetry with pen and paper, but her whole life became a poem and a song. And she did that amazing thing: she infused artistry and poetry into our national struggle. Just as the Father of the Nation had infused moral grandeur and greatness into the struggle, Mrs Sarojini Naidu gave it artistry and poetry and that zest for life and indomitable spirit which not only faced disaster and catastrophe, but faced them with a light heart and with a song on the lips and smile on the face. I do not think, being myself a politician which most of us are, that any gift was more valuable to our national life than this lifting it out of the plane of pure politics to a higher artistic sphere, which she succeeded in doing in some measure.

Looking back upon her life, one sees an astonishing combination of gifts. Here is a life full of vitality; here are fifty years of existence—not merely existence but a vital, dynamic existence—touching many aspects of our life, cultural and political. And whatever she touched she infused with something of her fire. She was indeed a pillar of fire. And then again, she was like cool running water, soothing and uplifting and bringing down the passion of her politics to the cooler levels of human beings. So it is difficult for one to speak about her except that one realizes that here was a magnificence of spirit and it is gone.

We shall, no doubt, for generations to come remember her, but perhaps those who come after us and those who have not been associated with her so closely will not realize fully the richness of that personality which could not easily be translated into spoken words or records. She worked for India. She knew how to work and she knew how to play. And that was a wonderful combination. She knew how to sacrifice herself for great causes. She knew also to do that so gracefully and so graciously that it appeared an easy thing to do and not anything entailing travail of spirit. If a sensitive person like her must suffer from the tremendous travail of spirit, no doubt she did, but she did it so graciously that it appeared that that too was easy for her. So she lifted our struggle to a higher plane and gave it a certain touch which I cannot think anybody else can give or is likely to give it in future.

Sir, I said she was a curious combination of so many things; she represented in herself a rich culture into which flowed various currents which have made Indian culture as great as it is. She herself was a composite both of various currents of culture in India as well as various currents of culture both in the East and the West. And so she was, while being a very great national figure, also truly an internationalist, and wherever she might go in the wide world she was recognized as such and as one of the great ones of the earth. It is well to remember that, especially today when through stress of circumstances we may occasionally drift into a narrow nationalism and forget the larger objectives that inspired the great ones who laid the foundations of our national movement.

The great Father of the Nation and this great woman have shaped our national movement so powerfully, not so much on the direct political plane, although she was active there and adequately functioned, but in those invisible planes which are so very important, because they shape the nation's character; because they mould ultimately its mental and aesthetic and artistic outlook; and without that mental, moral, aesthetic and artistic outlook, any success that we may gain may well be an empty success; because, after all, we seek freedom not merely because it is good in itself, but to achieve something else. We seek freedom to achieve a good life for our people. What is a good life? Can you imagine any good life which does not have an artistic and an aesthetic element in it, and a moral element in it? That would not be a good life; it would be some temporary phase of existence, which would be rather dry and harsh, and unfortunately, the world grows drier and harsher and more cruel. In our own experience of the last two years, political life has become a little more harsh, cruel, intolerant and suspicious and in the world today we see suspicion and fear all round, fear of one another. How are we to get over this? It is only through some experience of moral heights that we might overcome it, and that was the way shown to us by the Father of the Nation, or else the other way is to approach it from the human point of view, from the artistic and aesthetic point of view, and the human point of view is the forgiving point of view, is the point of view full of compassion and understanding of humanity and its failings as well as its virtues. And so Sarojini brought that human point of view, full of understanding, full of compassion for all who are in India or outside.

The House knows that she stood more than any single human being in India for the unity of India in all its phases, for the unity of its cultural content, the unity of its geographical areas. It was a passion with her. It was the very texture of her life. It is well to remember, when we sometimes fall into narrower grooves, that greatness has never come from a narrowness of mind, or again, greatness for a nation as for an individual comes from a wide vision, a wide perspective, an inclusive outlook and a human approach to life. So she became an interpreter in India of the various phases of our rich cultural inheritance. She became an interpreter in India of the many great things that the West had produced, and she became an interpreter in other parts of the world of India's culture. She became the ideal ambassador and the ideal link between the East and the West, and between various parts and groups in India. I do not myself see how we are to find the like of her now or in the future. We shall, no doubt, have great men and women in the future, because India even when she was low in the political scale, had never failed to produce greatness in her children. And now that India is free, I have no doubt that India will produce great men and women in the future, as she has done in the past and in the present; with our very eyes we have seen these great figures, and yet I doubt, while India produces great men and women, whether she will or can produce just another like Sarojini. So we think of her as a brightness, as a certain vitality and vividness, as poetry infused into life and activity, as something tremendously important and rich, and yet something which in terms of the material world is rather insubstantial, difficult to grasp and difficult to describe, as something which you can only feel, as you can feel beauty, as you can feel the other higher things of life. Maybe some memory of this will reach other generations who have not seen her and inspire them. I think it will, but I do not think they will ever feel it as we poor mortals have felt who had the privilege of being associated with her.

So, in making this reference in this House, I can only recount various ideas that come into my mind, and perhaps I recount them in a somewhat confused way, because my mind feels afflicted and confused as if an intimate part of it were cut off from it and because it is difficult to speak or to judge people for whom one has a great deal of affection. It was the affection of unity. It was the affection of one who even in his younger days was tremendously inspired by her speech and action and who during the succeeding decades grew more and more to love her and to admire her and to think of her as a rich and rare being. That rich and precious being is no more and that is sorrow for us, inevitably, and yet it is something more than sorrow. It is, if we view it in another light, a joy and triumph for us that the India of our generation produced such rare spirits as have inspired us and as will inspire us in the future.

Sir, it is customary when making such a reference to say that the sympathy and condolence of this House might be conveyed to the relatives of the person who has passed away. I say so and yet really the bond that held Sarojini to all of us here and to thousands and tens of thousands in this country was as close and great as the bond that held her to her own children or to her other relatives and so we send this message of condolence on behalf of this House. All of us really require that message ourselves to soothe our hearts.

A Radiant Figure[2]

Nearly three and a half year have gone by since Gandhiji passed away. The manner of his death was the culmination and perfect climax to an astonishing career. Even during his life time, innumerable stories and legends had grown around him and now he seems almost a legendary figure, one in the great line of India's sages and heroes and wise men. A new generation grows up to whom he is only a name, a great name to be revered but nevertheless a name. Within a few more years there will not be many left who have come in personal contact with him and had experience of that vivid, virile and magnificent personality. The legend will grow and take many shapes, sometimes with little truth in it. Succeeding generations will remember him and pay honour to him. As is India's way, we shall add him to our pantheon and celebrate the day of his birth and the day of his passing away. We shall shout *Jai* when his name is mentioned and, perhaps, feel elated that we have done our duty to him.

What gods there are, I know not; and I am not concerned about them. But there are certain rare qualities which raise a man above the common herd and make him appear as though he were of different clay. The long story of humanity can be considered from many points of view; it is a story of the advance and growth of man and the spirit of man; it is also a story full of agony and tragedy. It is a story of masses of men and women in ferment and in movement and it is also the story of great and outstanding personalities who have given content and shape to that movement of masses.

In that story Gandhi occupies and will occupy a preeminent place. We are too near him to judge him correctly. Some of us came in intimate contact with him and were influenced by that dominating and very lovable personality. We miss him profoundly, for he had become a part of our own lives. With us the personal factor is so strong that it comes in the way of a correct appraisal. Others who did not know him so intimately cannot, perhaps, have a full realization of the living fire that was in this man of peace and humility. So, both these groups lack proper perspective or knowledge. Whether that perspective will come in later years when the problems and conflicts of today are matters for the historian, I do not know.

[2] Foreword to D.G. Tendulkar's *Mahatma*, Pahalgam, Kashmir, 30 June 1951.

But I have no doubt that in the distant as in the near future this towering personality will stand out and compel homage. It may be that the message which he embodied will be understood and acted upon more in later years than it is today. That message was not confined to a particular country or a community. Whatever truth there was in it was a truth applicable to all countries and to humanity as a whole. He may have stressed certain aspects of it in relation to the India of his day and those particular aspects may cease to have much significance as times and conditions change. The kernel of that message was, however, not confined to time or space. And if this is so, then it will endure and grow in the understanding of man.

He brought freedom to India and in that process taught us many things which were important for us at the time. He told us to shed fear and hatred; he told us of unity and equality and brotherhood, of raising those who had been suppressed, of the dignity of labour and of the supremacy of things of the spirit. Above all, he spoke and wrote unceasingly of truth in relation to all our activities. He repeated again and again that Truth was to him God and God was Truth. Scholars may raise their eyebrows and philosophers and cynics repeat the old question: what is Truth? Few of us dare to answer it with any assurance; it may be that the answer itself is many-sided and our limited intelligence cannot grasp the whole. But, however limited the functioning of our minds or our capacity for intuition may be, each one of us must, I suppose, have some limited idea of truth as he sees it. Will he act up to it, regardless of consequences and not compromise with what he himself considers an aberration from it? Will he, even in search of the right goal, compromise with the means of attaining it? Will he subordinate means to ends?

It is easy to frame this question rather rhetorically, as if there was only one answer. But life is exceedingly complicated and the choice it offers is never simple. Perhaps, to some extent, an individual leading an isolated life may endeavour with some success to answer that question for himself. But where he is concerned not only with his own actions but with those of many others, when fate or circumstances have put him in a position where he moulds and directs others, what is he to do? How is a leader of men to function? If he is a leader, he must lead and not merely follow the dictates of the crowd, though some modern conceptions of the functioning of democracy would lead one to think that he must bow down to the largest number. If he does so, then he is no leader and he cannot take others far along the right path of human progress. If he acts singly, according to his own lights, he cuts himself off from the very persons whom he is trying to lead. If he brings himself down to the same level of understanding as others, then he has lowered himself, been untrue to his own ideal and compromised with Truth. And once such compromises begin, there is no end to them and the path is slippery. What then is he to do? It is not enough for him to perceive truth or some aspect of it. He must succeed in making others perceive it also.

The average leader of men, especially in a democratic society, has continually to adapt himself to his environment and to choose what he considers the lesser evil. Some adaptation is inevitable. But as this process goes on, occasions arise when that adaptation imperils the basic ideal and objective. I suppose there is no clear answer to this question and each individual and each generation will have to find its own answer.

The amazing thing about Gandhi was that he adhered, in the fullest sense, to his ideals and to his conception of truth; yet, he succeeded in moulding and moving enormous masses of human beings. He was not inflexible. He was very much alive to the necessities of the moment and he adapted himself to changing circumstances. But all these adaptations were about secondary matters. In regard to the basic things, he was inflexible and firm as a rock. For him, there was no compromise with what he considered evil. He moulded a whole generation and more and raised them above themselves for the time being at least. That was a tremendous achievement.

Does that achievement endure? It brought results which will undoubtedly endure. It also brought in its train some reactions. For people, compelled by circumstances to raise themselves above their normal level, are apt to sink back to even lower levels than before. We see something like that happening today. We saw that reaction in the tragedy of Gandhi's own assassination. What is worse is the general lowering of these standards for the raising of which Gandhi devoted his life. Perhaps, this is a temporary phase and people will recover from it and find themselves again. I have no doubt that, deep in the consciousness of India, the basic teachings of Gandhi will endure and continue to affect our national life.

No man can write a true life of Gandhi unless he is himself as big as Gandhi. So, we can expect to have no real and fully adequate life of this man. Difficult as it is to write a life of Gandhi, it becomes far more so because his life has been an intimate part of India's life for half a century or more. Yet, if many attempt to write his life, they may succeed in throwing light on some aspects of this unique career and also give people some understanding of this memorable period of India's history.

Tendulkar has laboured for many years over this book. He told me about it during Gandhiji's life time and I remember his consulting Gandhiji a few months before his death. Anyone can see that this work has involved great and devoted labour for many long years. It brings together more facts and data about Gandhi than any book that I know. It is immaterial whether or not we agree with the author's interpretation or opinion. We are given here a mass of evidence and we can form our own opinions. Therefore, I consider this book to be of great value as a record not only of the life of a man supreme in his generation but also of a period of India's history which has intrinsic importance of its own. We live today in a world torn with hatred and violence and fear and passion and the shadow of war hangs heavily over us. Gandhi told us to cast away our fear and passion and to keep away from hatred and violence. His voice may not be heard by many in the tumult and shouting of today but it will have to be heard and understood some time or other if this world is to survive in any civilized form.

People will write the life of Gandhi and they will discuss and criticize him and his theories and activities. But to some of us, he will remain something apart from theory—a radiant and beloved figure who ennobled and gave significance to our petty lives and whose passing has left us with a feeling of emptiness and loneliness. Many pictures rise in my mind of this man, whose eyes were often full of laughter and yet were pools of infinite sadness. But the picture that is dominant and most significant is as I saw him marching, staff in hand, to Dandi on the Salt March in 1930. Here was the pilgrim on his quest of truth, quiet, peaceful, determined and fearless, who would continue that quiet pilgrimage, regardless of consequences.

The tribal people of India are a virile people who naturally went astray sometimes. They quarrelled and occasionally cut off one another's heads. These were deplorable occurrences and should have been checked. Even so, it struck me that some of their practices were perhaps less evil than those that prevail in our cities. It is often better to cut off a hand or a head than to crush and trample on a heart. Perhaps, I also felt happy with these simple folk, because the nomad in me found congenial soil in their company. I approached them in a spirit of comradeship and not like someone aloof who had come to look at them, examine them, weigh them, measure them and report about them or to try and make them conform to another way of life.

I am alarmed when I see—not only in this country but in other great countries, too—how anxious people are to shape others according to their own image or likeness and to impose on them their particular way of living. We are welcome to our way of living but why impose it on others? This applies equally to national and international fields. In fact, there would be more peace in the world, if people were to desist from imposing their way of living on other people and countries.

I am not at all sure which is the better way of living. In some respects I am quite certain theirs is better. Therefore, it is grossly presumptuous on our part to approach them with an air of superiority or to tell them what to do or not to do. There is no point in trying to make of them a second rate copy of ourselves.

Now, who are these tribal folk? A way of describing them is that they are the people of the frontiers or those who live away from the interior of this country. Just as the hills breed a somewhat different type of people from those who inhabit the plains, so also the frontier breeds a different type of people from those who live away from the frontier. My own predilection is for the mountains rather than for the plains, for the hill folk rather than the plains people. So also I prefer the frontier, not only in a physical sense but because the idea of living near a frontier appeals to me intellectually.

MAULANA AZAD[3]

Mr Speaker, Sir: It has fallen to my lot often to refer in this House to the death of a colleague or a great man. I have to perform that sad duty again today in regard to one who was with us a few days ago and who passed away rather suddenly, producing a sense of deep sorrow and grief not only to his colleagues in Parliament but to innumerable people all over the country.

It has become almost a commonplace, when a prominent person passes away, to say that he is irreplaceable. That is often true; yet I believe that it is literally and absolutely true in regard to the passing away of Maulana Azad. We have had great men and we will have great men, but I do submit that the peculiar and special type of greatness which Maulana Azad represented is not likely to be reproduced in India or anywhere else.

I need not refer to his many qualities, his deep learning, his scholarship and his great oratory. He was a great writer. He was great in many ways. He combined in himself the greatness of the past with the greatness of the present. He always reminded me of the great men of several hundred years ago about whom I have read in history, the great men of the Renaissance, or in a later period, the encyclopaedists who preceded the French Revolution, men of intellect and men of action. He reminded also of what might be called the great quality of olden days—the graciousness, a certain courtesy or tolerance or patience which we sadly seek in the world today. Even though we may seek to reach the moon, we do it with a lack of graciousness or of tolerance or of some things which have made life worth-while since life began. It was the strange and unique mixture of the good qualities of the past, the graciousness, the deep learning and toleration, and the urges of today which made Maulana Azad what he was.

Everyone knows that even in his early teens he was filled with the passion for freeing India and he turned towards ways even of violent revolution. Soon after he realized that violence was not the way which would gain results.

---

[3] Speech in Lok Sabha on the death of Maulana Abul Kalam Azad, 24 February 1958.

Maulana Azad was a very special representative in a high degree of the great composite culture which had gradually grown in India. He, in his own venue, in Delhi or in Bengal where he spent the greater part of his life, represented this synthesis of various cultures which had flowed in and lost themselves in the ocean of Indian life and humanity, affecting and changing them and being changed themselves by them. He came to represent more specially the culture of India as influenced by the cultures of the nations of Western Asia, namely, the Persian culture and the Arabic culture which have affected India for thousands of years. In that sense, I can hardly conceive of any other person who can replace him, because the age which produced him is past. A few of us have some faint idea of that age which is past.

Change is essential lest we should become rooted to some past habit. But I cannot help expressing a certain feeling of regret that with the bad, the good of the past days is also swept away and that good was eminently represented by Maulana Azad.

There is one curious error to the expression of which I have myself been guilty about Maulana Azad's life and education. Even this morning the newspapers contained a resolution of the Government about Maulana Azad. It is stated that he went and studied at Al Azhar University. He did not do so. It is an extraordinary persistence of error. As I said, I myself thought so. Otherwise, I would have taken care to correct it in the Government resolution. The fact is that he did not study at Al Azhar University. Of course, he went to Cairo and he visited Al Azhar University. He studied elsewhere. He studied chiefly in Calcutta, in the Arabic schools as well as in other schools. He spent a number of years in Arabia. He was born there and he visited Egypt as he visited other countries of Western Asia.

We mourn today the passing of a great man, a man of luminous intelligence and mighty intellect with an amazing capacity to pierce through a problem to its core. The word 'luminous' is perhaps the best word I can use about his mind. When we miss and when we part with such a companion, friend, colleague, comrade, leader and teacher, there is inevitably a tremendous void created in our life and activities.

THE MESSAGE OF TAGORE[4]

All over India we have been celebrating the hundredth birth anniversary of Gurudeva. In many foreign countries also the centenary is being celebrated. Yet I

---

[4] From the Acharya's address to special Convocation of the Visva-Bharati during inauguration of the Tagore Centenary celebrations, Santiniketan, 9 May 1961. Courtesy: Rabindra-Sadan, Visva-Bharati.

think the celebration at Santiniketan has a deeper and a more intimate meaning not only because Gurudeva sanctified this place by his physical presence for many years but because he wished that the Visva-Bharati which he created should represent in some manner his spirit and his message. A seed was sown here, and those who are serving this institution as teachers and scholars and the many others who, though not directly associated with it, are influenced by it are, to some extent, its fruit. It is therefore proper that we should celebrate this occasion not merely with the pomp and ceremony of celebrations elsewhere but in a way peculiar to this institution. The teachers, the students and the scholars who are privileged to be associated with this institution have to try to live up to the message and to the ideals which Gurudeva placed before all of us. These ideals are not meant for a particular institution. They are meant for the whole of India and, in a measure, for the whole world. The Visva-Bharati is closely connected with those objectives and ideals, and it is proper that you should observe this day in a mood of rejoicing certainly, but also in a mood of introspection and with a degree of searching of the heart as to how far you have lived up to those ideals.

The Visva-Bharati came into existence in Gurudeva's time, and some years back it put on new garb of a university under our statutes and laws. It was made clear even at that time that the Visva-Bharati was not and should not be a replica of other universities in India. If the Visva-Bharati was to serve its special purpose it must function in its own way and in the manner laid down by Gurudeva. I hope, therefore, that whatever changes may take place in future, the Visva-Bharati will retain the essential stamp which Gurudeva gave it. For example, this mango-grove here has a definite meaning. It takes us back to the past of India, to the *ashrama* approach to education, and it also teaches us the virtues of simplicity. Today when we want the rapid advancement of education, we are inclined to think too much in terms of big halls, noble buildings and the like. These are necessary but if the spread of education depends on brick and mortar and is conceived in terms of these structures, its purpose is likely to be defeated. We have to think more of the human being whom we are to educate. If we think of the old *ashrama* way of teaching simply and economically, we will not only make rapid progress but be on a surer foundation.

Gurudeva was a rare kind of person to be born anywhere. In India he represented a multitude of things. The most dominant impression which one gets about him is that he was one in the long line of the ancient sages and *rishis* whom India has produced from time to time. Yet this tradition did not prevent him in the slightest from being a modern of moderns and making the whole world his field of thought and action. He was a great Bengali, but being a Bengali did not come in the way of his being a very great Indian. He was an intense nationalist, yet his nationalism did not come in the way of his widest internationalism. He broke down barriers which might limit his personality and his message was to break down barriers wherever they were—in our customs, in our thinking, in our lives, in our general functioning and in our traditions. I should like that aspect of his message to be remembered most of all, because unfortunately the people in India have grown up with all these barriers around them, which have come in the way of our unity, our homogeneity and our growth in the past and which will come in our way in future if we do not put an end to them. It has become essential for us to break down these barriers and that was a basic message of Rabindranath Tagore. Apart from the barriers of caste and race, the barriers that we create in our minds narrow our vision and our thinking and stunt us. In India we talk a great deal about our nationalism, and yet the fact is that we are narrow-minded and have not yet grown to the full degree of *rashtriyata*. We think in terms of many narrower needs at a time when even the idea of nationalism is becoming out of date. Therefore, we have not merely to repeat this great message but to try to live up to it.

I have a fear that in this year of Gurudeva's birth centenary his message and ideals might be swept away in the flood of words and eloquence and that we may imagine that we have done our duty by him. That is a dangerous delusion which comes over us often. I should like you specially here at Santiniketan and the Visva-Bharati to remember that the test of your homage is not what you may say about him but the way you live, the way you grow, and the way you act up to his message.

It has been a great privilege for me to be associated with this institution. The last time when I saw Gurudeva was about two or three years before his death. The tragic news of his death reached me when I was in Dehra Dun Jail. When I saw him last he spoke to me about Santiniketan and the Visva-Bharati and expressed a wish that I should serve it and help it in some way. His words remain with me always and I have often asked myself if I have carried out his wishes properly or if I have failed. Perhaps I could have done better. Anyhow I feel it my duty and privilege to be associated with this large family at the Visva-Bharati and I am grateful to those who have made it possible for me to be so associated. I look upon this institution as highly important for our country and even for other countries. I earnestly hope that it will prosper and carry on the traditions of Gurudeva.

Reflections

HISTORY AND CULTURE
IN NATION-BUILDING

On Understanding History[1]

I have come here to offer you a cordial welcome on behalf of the Government of India. As a Government we are naturally interested in many activities and as a Prime Minister I have to function on many stages and to say something on a variety of subjects. But I rather doubt if any subject would interest me more to listen to and sometimes even to speak on than the subject of history. I confess that being myself an amateur I feel a little overwhelmed when I meet a multitude of experts. Nevertheless, perhaps even an amateur has a place in the scheme of things and sometimes perhaps he may see the wood a little more and not be lost in the individual trees which an expert is apt to do.

Now, we talk of history, and people, I suppose, have numerous ways of thinking and looking at history. But whatever way you may have, whatever approach you may have, whether it is the old and completely out-of-date approach of a record of the doings of kings and battles and the like, or of social and economic progress, or of cultural progress, or the development of humanity as a whole, whether it is the history of a single country or a nation or it is viewed in the context of world history as it naturally must be, inevitably the basis of all that is an accumulation of facts and records and data. Otherwise, one simply builds one's idea of history on improvised knowledge without any accurate data. Therefore, a Historical Records

<hr>

[1] Inaugural address to the silver jubilee session of the Indian Historical Records Commission. New Delhi, 23 December 1948, *Jawaharlal Nehru: Selected Speeches*, vol. 1, 1946–9, pp. 353–8.

Commission is most essential for the building up of a proper history. This Historical Records Commission, which is celebrating its silver jubilee this year, is to be congratulated on this occasion on the work it has done in the past and on the work which I hope it is going to do with even greater fervour in the future.

Now, I do not know what many of you feel when you think about a historical subject. For my part I feel tremendously fascinated by and interested in the subject of history and my mind begins to wander a little trying to think of this long sweep and trying to draw not only interest, but inspiration or knowledge or understanding or all of them. I do not know if one always succeeds in getting that inspiration from it as a whole; one does sometimes find other aspects of it which are far from inspiring. In any event, one has to go back to it to understand the present and to try to understand what the future ought to be. They say that history never repeats itself. I suppose that is true. Nevertheless, to understand anything you have to go back to the roots of the forces and the various other happenings that are taking place today and they are the only possible data which you can have; otherwise you have to trust your imagination only.

History, as a famous writer has described it, is a record of the martyrdom of man. Perhaps so. It is also a record of repeated resurrections after every crucifixion. So you see this process of martyrdom and crucifixion of man, and resurrection following it, in interminable succession. You may consider history as the onward march of humanity, of the human spirit, and yet sometimes we are pulled back by seeing how that onward march is suddenly arrested and thrown back.

Now, every age, I suppose, thinks that it is an age of transition. Nevertheless, I suppose there is an element of truth in our thinking that the present age we live in is peculiarly an age of transition and change: at any rate the problems we have to face appear to be far bigger and acuter than any other problems, partly because of the extent of the problems and because every problem now becomes a world problem. It is quite impossible today to think of current events or of history in the making in terms of any one nation or country or patch of territory; you have inevitably to think in terms of the world as a whole. You may, of course, and you should, think of each of the smaller aspects of that larger picture; you may examine them more closely. But the whole conception of the history of a country being the names of a large number of kings and emperors, and our learning them by heart, I suppose, is long dead. I am not quite sure whether in the schools and colleges of India it has ceased to exist or not, but I hope at any rate that it is dead, because anything more futile than children's study of the record of kings' regions and battles I cannot imagine.

The other aspect of history which has come much more to the forefront—the social aspect of history, the development of the social organism—involves much closer research into the daily lives of the common man. Maybe in family budgets a hundred or a thousand years ago, there were a hundred and a thousand and one things which make us realize something of what the life of humanity was in the past age. It is only then that we can really clothe the dry bones of history with life, flesh and blood. I must confess that even now, in spite of this acknowledged new approach, most of the books on history and papers on history that appear, interesting though the subject matter may be, appear to me to be quite singularly lifeless and dead. They are just the dry bones; there is no flesh and blood in them. And I suppose the only way really to read, write or understand history is to evoke in the mind a picture of a living society functioning, thinking and having all the virtues and failings which the human being has possessed, and gradually changing whether in the direction of progress or in some other. For that too, I suppose, two things are necessary: one, of course, a much more intimate knowledge of detail which this Commission should collect and supply, and the other is a co-ordinating type of mind which is capable of clothing that detail in proper garb and giving it a semblance of life. I hope that this Historical Records Commission and the eminent historians associated with it who will collect material or write papers and essays and books on it will always try to think of two things. One is that they should not always write only for their brother historians. There are other people also outside their charmed circle who ought to be approached. I say this, because the average technical or scientific paper is so very much meant, or at any rate it looks as if it were meant, for the charmed circle of people who are interested in a specifically narrow aspect of a particular question that it loses all interest for the wider public. Now, surely a Commission like this, as all other Commissions, should try to function in a larger atmosphere and try to appeal to the minds of the larger public—the intelligent or semi-intelligent public. It appears to be a different species of approach and a different species of writing to go on with popularization which means a deviation from scholarship. I do not think there is any necessary conflict between real scholarship and a popular approach. I find in such papers and articles that I sometimes see rather an attempt at unconsciously forgetting the fact that a larger public has to be or should be addressed. I do not think that is good, because you isolate yourself from that larger public. You do not get their backing, and that larger public cannot benefit by your labours. Secondly, any subject that you may investigate—although necessarily you investigate a particular subject—might generally be viewed in relation to a larger whole. Otherwise, it has no real meaning except as some odd incident which might interest you. Because, if there is to be an understanding, there must be an understanding of every subject in that relationship. It has no meaning otherwise. Now, once you start on this question of the relationship of events to one another it opens out an enormous field, because everything is related to everything else: nothing is isolated. Every aspect of life is related in some way or other to another aspect, and every aspect of life in one nation is related to other national lives. It was so to some extent even in the past. But in the present age this is so obvious, because of all kinds of factors which bring nations close to one another even though they might not love one another. So that, it is in relation to that that each small item should be viewed; also I would say, though perhaps that involves a much more difficult undertaking, how far this can be related to, shall I say, an integrated view of history. Whether history can be considered in that sense or not I do not know. But the human mind always tries to understand things in an integrated way. Otherwise, they have no significance and we have to arrive at the conclusion that things that happen have no connection with each other and happen in an odd, haphazard way. Looking at it in that integrated way, one has to think what history is—a record of human progress, a record of, shall I say, the struggle of the advancement of the human mind, of the human spirit, towards some known or unknown objective. It becomes a very fascinating study. Whether it is ultimately true or not, nevertheless, it does give some string to connect all the separate incidents. Originally history was taught, I suppose, purely on political lines. And with that were associated, of course, many other aspects, religious, and to some extent cultural also.

Then a great deal of stress was laid on the economic aspect which undoubtedly is exceedingly important. Nobody has ever said that the economic aspect is the sole aspect—that would be absurd—but it is an important aspect and in the larger sense it would cover the cultural aspect too. But quite apart from these individual and separate aspects of history, I suppose there is something which I cannot define, some attempt to understand what all this sweep of history means, where possibly it is leading to, or whether it has any meaning at all or not. Ultimately, I suppose, practically all the problems we have to face in the world can be put in a sentence or two. They are problems of relationships: the relationship of the individual with the individual, the relationship of the individual with the group, and the relationship of groups. Almost every political, cultural or personal problem can be brought within that sentence, and it is these gradually changing relationships that give meaning to the social organism and ultimately to the national and international life that we see around us.

I am rather casually throwing out ideas before this very learned audience so that this Historical Records Commission may try to relate their work, in so far as